GERMAN STUDENTS'
WAR LETTERS

GERMAN STUDENTS' WAR LETTERS

Translated and Arranged from
the Original Edition of Dr. Philipp Witkop

A. F. Wedd

FOREWORD BY JAY WINTER

Pine St Books

Originally published 1929 by Methuen

First Pine Street Books paperback edition published 2002
Foreword copyright © 2002 University of Pennsylvania Press
All rights reserved
Printed in the United States of America on acid-free paper

10   9   8   7   6   5   4   3   2   1

Pine Street Books is an imprint of
University of Pennsylvania Press
Philadelphia, Pennsylvania 19104-4011

Library of Congress Cataloging-in-Publication Data

Kriegsbriefe gefallener studenten. English
  German students' war letters / translated and arranged from the original
edition of Dr. Philipp Witkop [by] A. F. Wedd ; foreword by Jay Winter.
    p.   cm.
  Originally published : [London] : Methuen, 1929
  Includes bibliographical references
  ISBN 0-8122-1816-7 (pbk : alk. paper)
  1. World War, 1914–1918—Personal narratives, German. 2. Soldiers—
Germany—Correspondence. 3. Students—Germany—Correspondence.
I. Witkop, Philipp, 1880–1942. II. Wedd, A. F. (Annie F.). III. Winter, J. M.
IV. Title.
D640.A2 K76   2002
940.4'8243—dc21

2002075444

FOREWORD
Philipp Witkop and the German "Soldiers' Tale"

JAY WINTER

There has been a burst of interest in recent years in "war litera-ture," understood as a genre of writing in which soldiers display the authority of direct experience in telling their "truth" about war and combat. In the process, they offer reflections on much else besides—on comradeship and masculinity, on the image of the enemy, on national sentiment, on the burden of survival when so many others failed to come back, and on the "lies" that those who weren't there told about those who were.

Much of this discussion centers on memoirs written long after the Armistice of 1918, but it also refers directly to a vast body of evidence published during and after the war derived from sol-diers' letters. To Samuel Hynes, these letters were "war memoirs of the dead."[1] This massive body of correspondence is an essen-tial but relatively unexplored part of the cultural legacy of the Great War.

Never before had soldiers created such an avalanche of letters and postcards. Estimates vary, but the number of items sent by soldiers to their families in wartime must be calculated in the tens of millions. Most such items were ephemeral; indeed, the British army had a standardized form for soldiers to tick off boxes as to their being well, in good spirits, and so on. Censor-ship lay behind this effort to restrict soldiers' comments to the absolutely anodyne; officers were obliged to read handwritten missives and eliminate any information potentially of value to the enemy. But the sheer deluge of letters written home defeated army efforts to sanitize correspondence. To be sure, soldiers engaged in their own form of self-censorship and took pains to shield parents and others from some disagreeable features of war. What is striking, though, is how much of the ugliness of war was portrayed in soldiers' letters to family members in wartime.

It is simply untrue, therefore, to say that civilians did not know how bad trench warfare really was. The men who fought told them what it was like, and though some elements—especially smell—were un-transmissible, there were other features of combat which correspondents conveyed time and again.

The publication of this volume of German soldiers' letters is therefore timely, in that it enables us to explore facets of the cultural history of the war receiving increasing comparative scholarly attention. Much of this historical work is based on British texts, both ephemeral ones and those that have entered the literary canon, like Robert Graves's *Goodbye to All That* or Siegfried Sassoon's *Sherston's Progress*. Paul Fussell has developed a highly influential interpretation of "modern memory" as a style of ironic thinking and writing about war that emerged in war books about the 1914–18 conflict and came to infuse literary culture throughout the twentieth century.[2] In addition, Samuel Hynes has written movingly of what he terms "the soldiers' tale."[3] Here the singular is crucial, for it embodies another interpretation based on Anglo-Saxon texts, starting with the Great War and moving through the century, disclosing a certain kind of laconic prose, a refusal to bandy about the "big words" of noble and ignorant sentimentality when describing war. Following Tolstoy, Hynes wants to see what soldiers said about the "actual killing," the cutting edge of battle.

The problem is that for Fussell and Hynes, and for the generations of students who have encountered their work, the issues raised here have been encapsulated, perhaps insulated, in an Anglo-Saxon cultural environment. In effect, they have not really followed Tolstoy to Europeanize the story of cultural responses to war. They have not engaged with the work of thousands of Europeans who served in the Great War and who developed their own distinctive voices un-assimilable into the Anglo-Saxon "soldiers' tale," let alone into the Anglo-Saxon version of "modern memory."

On the other side of the fence, the German "soldiers' tale" has also been separated from that of other soldiers on the other side of the line. That Hitler was a soldier of the Great War, and proudly wore the uniform of the private soldier as a badge of honor, explains some of the difficulty. The shadow of the Nazis and the problem of the "brutalization" of Great War veterans have made it difficult for us to separate the cultural history of their military participation in the 1914–18 conflict from the Nazi seizure of power. The one seems to have prepared the other. The work of George Mosse and Klaus Theweleit has enriched our understanding of both the "myth of the war experience"[4] and the "male fantasies"[5] associated with it in Germany, but their interpretations do not obtain when applied to British and French evidence. Consequently they have enhanced the sense of a cultural *Sonderweg*, which though intrinsically comparative as a category is usually framed in such a way as to separate the German story from all others.

This is no longer a tenable position. It is time to bring the cultural history of the Great War into a fully European framework.[6] For this reason, among others, this new edition of Philipp Witkop's collection of German soldiers' letters helps inaugurate a new phase in the unfolding of a fully European cultural history of the Great War. Having these texts in print, available for critical investigation by a new generation of scholars, will make truly comparative discussion of many themes possible.

Perhaps the most intriguing of them all is the study of what Hynes calls the "soldiers' tale," but applied to all combatant populations. Now that German cultural historians have emerged from the shadow of the Nazi experience to confront the Great War as more than a prelude to still worse events, we are in a position to begin to pose the question as to the commonality of language in the letters and memoir literature produced by millions of men who fought on both sides of the Great War.

A number of pioneering works have pointed the way forward toward this comparative project. Bernd Ulrich has provided an authoritative account of the nature of German soldiers' correspondence, both published and unpublished.[7] A group of studies has emerged from a team in Stuttgart, Düsseldorf, and Tübingen working on facets of wartime cultural history, including the publication of soldiers' letters.[8] The riches of the Bibliothek für Zeit-geschichte in Stuttgart have provided much of the material on which this research rests. German trench newspapers are now the subject of active research.[9] Aribert Reimann has used the procedures of historical semantics pioneered by Reinhard Koselleck to show both the deep affinities and striking differences in German and British correspondence between soldiers and their families during the Great War.[10] His selection of materials was different from that adopted during and after the war by Philipp Witkop, the editor of the volume here introduced. Reimann is interested in "everyman," and the more ordinary the language the better. As we shall see, Witkop was much more interested in capturing what Aleida and Jan Assmann have termed "cultural memory," that is, a set of codes in which educated men and women place their stories in a literary, aesthetic, and philosophical framework. Those codes were defined as national in character, with deep resonances in German literary and religious life.

POLITICS

The search for "cultural memory" was (and remains) an intensely political quest.[11] To uncover it we must explore the construction, adaptation, and circulation of texts about significant historical events, initially produced by those directly engaged in them, but codified in an archive of words, sounds, and images accessible to later generations. Soldiers' letters form one such archive of cultural memory. Given the life history of such narratives, the engagement of those who construct narratives with those who disseminate them almost always involves questions of political aims and political conflict. Cultural authority and political authority are rarely unrelated, and this is especially true in the case of narratives about war.

Within this archive of "cultural memory," one salient narrative is the story of the idealism and national unity that unfolded at the outbreak of war in 1914. The fact that major opposition to the declaration of hostilities was muted is incontestable. More controversial is the way the narrative posited that a broadly unified response to the outbreak of war in August 1914 disclosed essentially German forms of cultural memory, understood in a Hegelian manner as the unfolding of an intrinsically German "spirit" (*Geist*), which transcended region, religion, class, and politics. This notion was self-consciously constructed while the war was very young and served as the ideological framework within which to place the rough consensus that emerged in 1914 that Germany was fighting a defensive war not of her own making. That the story of Germany's defensive response to the war crisis was mostly mythical takes nothing away from the force of the belief,[12] nor from its utility as a rallying cry to renew the war effort during periods of war weariness in 1917 and 1918.

Witkop's collections of soldiers' letters were foundational texts of this myth of "war enthusiasm" termed the *Augusterlebnis*, the experience of national exhilaration during which all political parties rallied around the flag. Now we know that this popular mood was neither homogeneous nor enduring. Panic, anxiety, and stoicism matched patriotic fervor in Germany as it did in all other combatant countries. Concentrating on student rallies or on urban photography is misleading; these orchestrated events, duly recorded in newsreel film, tended to naturalize what was artfully and systematically constructed as an ideology. And what was seen in Berlin tells us little about what happened in other towns, with large working-class populations, or in the countryside, where the harvest was underway. Immovable pacifism and exhilarated patriotism were by no mean the only forms of response to the outbreak of war; all myths, including this one, simplify reality.

Given its emotive force, this story about German national identity in 1914, flowering in the idealistic spirit of sacrifice particularly expressed by the young, became part of the archive of German cultural memory almost as soon as it appeared.[13] Many anthologies of soldiers' letters were published during and after the war in order to deepen and to perpetuate this myth. During the war, the army was favorably disposed to this kind of publication, and in the Weimar Republic successive state ministries of education continued to cultivate (and subsidize) this perspective.[14] The Nazis too had their reasons for disseminating this story, though their motives for doing so were entirely different.

The most prominent figure who took on this editorial task

during and after the 1914–18 war was Philipp Witkop, professor of modern literature at Freiburg, a friend of Thomas Mann, and an expert on German lyric poetry.[15] He was a poet in his own right, a distinction that did not find favor in the hearts of some of his Freiburg colleagues of a more "scientific" disposition. Of direct relevance to his later work, though, was his parallel interest in workers' education, on which subject he published his first book. As Wolfgang Natter has shown, here in this early work are the seeds of Witkop's anthologies, which also took as their function the elevation of a reading public to a higher cultural and spiritual level of existence.[16] Nurturing *Bildung* is one way to describe his lifetime mission. Another way of putting it is to say that his business was the dissemination of texts disclosing (while constructing) German cultural memory.

First in 1916 in a collection of German soldiers' letters, both of those who had died and of those who were still alive, and then in 1918 in a collection of fallen soldiers' letters, Witkop made selections that constructed a highly idealized portrait of the German soldier. By choosing student letters, he projected onto the mass of German soldiers the taste for philosophical prose and poetry he spent his own professional life exploring. He believed that soldiers in 1914 were reaching out for spiritual guidance, and had found in the Bible, in Goethe, and in Nietzsche—in particular in *Thus spake Zarathustra*—the stuff of which stoicism and sacrifice had been made. Such a claim about soldiers' sensibilities was not original; it drew on celebrated cases of artists who volunteered early in the war, like Otto Dix and Franz Marc.[17] The problem was that Witkop's project suggested that these unrepresentative soldiers stood for the army as a whole. The fact that both Dix and Marc, among others, shed their early idealism in the mud and detritus of the trenches was never fully acknowledged.

Witkop's Hegelian sleight of hand—taking elites as representative of the nation as a whole—was an intrinsic part of the project of constructing a specifically German cultural memory out of the upheaval of the Great War. If spiritually minded soldiers carried the *Geist*, the spirit of the German *Volk* or people, then an exploration of their letters would take on the features of cultural anthropology: Germany—the true Germany, the ideal Germany—was in essence what these soldiers said and did. Another way of putting the same point is to say that those who expressed their Germanness in an idealistic form, either in writing or in military deeds, were to Witkop and people like him "seers," visionaries, who could conjure up the outlines of the life and pulse of a nation in a way no materialist could do. They pointed the way to a better future, one worthy of the sacrifices of so many idealistic young men.

Witkop worked to bring together these spiritual "leaders" of the German nation and the rest of the army in two ways. The first was by organizing courses in higher education within the army itself; soldiers were granted two weeks' furlough to attend.[18] The second was by providing articles and commentary in one of the army's official newspapers, the *Kriegzeitung der 7 Armee*, which he helped edit. This publication must be distinguished from trench journals, cyclostyled or mimeographed by soldiers at the front, frequently using "borrowed" equipment and whatever paper was not nailed down. The cost of these newspapers was minimal, paid by small groups of men who knew each other and shared the same sense of humor and grievances. The life expectancy of the newspapers was even shorter than that of the editors and readers. They came and went and sometimes came again.[19] The glossy periodicals published at the army's expense for separate army groups bore no resemblance to the bottom-up journalism produced in the German army and in other combatant forces. They were *dirigiste* in character, presenting to soldiers what the Army High Command believed they should think about the war.[20]

Witkop's war service was within the cultural apparatus of the German army. He was a patriot and a liberal intellectual. His commitment to collecting soldiers' letters in wartime was intended to honor all those who had fought. But his goal was also to preserve and perpetuate the idealism of those who had volunteered for duty during the first days and weeks of the war and to show how deeply ingrained in the German nation as a whole were the values of these young men, many of whom were students. Such men were subject to conscription, but could come forward to serve even before they had been called. About

100,000 men did so, including about 10,000 German Jews.[21] To understand fully the nobility of these men, Witkop urged us to turn to their letters.

In 1916, Witkop brought out the first of his edited anthologies under the title *Kriegsbriefe deutscher Studenten* (War Letters of German Students). In 1918 he published a slightly longer edition—this time 153 rather than the 114 pages in the 1916 collection—with a new title, *Kriegsbriefe gefallener Studenten* (War Letters of Fallen Students).

Ten years later, at the tenth anniversary of the Armistice, Witkop published a much expanded collection of letters, from which the English translation we introduce here was made. This 1928 German edition was reprinted and, after the Nazis came to power, weeded to remove some Jewish and pacifist voices among the letter-writers anthologized in it. Witkop never joined the Nazi party and tried to resist these efforts to "cleanse" his book. He failed, and died of natural causes in 1942. Estimates of the circulation of the war letters project are hard to pin down, but the figure of 200,000 sales in the interwar years appears to be approximately reliable.[22]

The English edition of this text, a reduced version of the 1928 German edition, was produced in 1929. Of the 131 soldiers whose letters are included in Witkop's German edition, 95 were selected for the English edition. In addition, the order was changed and some passages deleted. A comparison between the texts suggests that such editorial changes were made arbitrarily and without any substantial effect on the integrity or the message of the volume as a whole.

The introduction was written by the translator, Annie F. Wedd. An established translator and editor, she occupied no significant literary or political position. In effect, the letters were taken to speak for themselves. Her brief introductory comments set the stage in a straightforward way. She believed that the German nation had been unfairly blackened in wartime as a population of barbarians. Students, she argued, had been able to escape from militarism, and mixed the language of romance and duty in equal parts. She found these letters a good antidote too to the "squalor of much recent War literature." The reference is clearly to Remarque's *All Quiet on the Western Front*, first serialized in 1928 and published a year later. *All Quiet* was a publishing phenomenon, enjoying a commercial success spilling over to many other publications on the Great War, including this one. To recall, with Wedd, that the German men who had fought in the war had believed in something, and had retained their vision of idealism and duty even unto death, would be an aid to international understanding. In effect, the letters were written by men who would not be out of place in British society, in American society, or wherever civilized values were cherished. This form of international cultural solidarity infused League of Nations sentiment until the Nazi seizure of power in 1933. Then a different soldiers' tale came to the fore, also tapping letters like those collected by Witkop, but eclipsing the vision with which the project had begun twenty years before.

CONSOLATION

Now that we have some idea why this volume was produced, and what political and cultural issues surrounded its initial and later publication, we can turn to the question of its intended audience. This volume was clearly aimed at a population in mourning. Witkop got permission during the war from the Army to write to the families of men who had died on active service and to ask them to contribute letters to his project. He received thousands of replies. We can imagine the difficulty parents or wives had in sifting through the papers of their son or husband and making a gift of the letter to Witkop and through him to the nation.

Here we reach the intersection of politics and bereavement. The entries in the book resemble gravestones, in a general way. There is the name, and instead of military rank, there is his academic affiliation. Then follows the date and place of his birth and his death. So far the parallel with a grave site similar to that used in other similar ventures, for instance, Laurence Housman's *War Letters of Fallen Englishmen*. Housman's identification also includes the service arm and rank, which Witkop's book avoids. Still, the similarity to a cemetery stone is clear.

What both editions add, of course, is a letter or several letters.[23] This practice helps establish the individuality of the soldier who died; without such special individuation, he would fade into an army of the dead and therefore into oblivion. Thus these books offer two services to bereaved families. For those whose sons or husbands or brothers had no known grave, these pages provide a kind of surrogate resting place his remains never had. And second, the text of the letters does more than just list his name, date of birth, and date of death. It is a kind of portrait, like those found in East European cemeteries. The letters construct a snapshot of the mind of the fallen soldier. The prose comes to stand for the man himself, his nobility, his beliefs, his aspirations. It is as if he wrote his own epitaph.

The parents of Friedrich Steinbrecher wrote to Witkop on precisely this point. They thanked him for having "erected a memorial" for their son. "We cannot have his grave decorated," they noted, "since his last resting place is unknown." As Natter has shown, Witkop's mission was to give his book the character of "a cemetery of honor, a monument of honor that these young fallen have built for themselves; a national book of edification, to which we, to which our grandchildren, will return over and over again, touched, with respect, love, and gratitude."[24]

The task of producing such a book as Witkop's or Housman's was clearly a tribute of an older generation to a younger one. The editors did not fight, and they recognized a debt to those who did, to make something better in the world after the war. These collections of letters were therefore moral promissory notes, statements of an indebtedness that could never be fully discharged. These men had given everything; how small, though real, a tribute it was to gather together the letters of such men in a volume of collective mourning and collective remembrance.

There is every indication that Witkop edited the letters for publication, but precisely how this was done is not specified. Censorship operated on several levels. The first was in the initial drafting of the letter. Soldiers were well aware of the army censors' sensibilities and may have limited their griping or caustic remarks accordingly. In addition, there is the censorship of the men themselves with respect to their families' sensibilities. Here too there is great variation but, as we have already noted, social conventions probably constrained the content of the letters. If we add to these two constraints the editorial hand, invisible to the book's readers at least, then it is clear that we are confronting not "raw evidence" but constructed representations of war and of warriors.

For historians the value of this collection resides in part in its disclosure of the erection of a narrative, a story about the war that privileged what was understood to be direct, unvarnished, experience. Censorship and editorial arrangement of letters in this volume undermine this claim, which we shall analyze in a moment. The soldiers' tale is as mediated as any other kind of narrative, only more so in the case of German soldiers in an authoritarian state at war.

Instead of a kind of unmediated source about the war *wie es eigentlich gewesen war*, war as it really was like, what we encounter in this collection of letters is the elaboration of a set of representations of war and warriors by those who went through it as combat soldiers.

What do we learn of the "men of 1914" from these letters? First, we see them as fully aware of the evils of war. Indeed, the language many of them use is that of soldier pacifists, people who took up arms in defense of their country, but who—after what they had seen—would willingly take up arms against war itself. One soldier wrote that war is "a very, very evil thing," but one that must be faced out of duty to one's nation. And then, the writer insisted, after peace is restored, "I have firmly resolved, if I do come back, to do everything in my power to prevent such a thing from ever happening again in the future." These sentiments voiced by Franz Blumenfeld, a student of law killed on the Somme at age twenty-three in 1914, were repeated time and again by the men whose letters Witkop collected. To Karl Josenhans, a student of theology, killed in the Argonne in 1915, aged twenty-three, war was "a degrading thing," and, though Germans were not to blame for it, its cruelties were "sickening." To Robert Otto Marcus, a medical student from Munich, this was not war at all, but "abominable, cruel, wholesale assassination . . . unworthy of human beings." Richard Schmeider, a student of philosophy in Leipzig, told his parents that "There are moments when even the bravest soldier is so utterly sick of the whole thing that he could cry like a child. When I heard the birds singing at Ripont, I could have crushed the whole world to death in my wrath and fury." Here is the mental world of thoughtful German soldiers, utterly remote from the worship of war.

The second representation of the soldier that emerges out of these letters is deeply romantic and sentimental. Walter Roy, a student of medicine from Jena, wrote his parents a farewell letter before the attack in which he was killed in April 1915, thanking them "for all the sunshine and happiness in my life." Ludwig Franz Meyer wrote a poem to his mother from the Eastern front, saying that, whatever hardships he faced, his mother had most to bear. Willi Bohle wrote home in April 1917: "Darling Mother, darling little Mother, and you too, my brother and sister, I am ready to endure anything for your sakes, so that you may never see what ruined villages and shell-destroyed fields look like; so that you may never learn what the word *war* really means."

The third representation is that of the Christian soldier. Religious sentiment appears regularly in this collection. Heinz Pohlmann, a philosophy student from Berlin, said farewell to his parents and urged them not to lament, for he felt "safe in the Hands of God." Johannes Haas, a student of theology from Leipzig, actually had the time and presence of mind to write to his parents to thank them for "having led me to the Saviour," and then, while fatally wounded on the field of battle, to tell them, "I think I am dying. I am glad to have time to prepare for the heavenly home-coming." In Hungary, Walter Schmidt, visited the Virgin of Timosaora: "Here in the heart of the Mother of God the suffering find comfort and succour and the afflicted a refuge!"

There are letters about Christmas truces and a kind of Christmas spirit laced with nostalgia for home. Martin Müller, killed on the Somme in 1916, described the way in 1914 "The Holy Night sank softly down upon the earth." He heard the sounds of "Silent Night" and then enjoyed a Christmas tree in the trenches, decorated by a Coblenz Pioneer with "angel's hair," "little bells and gold and silver threads." Hugo Müller's Christmas in 1915 was more modest, though festive: "even the rats and mice had a share in the celebration, nibbling the cake crumbs and the eel's skin." Hans Spatzl wrote his parents in December 1916 that "I am looking forward to Christmas even more than I did last year, for I am in hopes that the dear Christ Child may have mercy upon us. . . . We shall not rise without having received a gift."

Peace-loving, sentimental, religious in a kind of ecumenical spirit: these are the facets of the soldiers' temperament described in these letters. In short, we are in the world before the war, transposed into a landscape of which no one had even dreamed before 1914. Here is the drama of these letters: decency confronted but not overwhelmed by fire and steel.

What was new and odd about the landscape of industrialized warfare, dominated by machines and metal, is the subject of other soldiers' comments. Here is a world of work, though in an assembly line of human destruction. Helmut Zschuppe saw all hell break loose in artillery fire, producing jagged and lethal metal fragments "in a fantastic manner such as no power on earth could devise." Hugo Müller wrote home of uncanny sights, of having confronted "a human hand with a ring on one finger" or of having to use his shovel to scrape away the brains of a comrade, killed the day before by a shell that had decapitated him. Adolf Stürmer couldn't look at a corporal in his unit, killed that very day, and whose face was "so set, pale and covered with blood"; "only that morning we had sat together, chatting and laughing." Friedriche Oehme wrote of villages that looked as if they had emerged from Dante's "Inferno," and of men "crazy with fear" going into battle. After three days in the line, his men were "frozen, dead-tired, and broken down by shell-fire." Gerhard Gürtler's men hear nothing in the front line but "the drumfire, the groaning of wounded comrades, the screaming of fallen horses, the wild beating of their own hearts, hour after hour, night after night." And even out of the line, "their exhausted brains are haunted in the weird stillness by recollections of unlimited suffering." Having been awarded the Iron Cross while convalescing in hospital, Helmut Schuppe thought the cross itself was "made of shell-splinters—black blood congealed on a yellowish dead face with open mouth—bandages encrusted with pus—the strangled cries of hoarse voices—flaccid, gangrened flesh on the stump of a leg."

To some soldiers, exposure to extreme violence was "purifying and deepening"; this was Hero Hellwich's conclusion. But to others it was a school in disenchantment. "The war which began as a fresh youth is ending as a made-up, boring, antiquated actor" called Death. "When one has seen how brutal, how degrading war can be, any idyllic interval comes like a reprieve from the gallows," wrote Friedrich Georg Steinbrecher in November 1916. And his reprieve was up five months later.

As, at one time or another, was that of every single soldier whose letters were published in this volume. What we hear are the voices of those whose sole legacy lay in the letters they sent home. Herein resides the poignancy—and the power—of this collection. The letters were written not for publication but to strengthen the ties between a soldier and his family, for the defense of which he had gone to war in the first place.

EXPERIENCE

These images of war and of the soldiers' temperament were drawn from an unrepresentative sample of the army or the German population as a whole. These are highly educated men, many were officers, and their letters are clustered in the early part of the conflict. But what gave their testimony power and a more general purchase was the sense that they had had access to an experience the rest of the world did not know.

It is in this notion of "war experience" that we can see the most striking legacy of these and other writings about the Great War. These letters were constructed as a window onto a special world, an odd world of the familiar and the unfamiliar mixed in equal parts. The letters disclosed the exposure of soldiers to a level of extreme violence and suffering that most of us never approach; their passage through the crucible of war gave their voices reverberations which seemed to come from another world. They represented those who had gone through war as an "inner experience," something extraordinary, something overwhelming, a secret that only they could know. The religious overtones are hard to miss.[25]

For this very reason, the concept of "experience" emerging from soldiers' letters is an essentialist one. That is, experience is a thing—fixed, immutable, separate from the man or woman who had it. The soldier writing home has gathered some fragments of this "experience" and tries to convey it in a kind of prose which would enable his loved ones to grasp where he is and what he is. The quasi-sacred nature of these letters arises out of this externalized sense of what is "war experience." That is why proprietary possession of these letters was a matter of political importance in the inter-war years. They disclosed what the war "meant" in a way that only those who had fought could know.

It is crucial, though, to see that the publication of such letters introduces a second meaning to "experience," one that is central to the ways such collections were mobilized in the decades after they were written. As Joan Scott has argued, experience is not something that individuals have, but something out of which the individual's sense of self emerges. Experience is therefore not "the authoritative (because seen or felt) evidence that grounds what is known," but rather the social construction of knowledge by people who define themselves in terms of what they know.[26] Experience from this point of view is constituted by subjects, and thus highly volatile; it changes when identities change, and has no inert, external, objective existence outside of the people who contemplate it. Experience is thus ascriptive, not descriptive.

This second sense of "war experience" helps us see how it was that Witkop's project, steeped in German idealism, could just as easily be interpreted and used as an internationalist or even as a pacifist tract, and a few years later be published, with some emendations to be sure, by the Nazis as a paean to the German martial spirit. The text itself went through both stages. First, the letters were published as unvarnished experience. The letter writers were privy to a truth; their experience was something they and they alone had had. But over time their "war experience" became the constitutive material out of which new political and social identities emerged. The "experience" did not change; just its location. Subjects do not reach out to grasp experience in the external world; they construct experience internally, as part of their sense of who they are.

This double level of "experience" brings us back to Hynes's "soldiers' tale." Much writing about war has this duality to it. The stories soldiers relate tell us something of what they have been through, but the act of narration tells us who they are at the time of the telling. Later on, the experience changes as the narrator's life changes. Since identities are not fixed, neither is "experience." It is the subject's "history," expressed at a particular moment in the language of the subject.[27] That language is not universal; it is particular, localized, and mostly regional or national in form.

The "soldiers' tale" is the framework within which knowledge about war is constructed by men whose identities were defined for them by what they had seen. Those who write the stories tell us who they were and who they have come to be. This process of change, these personal odysseys, do manifest some universal elements. But in conclusion it may be useful to show that we must differentiate between and among national and other forms of the soldiers' tale. The German "soldiers' tale" stands alongside other similar national narratives, but it is not identical to them.

Here is Hynes's opening description of what he means by the "soldiers' tale":

> In the title of this book, *Soldiers'* is plural and *Tale* is singular. I have imagined that if all the personal recollections of all the soldiers of the world's wars were gathered together, they would tell one huge story of men at war—changing, as armies and weapons and battlefields changed, but still a whole coherent story. Such an entire tale can never exist: the men who could tell it are mostly dead, and while they lived they were inarticulate, or unlettered, or simply distracted by life, so that their wars were left unrecorded. Nevertheless, that notional tale is my subject: what happened in war, one man at a time; who the men were who told war's separate stories and what their stories tell us (and don't tell us) about war; and how the experience of war has changed in our century, as one war has followed another.[28]

Even a cursory glance at this volume of German students' letters is sufficient to expose the need to nuance this claim about a universal "soldiers' tale." The particular inflections and references embedded in these letters disclose a national archive of meanings which are not the same as those linked to other national groups. The language of spirituality is distinctive; so are codes of emotional expression. Anyone who has written a poem for a German family birthday party will know how different it is from a French or British or American occasion of the same kind.

If it is true that experience constitutes identities and that experience changes as subject positions shift over time, then no one "soldiers' tale," no one meta-narrative of "war experience" can be said to encompass them all. Accepting the idea that experience is not external to the story-teller, something he or she has as a property, but rather a part of his or her subjectivity, has other advantages as well. It will allow us to incorporate the voices of women into the narrative of war; as it stands Hynes's "soldiers' tale" is irredeemably masculine. The "soldiers' tale" is about war experience, to be sure. But in the dual sense of the term used here the notion "war experience" cannot be restricted to those who bore arms. Women told "truths" about war of no less value or significance than the "truths" embedded in collections such as Witkop's.[29]

Even if we restrict our attention to the writings of men in uniform, it is evident that we need a much more multivocal approach to soldiers' tales in order to register the ways different cultural archives inform story telling, and how story telling becomes part of different cultural archives. Only then will the many forms of the soldiers' tale emerge as poignant, distinctive and powerful elements of national cultural histories.

NOTES

1. Samuel Hynes, *A War Imagined: The First World War and English Culture* (London: Bodley Head, 1990), 209.

2. Paul Fussell, *The Great War and Modern Memory* (New York: Oxford University Press, 1975).

3. Samuel Hynes, *The Soldiers' Tale: Bearing Witness to Modern War* (New York: Penguin, 1997).

4. George L. Mosse, *Fallen Soldiers: Reshaping the Memory of the World Wars* (New York: Oxford University Press, 1990).

5. Klaus Theweleit, *Male Fantasies*, 2 vols., trans. Stephen Conway in collaboration with Erica Carter and Chris Turner; foreword Barbara Ehrenreich (Minneapolis: University of Minnesota Press, 1987–79).

6. See the programmatic statement by the comité directeur of the research center of the Historial de la Grande Guerre in Jean-Jacques Becker et al., *Guerre et cultures: 1914–1918* (Paris: A. Colin, 1994).

7. Bernd Ulrich, *Die Augenzeugen: Deutsche Feldpostbriefe in Kriegs-und Nachkriegszeit 1914–1933* (Essen: Klartext, 1997). See also Ulrich, "Feldpostbriefe des Ersten Weltkrieges—Möglichkeiten und Grenzen einer alltagsgeschichtlichen Quelle," *Militärgeschichtliche Mitteilungen* 53 (1994); Ulrich and Benjamin Ziemann, eds., *Frontalltag im Ersten Weltkrieg: Wahn und Wirklichkeit: Quellen und Dokumente* (Frankfurt am Main: Fischer, 1994); and Ulrich, *Krieg im Frieden: die umkampfte Erinnerung an den Ersten Weltkrieg: Quellen und Dokumente* (Frankfurt am Main: Fischer Taschenbuch Verlag, 1997).

8. Gerhard Hirschfeld and Gerd Krumeich with Irina Renz, eds., *Keiner fühlt sich hier mehr als Mensch: Erlebnis und Wirkung des Ersten Weltkriegs* (Essen: Klartext, 1993).

9. See Rob Nelson, "German Soldiers' Newspapers of the Great War," PhD dissertation, Cambridge University, 2002.

10. Aribert Reimann, *Der grosse Krieg der Sprachen: Untersuchungen zur historischen Semantik in Deutschland und England zur Zeit des Ersten Weltkriegs* (Essen: Klartext, 2000).

11. I base these remarks in part on the work of Aleida and Jan Assmann, and in particular on Jan Assmann and Tonio Holscher, eds., *Kultur und Gedachtnis* (Frankfurt am Main: Suhrkamp, 1988), as well as Aleida Assmann's unpublished paper, "Gedächtnis als Leitbegriff der Kulturwissenschaften." I owe much to the Assmanns' stimulating discussions of this theme in their Yale University seminar on Cultural Memory, held in the spring term 2002.

12. The literature on this subject is overwhelming. For differing points of view see Stig Forster, ed., *Moltke: von Kabinettskrieg zum Volkskrieg: eine Werkauswahl* (Bonn: Bouvier, 1992); Manfred F. Boemeke, Roger Chickering, and Stig Forster, eds., *Anticipating Total War: The German and American Experiences, 1871–1914* (Cambridge: Cambridge University Press, 1999); Niall Ferguson, *The Pity of War* (London: Penguin, 1998).

13. Jeffrey Verhey, *The Spirit of 1914: Militarism, Myth, and Mobilization in Germany* (Cambridge: Cambridge University Press, 2000).

14. Wolfgang G. Natter, *Literature at War, 1914–1940: Representing the "Time of Greatness" in Germany* (New Haven, Conn.: Yale University

Press, 1999), III. This excellent study has the only extant extended discussion of Witkop's publications in the context of German war literature as a whole.

15. Philipp Witkop, *Die Anfange der neueren deutschen Lyrik* (Leipzig: Teubner, 1908); Witkop, *Die neuere deutsche lyrik* (Leipzig: Teubner, 1910–13); Witkop, *Gottfried Keller als lyriker* (Freiburg: B.C. Troemers Universitäts-buchhandlung, 1911).

16. Natter, *Literature at War, 1914–1940*, 92ff.

17. On Dix, see Linda F. McGreevy, *Bitter Witness: Otto Dix and the Great War* (New York: Peter Lang, 2001), 163–65. On Marc see Klaus Lankheit, ed., *Franz Marc im Urteil seiner Zeit: Einfuhrung und Erlauterende* (Cologne: M. DuMont Schauberg, 1960) and in general Roland N. Stromberg, *Redemption by War: The Intellectuals and 1914* (Lawrence: University of Kansas Press, 1982).

18. Natter, *Literature at War*, 94.

19. The finest collection of these newspapers is in the Bibliothek für Zeitgeschichte in Stuttgart.

20. On these newspapers, see Nelson, "German Trench Newspapers"; for an alternative view see Anne Lipp, "Friedenssehnsucht und Durchhaltebereitschaft: Wahrnehmungen und Erfahrungen deutscher Soldaten im Ersten Weltkrieg," *Archiv für Sozialgeschichte* 36 (1996): 279–92, and Lipp, "Heimatwahrnehmung und soldatisches 'Kriegserlebnis,'" in Gerhard Hirschfeld, Gerd Krumeich, Dieter Langewiesche, and Hans Peter Ullmann, eds., *Kriegserfahrungen: Studien zur Sozial- und Mentalitätsgeschichte des Erste Weltkrieges* (Essen: Klartext, 1997), 225–42. On trench journalism in British and French forces respectively, see J. G. Fuller, *Troop Morale and Popular Culture in the British and Dominion Armies, 1914–1918* (Oxford: Clarendon Press, 1990), and Stéphane Audoin-Rouzeau, *Men at War, 1914–1918: National Sentiment and Trench Journalism in France During the First World War*, trans. Helen McPhail (Providence, R.I.: Berg, 1992).

21. Jay Winter, "All Quiet on the Eastern Front: German and Austrian Jews, the Eastern Front, and the First World War," *14–18*, no. 3 (2000): 25–53.

22. Manfred Hertlin and Michael Jeismann, "Der Weltkrieg als Epos. Philipp Witkops "Kriegsbriefe gefallener Studenten,'" in Hirschfeld, Krumeich, and Renz, eds., *Keiner fühlt sich hier mehr als Mensch*, 175–98.

23. On the two collections, see Neil Jacob, "Representation and Commemoration of the Great War: A Comparative Study of Philipp Witkop's *Kriegsbriefe gefallener Studenten* (1928) and Laurence Housman's *War Letters of Fallen Englishmen* (1930)," *Irish History* (2002).

24. As cited in Natter, *Literature at War*, 108–9.

25. See Ernst Jünger's version of this sense of "inner experience" in Richard Winter, ed., *Der Krieg als inneres Erlebnis: Auszuge aus den Schriften Ernst Jungers* (Bielefeld: Velhagenand Klasing, 1941).

26. Joan W. Scott, "The Evidence of Experience," *Critical Inquiry* 17 (Summer 1991): 780ff.

27. Scott, "The Evidence of Experience," 793.

28. Hynes, *The Soldiers' Tale*, xii–xiii.

29. For some examples, see Margaret R. Higonnet, ed., *Nurses at the Front: Writing the Wounds of the Great War* (Boston: Northeastern University Press, 2001); and Higonnet, *Lines of Fire: Women Writers of World War I* (New York: Plume, 1999).

INTRODUCTION

THE Letters contained in this volume have been selected from a larger collection published early in the present year by Professor Philipp Witkop of Freiburg-in-Baden, who had himself a choice of about 20,000 placed at his disposal by relatives and friends of the fallen, through the German Ministry of Education.

In his Foreword to the German edition Professor Witkop points out that already, only ten years after the end of the World War, the remembrance of those who made the Supreme Sacrifice is in danger of growing dim and of being soon confined to mere memorials in bronze and stone. As an antidote to this tendency to oblivion and as a reminder of the objects for which these young lives were offered up, Professor Witkop published the Letters.

The impression made upon the readers to whom they are now presented may be slightly different but perhaps even more desirable. Many English people have been accustomed to think of the German army as a horde, if not of actual barbarians, yet of primitive, unreasoning automatons, blindly obeying the orders of slave-drivers with whips and revolvers.

Conscription did of course exist in pre-war Germany, but the better educated were able, by passing an examination, to reduce the period of service from three years to one, while students were often allowed to defer even this short period until after the completion of their University course. Thus many of those who volunteered during the War had altogether escaped the brutalizing influence of the 'blood and iron' militarism which prevailed under the old system. To this category the writers of these letters belong. They are all young University men, studying for every variety of profession—philosophy, theology, medicine, law, engineering, and so on. Thoughtful, poetic, romantic, religious youths for the most part, they hate war in itself and shrink from the bloodshed, the dirt, the terror and the privations ; yet to not one of them is there ever any question of where their duty lies : the Fatherland has need of its sons, and as a matter of course they must answer the call.

To readers disgusted with the squalor of much recent War literature this book will come as a relief. Horrors are inevitable in any account of life in the trenches, but in the majority of these letters there is to be found at least an attempt to realize the meaning of it all, to rise above the mud and the blood, the hardships and dangers. The writers look forward to a regeneration of their country, and ultimately of the world, through their suffering. They willingly and gladly offer up their lives, and repeatedly declare that even defeat would be preferable to a victory which should fail to attain this object. Moreover the descriptions given and the sentiments expressed gain immensely in value from the fact that they were recorded at the very moment or immediately after they were experienced, and also without a thought of publication ; while a pathetic interest is added by the knowledge that in every single case the writer was subsequently killed or died of wounds.

Professor Witkop expresses the hope that the Letters may form a living memorial by means of which these Sons of the Fatherland may survive in the remembrance of their fellow-countrymen as an example of devotion to duty, of self-sacrifice and patriotism, and as a spur towards the realization of the ideals which they cherished. Should they at the same time help towards the establishment of justice and a better understanding between nations, then indeed, in the words with which Professor Witkop ends his Introduction, the writers' last will and testament will have been carried out and ' their death will not have been in vain '.

A. F. WEDD

June 1929

GERMAN STUDENTS' WAR LETTERS

WALTER LIMMER, Student of Law, Leipzig

Born August 22nd, 1890, at Thiergarten, near Plauen in Vogtland.
Died September 24th, 1914, of wounds received September 16th, near Chalons-sur-Marne.

Leipzig (still, I'm sorry to say), *August 3rd,* 1914.

HURRAH ! at last I have got my orders : to report at a place here at eleven o'clock to-morrow. I have been hanging about here, waiting, from hour to hour. This morning I met a young lady I know, and I was almost ashamed to let her see me in civilian clothes. You too, my good Parents, you will agree that I am right in saying that I don't belong in this peaceful Leipzig any more. Dear Mother, please, please, try to keep constantly before your mind what I have realized, in the midst of conflicting emotions, since I said good-bye to you yesterday, namely that if at this time we think of ourselves and those who belong to us, we shall be petty and weak. We must have a broad outlook and think of our nation, our Fatherland, of God— then we shall be brave and strong.

Leipzig, August 7th, 1914.

After all, I am glad that we have stopped here a few days longer. It has given me time to put my thoughts in order and get them thoroughly under control again. Every soldier must, to start with, be, as I was a week ago, oppressed by the first mental picture of horrors which are no longer mere possibilities, but actually approaching realities ; and on the day of the first battle the feeling of dread is bound to try and get possession of one's heart again, but now it won't find us shaky or unprepared. I personally have entirely regained my self-possession. I have thought out my position as if I had already done with this world—as if I were certain of not coming home again ; and that gives me peace and security. Dear Father, good Mother, beloved Brothers and Sisters, please, please don't think me cruel for saying this, but it would be a good thing if already you too would, with brave hearts and firm self-control, get accustomed to the idea that you will not see me or any of my brothers again. Then if bad news does come, you will be able to receive it much more calmly. But if we all do come back, then we can accept that joy as an unexpected and all the more gracious and glorious gift of God. You will believe that I really mean this. The matter is much too sacred to me for me to be capable of merely making phrases in what I have just said.

In any case I mean to go into this business ' like Blücher '. That is the simple duty of every one of us. And this feeling is universal among the soldiers, especially since the night when England's declaration of war was announced in the barracks. We none of us got to sleep till three o'clock in the morning, we were so full of excitement, fury, and enthusiasm.

(2)

It is a joy to go to the Front with such comrades. We are bound to be victorious ! Nothing else is possible in the face of such determination to win. My dear ones, be proud that you live in such times and in such a nation, and that you too have the privilege of sending several of those you love into this glorious struggle.

In the train.

Our march to the station was a gripping and uplifting experience ! Such a march is hallowed by its background of significance and danger. Both those who were leaving and those who remained behind were beset by the same thoughts and feelings. It seemed as if one lived through as much in that hour as ordinarily in months and years. Such enthusiasm !—the whole battalion with helmets and tunics decked with flowers—handkerchiefs waving untiringly—cheers on every side—and over and over again the ever-fresh and wonderful reassurance from the soldiers : ' *fest steht und treu die Wacht am Rhein !* ' This hour is one such as seldom strikes in the life of a nation, and it is so marvellous and moving as to be in itself sufficient compensation for many sufferings and sacrifices.

South of Chalons, September 9th, 1914.

This ghastly battle is still raging—for the fourth day ! Up till now, like most battles in this war, it has consisted almost entirely of an appalling artillery duel. I am writing this letter in a sort of grave-like hole which I dug for myself in the firing-line. The

(3)

shells are falling so thick to-day, both before and behind us, that one may regard it as only thanks to the special mercy of God if one comes out of it safe and sound.

Attigny, September 20th, 1914.

MY DEAR, GOOD PARENTS AND BROTHERS AND SISTERS,—

Yes, I can hardly believe it myself, but it's true : I am on my way to you and home. Oh, how happy I am to see a brighter world again, instead of that world of horror ! At last I am free from that secret dread which always haunted me, that I should never see you and your world again, for Fate has presented me with the hope that, unless some unforeseen obstacle should arise, I shall look into your dear eyes once more.

[Four days later he died of tetanus in the Military Hospital at Luxemburg.]

BENNO ZIEGLER, Student of Medicine, Freiburg in Baden

Born May 29th, 1892, at Ueberlingen.
Killed October 8th, 1914, near Annay.

At the Front, September 14th, 1914.

IF only the hand of God, which up till now has graciously led me unscathed through all fatigues and dangers, continue to protect me, it shall not be my fault if I too am not a Man when I come home.

I am counting more than ever on that, for truly the war-horror seems to have reached its climax. O God ! how many have those hours been when on every side gruesome Death was reaping his terrible harvest. One sees someone fall—forward on his face —one can't immediately recognize who it is—one turns the blood-covered face up—O God ! it's you ! Why had it to be just *you* ! And how often that happened ! At such moments I had but one picture before my mind's eye. I saw you, my dear, good Father, as you laid your hand in blessing upon my head—beside your bed it was, on the morning when I thought I must go—and you prayed for God's mercy on me. Father ! your blessing has helped me ! It was that which has made me strong, stronger than my comrades—for there have been times when I have been able to comfort and encourage them—I, the weakling !

Such a good comrade, one of them was—a head-teacher from Landeck. He went into action with us the very day he came out of hospital. As a

(5)

Lance-Corporal he was allowed, for the first time, to lead a whole half-platoon, and he was so proud ! ' The second half-platoon will follow me. Forward ! ' he cried. ' Always forward ! ' And at that very moment a shell-splinter carried away the lower part of his thigh. He lay there, on one side, for four hours, lay and nearly bled to death. At last somebody happened to notice him lying there. The battle was still going on. The enemy's rifle-bullets were still whizzing from the edge of the wood. Nobody wanted to leave a position of safety to fetch him in. I dared to do it. The man who had found him went too, and we carried him on his coat into safety. I bound him up, and the same night four of us carried him six miles to the Field Hospital. He gave me a silk shirt and his favourite pipe as a thank-offering. Poor chap ! he will probably have to have his leg amputated at the knee. Such isolated instances make more impression upon one than a fight against a whole French Army Corps.

WILLI BÖHNE, Student of Chemistry, Freiburg in Breisgau

Born April 11th, 1895, at Elberfeld.
Killed October 24th, 1914, near Lille.

October 16th, 1914.

DEAR PARENTS, BROTHERS AND SISTERS,—

At the moment I am lying in the straw, having just put away the tasty dinner provided by the field-kitchen, and am smoking one of some ' Love-Gift ' [1] cigars which have just been issued. But — —

October 20th.

Here is a long pause, by no means so insignificant, however, as those two dashes. What I was going to say was : but the dinner break is over and we must get back to work. Work ? Yes, if you could only see us at it ! We are simply nothing but moles ; for we are burrowing trenches so that the Herren Engländer shan't break through here. One has to do all sorts of things like that, things one had no idea of before, but one doesn't mind. We manage to make ourselves quite snug here, too. We have constructed dug-outs in which we can lay our weary heads at night and slip into to be out of the way of shrapnel. We also get a sip of wine now and then,

[1] This was the name given to presents sent by anonymous donors in Germany for distribution among the troops at the Front.

for some of our patrols have brought quite a lot of bottles of red wine with them !——

[Below in a different hand.]

I take the liberty of completing this letter begun by your dear son and brother, who is unable to finish it himself, being wounded. In order to break the news to you I respectfully inform you of this. Be prepared for the worst. The bullet which struck this hero was aimed only too well, for it killed him. Comfort yourselves with the knowledge that he died the finest of all deaths—a hero's death for the Fatherland.

With friendly greetings,
A Comrade, who means this kindly.

MARTIN DRESCHER, Student of Philosophy, Berlin

Born June 22nd, 1893.
Died November 3rd, 1914, of wounds received at Cherburg.

THAT was a day which I shall never be able to think of without horror—the 21st of October. Our guns had not come up and we had to march against enemy artillery, infantry and machine-guns—no, not march, but advance by leaps and bounds. We never even had a chance to fire ; it was a case of running the gauntlet. Then in the evening we had to dig ourselves in. The minutes mounted up to hours. A little remnant of our company got together. I had got shifted into another company. There was a deathly silence ; burning villages all round ; the groans of the slightly and dangerously wounded ; and on top of that to have to dig a man-deep trench ! At two o'clock I was still helping search for our badly-wounded Platoon-Commander.

So it goes on from day to day : alternately awful marches and then a whole day's inactive vegetating ; heat and cold ; too much to eat and then a long spell of hunger. One talks about nothing but these material things and about the question of whether we shall be dead to-morrow or not. I have made up my mind to it pretty well. At first, of course, I trembled ; the will to live is bound to be so strong ; but the thought of immortality is a sublime compensation. And even though I do not hold the ordinary belief in personal immortality, yet last night

2 (9)

I was cheered by the sight of the glittering stars and other remembrances and things I have noted in old days, especially out of Goethe, which have brought me back to the conception of a Universal Spirit into which the individual soul is absorbed. And I can now listen more calmly to the shells screaming overhead. I am firmly convinced that I, that is my soul has not lived just this one life, and that it will live over and over again—how I don't attempt to imagine, for that is useless. Thus I am calm and resigned.

FRIEDRICH (FIDUS) SOHNREY, Student of
Political Economy, Berlin

Born December 21st, 1887, at Möllenden.
Killed November 8th, 1914, near Clamecy.

In the Trenches near Clamecy, October 24th, 1914.

I GO every day into the village here to see a family
with six children. The father is in the war. The
woman says that he is a Reserve Dragoon. She
innocently believes that he has not yet been under
fire, but she has had no news for two months. She
sheds tears when she tells me that and hears that
we get letters from home every day. I get hot water
there so as to have a good wash after four days'
interval, but I can't stop too long, as suspicious
scratchings on the part of the children indicate
undesirable house-mates.

One does feel sorry for these poor people, who
have hardly a stitch of underclothing to change into,
not to speak of anything to eat—nothing left but
potatoes, and the woman is always tearfully asking
me how much longer she and her children will have
to go on living like that. She is always lamenting
over the war : ' C'est triste pour nous et pour vous.'
She lays the blame for it on the English and curses
them. It makes her very unhappy when I tell her
that we are making preparations for the winter and
shall probably spend Christmas in the village. She
just sobs helplessly. By way of thanks I leave her
some bread and army biscuit, which the children
fall upon with shouts of delight. The youngest is

(11)

five months old. It is true that one cow has been left in the village, by order of the Area-Commandant, to supply milk for the babies, but even so that is little enough. On the second day I gave each of the children two sous. The woman was very much pleased and touched by my sympathy. She followed me to the door and assured me that her house was always ' à votre disposition '.

We all pity these poor people, who are clinging to the last remnants of their former happy existence, though in constant danger of seeing all their possessions burnt and smashed up by their own artillery, and I hardly think that a single one of our soldiers would treat them with anything but friendliness. Many of the men habitually give them some of their bread. The inhabitants of the place gather round our field-kitchens regularly to collect their tribute. So we are seeing to it that our enemies' belongings do not starve. Kindliness is probably that part of the German character from which it derives its greatness. ' It is the German soul, that makes a sick world whole '—and no doubt that means the German heart.

ALFRED BUCHALSKI, Student of Philosophy, Giessen

Born October 24th, 1891, at Bromberg.
Killed November 10th, 1914, near Kortekeer.

Before Dixmuide, October 28th, 1914.

WITH what joy, with what enthusiasm I went into
the war, which seemed to me a splendid opportunity
for working off all the natural craving of youth for
excitement and experience ! In what bitter disappointment I now sit here, with horror in my heart !
And in violent contrast to this, with what deep
satisfaction I breathe in, with this precious air, that
life of which hundreds have been deprived !

How shall I ever properly describe to you the
experiences of the last few days ? I should like to
give you a complete picture of the whole battle,
but only little isolated incidents thrust themselves
into the foreground. It was ghastly ! Not the
actual shedding of blood, nor that it was shed in vain,
nor the fact that in the darkness our own comrades
were firing at us—no, but the whole way in which a
battle is fought is so revolting. To want to fight and
not even to be able to defend oneself ! The attack,
which I thought was going to be so magnificent,
meant nothing but being forced to get forward from
one bit of cover to another in the face of a hail of bullets, and not to see the enemy who was firing them !

Certainly I hope to get used to this sort of warfare,
and that I may yet get a chance of carrying out the
order : ' Forward, at the enemy ! ' If one could
only accomplish something, then, no doubt, the
bullets wouldn't hurt so much !

RUDOLF FISCHER, Student of Philosophy, Heidelberg

Born December 8th, 1892, at Freiburg i. Baden.
Killed December 1st, 1914, near Vermelles.

Bauvin, November 18th, 1914.

I THINK that you imagine our life as much worse than it is. If it is cold, we have overcoats, tents and blankets ; if the ground is hard, we have plenty of straw ; if we are thirsty, there is coffee, and on rare occasions wine ; if we are hungry, there are fried potatoes (great delicacies when nothing else is to be had), boiled potatoes when, as is usually the case, one can't hunt up any fat ; and besides that the not-bad field-kitchen food. When the post arrives there is a real feast for both the heart and stomach, especially the heart.

The things one has to go without are made up for in many ways of which I did not dream. Never before have I been so inspired to meditation by the sight of the starry heavens ; never lived so close to Nature. Morning, evening, noon, night mean something here. To-day, for instance, there had been a frost and it was a cold, misty, winter's morning. I went with Joseph round to the other side of the village to the baker's. The sun was just rising in a wintry-red sky. Other men were going across the field to fetch bread. It was quite home-like—the white-veiled landscape, the groups of fields and trees and the pretty village, the cold, fresh air.

Spiritually I am pretty well all right again and

(14)

proud to be allowed to help and to fight for parents, brothers and sisters, for the dear Fatherland and for all that has stood highest in my estimation—for we are fighting for poetry, for art, for philosophy and culture. It is tragic but magnificent.

The whole life here at the front is permeated with a sublime solemnity. Death is a daily companion who hallows everything. One no longer receives him with pomp or lamentation. One treats His Majesty simply and plainly. He is like many people whom one loves even though one respects and fears them. Nobody will come through this war without being changed into a different person.

So be happy in Freiburg as we are at the Front.

RUDOLF MOLDENHAUER, Student at the High School of Commerce, Munich

Born March 18th, 1894, at Munich.
Killed December 13th, 1914, near Peronne.

Halle, near Peronne, December 9th, 1914.

. . . When we have the treat of a beautiful sunset over the watery marshes of the Somme ; when a beautiful, cold, December morning breaks through the mist of dawn and the red clay of the trench glows in the sunshine : then we are happy and rejoice like children over the beauty of it. We watch our men in their field-grey uniforms ; they come out of the dug-outs, stretch themselves, wash themselves and clean their rifles. They look out over the edge of the trench with shining eyes, and their bodies seem to be bursting with health and fitness. They are all young, full of joy in Nature, are living parts of that most wonderful whole—a nation developed into full beauty, goodness, and strength.

FRANZ BLUMENFELD, Student of Law, Freiburg i. Br.

Born September 26th, 1891, at Hamburg.
Killed December 18th, 1914, near Contalmaison.

Freiburg, August 1st, 1914.

. . . If there is mobilization now, I must join up, and I would rather do so here, where there would be a chance of going to the Front quite soon, than in Travemünde, Hamburg or Bahrenfeld, where we should probably be used only to defend the Kiel Canal. And I can't think of anything more hateful than to be forced to sit at home doing nothing when there is war and fighting out there.

You must not imagine that I write this in a fit of war-fever ; on the contrary, I am quite calm and am absolutely unable to share the enthusiasm with which some people here are longing to go to war. I can't yet believe that that will happen. It seems to me impossible, and I feel sure that things will go no further than mobilization. But if it does start then you will understand that I can't stop anywhere here. I know too that you are a dear, good, sensible little Mother, and would not wish that your sons should show cowardice in the face of great danger and stay prudently behind.

September 23rd, 1914 (in the train, going north).

. . . At the moment we are sitting in the train. Where we are going we are not told, but we take for granted that it is to Belgium. We are supposed to

(17)

be in for a thirty hours' journey. Now we are north of Trèves, I think in the Eifel, in most beautiful country. The sun is shining too and everything looks so peaceful. The contrast to the desolation in Lorraine, with all the military activity and the incessant rain, is incredible. But even yet one can't realize the war in earnest, and I keep catching myself simply enjoying all the novel impressions.

You can't imagine the purely artistic, marvellous fascination of this constantly changing, unaccustomed picture. Last night, for instance, the scene round a big table in the living-room of a peasant's house in Lorraine : infantry and artillery all mixed up together in the wildest confusion, one in a helmet, another with his cap on the back of his head or half over his face, all more or less unshaved, smoking, eating, and sleeping. Round the walls one or two more ; others sitting on the floor asleep. And in the midst of all this, two old peasant women busy cooking a little soup and making coffee, poor and humble and delighted with the few coppers which they afterwards got from the soldiers for all their trouble. I learn more about the people like this than from all my lectures and touring-companies.

In the train, September 24th, 1914.

My dear, good, precious Mother, I certainly believe and hope that I shall come back from the war, but just in case I do not I am going to write you a farewell letter. I want you to know that if I am killed, I give my life gladly and willingly. My life has been so beautiful that I could not wish that anything in it had been different. And its having been so beautiful was thanks above all to you, my dear, good, best of Mothers. And for all your love, for all that you have done for me, for everything, everything, I want to thank you and thank you. Really you can have no idea how keenly I have realized just lately how right you were in your way of bringing me up—I was not entirely convinced of the wisdom of some things before, for instance as regards the importance of physical training—how absolutely right and good.

But not only for the way in which you brought me up do I thank you, but for everything, everything —for the life you gave me, and above all for being just what you are. Oh, but you know, without this letter, and much better than I can write it, how I feel.

Then I want to write to you about something else, which, judging from bits in your letters, you haven't quite understood : why I should have volunteered for the war? Of course it was not from any enthusiasm for war in general, nor because I thought it would be a fine thing to kill a great many people or otherwise distinguish myself. On the contrary, I think that war is a very, very evil thing, and I believe that even in this case it might have been averted by a more skilful diplomacy. But, now that it has been declared, I think it is a matter of course that one should feel oneself so much a member of the nation that one must unite one's fate as closely as possible with that of the whole. And even if I were convinced that I could serve my

Fatherland and its people better in peace than in war, I should think it just as perverse and impossible to let any such calculations weigh with me at the present moment as it would be for a man going to the assistance of somebody who was drowning, to stop to consider who the drowning man was and whether his own life were not perhaps the more valuable of the two. For what counts is always the readiness to make a sacrifice, not the object for which the sacrifice is made.

This war seems to me, from all that I have heard, to be something so horrible, inhuman, mad, obsolete, and in every way depraving, that I have firmly resolved, if I do come back, to do everything in my power to prevent such a thing from ever happening again in the future. . . .

October 14th, 1914 (in Northern France).

. . . One thing weighs upon me more from day to day—the fear of getting brutalized. Your wishing you could provide me with a bullet-proof net is very sweet of you, but strange to say I have no fear, none at all, of bullets and shells, but only of this great spiritual loneliness. I am afraid of losing my faith in human nature, in myself, in all that is good in the world ! Oh, that is horrible ! · Much, much harder to bear than being out-of-doors in all weathers, having to get one's own food, sleeping in a hay-loft —I don't mind any of those things. It is much harder for me to endure the incredibly coarse tone that prevails among the men here.

The sight of the slightly and dangerously wounded,

the dead men and horses lying about, hurts, of course, but the pain of all that is not nearly so keen or lasting as one imagined it would be. Of course that is partly due to the fact that one knows one can't do anything to prevent it. But may it not at the same time be a beginning of a deplorable callousness, almost barbarity, or how is it possible that it gives me more pain to bear my own loneliness than to witness the sufferings of so many others? Can you understand what I mean? What is the good of escaping all the bullets and shells, if my soul is injured? That is how they would have expressed it in old days. . . .

November 5th, 1914.

. . . I am glad to say that the feelings of those days have quite disappeared. Much that certainly wasn't a passing mood is really better. Anyhow, I get on much better now with my comrades, and that is a great thing. Some of them certainly are very quarrelsome and grumbling people, but there are at least two who are splendid fellows.

Another thing that helps is that we now have Mecklenburg Jaegers on the road behind us. Every time I pass them it quite cheers me up. To hear the good old dialect does me no end of good, and then what fine, wonderful chaps they are! Always quietly cheery, helpful, brisk, and extraordinarily friendly both with one another and with everybody else.

December 2nd, 1914.

. . . For the rest, we neither shoot nor are shot at much. Our occupations consist chiefly in sleeping, eating, playing chess (the others play cards), writing letters and reading the paper.

You see, it is quite a pleasant life ! Especially in the evening in our ' sitting-room ', when a small candle is burning on the table and everybody is sitting round smoking or enjoying the good things which the post has brought. Behind, in the corner, one of us is making coffee on the little stove, another is drying his stockings, a third perhaps warming up potatoes ; when in addition somebody is making music on a mouth-organ and the others softly or loudly humming the same tune, really it can be astonishingly snug and pleasant.

Honestly I have now got so used to the life here that I am extremely sorry that I wrote you such a miserable letter at first, simply because I was suffering from the quarrelsome ways of the men. Now I get on quite well with the others, and it seems to me, too, that they have become much more bearable. Sometimes I even persuade myself that this is partly due to my influence.

EMIL ALEFELD, Technical Student, Munich

Born December 12th, 1892, at Darmstadt.
Killed December 20th, 1914, in Flanders.

Strassburg, October 8th, 1914.

A LOT of men I know are off too by the next transport. We are looking forward to it. God will protect us. I have not been able to accomplish enough
in the world yet, though of course it is possible that
my country may disappoint me in many ways after
the war, and that we may owe our victory merely
to the fact that our enemies are much worse than we
are. I comfort myself with that reflection, in case
the Almighty should have issued a grave decree
concerning me. But all the same we—I use the
word in the narrowest sense of the few people with
ideals—are Germans ; we are fighting for our
country and are shedding our blood in the hope that
the survivors may be worthy of our sacrifice. To me
it is a battle for an idea—the Fata Morgana of a pure,
true, honourable Germany, free from wickedness
and deceit. And if we go under with this hope in
our hearts, that is perhaps better than by a great
effort to have won a victory and then to see that it
was only an outward triumph without any spiritual
benefit.

Strassburg, November 30th, 1914.

When I shall get away I don't know now, perhaps
in five days, perhaps not for a fortnight. And if I
knew for certain that I should not come back, I

should go all the same ; not with *that* enthusiasm which I felt at Mülhausen, when I believed that our nation had been suddenly ennobled by the war ; my present enthusiasm is different : I will fight and perhaps also die for my belief in a finer, greater, worthier Germany, from which all wickedness and self-seeking are banished and where faith and honour have been reinstated in their old places. We are far, very far, from that. We are still a nation of weak, self-seeking people, not of real ' men '. Yes, no doubt I have become more in earnest because I see that so many people have not.

WERNER LIEBERT, Student of Law, Leipzig

Born June 14th, 1892, at Dresden.
Killed May 10th, 1915, near Givenchy.

Morning of December 4th, 1914.

MY DEAR, DEAR PARENTS,—

Your letter of the 26th brought me the sad certainty that my dear brother had died a hero's death for Germany's victory. The post came early this morning.

My pain is inexpressible. I am not to be comforted. I can't yet realize that I shall not see Hans or hear his voice again. The thought that the dear fellow, who went off so full of joy and hope, will never again see that home and those dear ones for whom he was no doubt longing just as I am, is intolerable. Of you and your sorrow I cannot think without tears.

Only one thing comforts me a little : since I have known that my dear brother is no more, a wonderful change has taken place in me. I suddenly believe in immortality and in a meeting again in the other world. Those conceptions were empty words to me before. Since the day before yesterday they are objects of firm faith. For it cannot be that death should part one for ever from those one loves. What would be the use of all love and affection, which are the most beautiful flowers in human life, if they were to be destroyed for ever in an instant ? This is certainly but a small consolation for the fact that the poor fellow has been deprived of all his life's happiness. How beautiful life is one only realizes out here, where one has constantly to risk losing it.

3

KURT SCHLENNER, Student of Law and Political Economy, Berlin

Born April 21st, 1895, in Berlin.
Killed December 21st, 1914, before Ypres.

Bergen op Zoom, December 9th, 1914.

. . . It is obvious that many of one's impressions of the war must be painful, but perhaps I have written too much about that kind. It is just as obvious that, on the other hand, there is much that is glorious and wonderful. The finest thing of all is the marvellous comradeship at the Front, fresh instances of which are always gladdening one's heart. First of all there is the universal comradeship which runs through the whole German army and is shown by our all calling each other ' Du '.

The other night in Amersfeld I was on guard in wonderfully beautiful, bright moonlight, in the road outside our quarters and was amusing myself by smoking and singing. Columns kept passing, sometimes Artillery, sometimes Army Service Corps. ' Good evening, Comrade ! ' they all called out to me as they went by. Once a door on the other side of the road opened and a Pioneer or somebody called out, ' Hi, Sentry ! ' and almost at the same moment I found a glass of beer in my hand.

These are little things, but they show a comradeship which warms one's heart. It makes so many things easier. I think that this alone must give us a great pull over the motley crew of enemies facing us. Over there every man must first have a look to see

(26)

whether the comrade appearing before him is of his own race or not—one could not very well respect a nigger as a comrade.

Even more important than this general relation is the personal comradeship between man and man among those who are constantly dependent on one another. No test enables one to divide people up into good and bad so easily as that of comradeship. Anybody who on a night-march, where there is no road, thinks only of himself and plunges along after the man in front of him without caring whether the man behind him can get along too—well, we call him a *bad* comrade. Anybody who, in spite of his own difficulties, still finds time to help the man in front of him out of a shell-hole and to warn the man behind him of what's coming, is simply a *good* one.

One can draw delicate distinctions too when a big load of parcels from home comes in. The bad comrade gives away only what he doesn't want, and only the worst because he can treat himself to something better ; the good one shares everything equally, and even prefers to eat the outside of the cake himself and give away the middle. It is a fine thing though that, whereas in Satzkorn in the training-camp there were quite a lot of ' bad ', the race is now nearly extinct, for the war forces us to draw nearer to one another as each one sees how much he depends on others.

The test of comradeship enables one also to look into the very depths of each one's soul, and then one sees how much, in civil life, was only outward show. On the other hand one recognizes the wonderfully

(27)

sound kernel which may be hidden beneath a most unprepossessing exterior. The finest example of this is, to my mind, my dear comrade G., an ordinary private. He really looks an awful fool and his manner is awkward and retiring, but all the same, in the course of long conversations in the trenches and in billets, I have been able to look into the depths of his soul and have seen what efforts and aspirations there are in the man, and on what an infinitely higher level he stands than by far the greater number of those who call themselves educated.

KARL ALDAG, Student of Philosophy, Marburg

Born January 26th, 1889, at Obernkirchen.
Killed January 15th, 1915, near Fromelles.

Flanders, November 11th, 1914.

On the 14th we joined the Regiment and were divided up among the different companies. That night we marched into a village that had been taken by a Bavarian regiment. We relieved the Bavarians. It was a very far-advanced position, not fortified and very dangerous, as soon appeared.

The fun began on the first day about noon, when shells and volleys of infantry-fire simply poured into the village. We took refuge in the cellars, but as the attack came nearer, we had to go out to defend the place. We had no trenches or any other kind of cover and were fully exposed to shell-fire the whole afternoon. Those were difficult hours, full of fear and horror. In the evening the firing started again and lasted till about half-past nine. The contrast with the peacefully falling shades of evening was terrible and melancholy ; the stars shone so quietly and brilliantly down upon the battle—that really was beautiful.

On October 19th they attacked. Artillery-fire from three sides. The infantry got so near that we could hear their words of command. Then suddently our guns started, and that stopped them. Then a merry firing began ; they suffered heavy losses, and soon all was quiet. If they had been a little bolder we should have been done for that day.

(29)

We were standing in a horseshoe, but all the same our casualties were slight. I can't describe my frame of mind on that afternoon. Not for a moment did I feel any fear of death ; one simply abandons oneself to fate—if one is going to be hit, one will be hit.

The French didn't attack again after that, though they fired on us often and violently, especially the English naval-guns, which make a terrific noise. We made ourselves a safer, properly fortified position. We also established an interesting advance-post of twenty-four men. It was only 150 yards from the enemy, and to get to it one had to cross the French line of fire, so it could not be relieved by day-light. The enemy artillery was firing from close in front of us, and on our left-rear was enemy infantry. When I was up there, fighting was going on during the day and we couldn't be relieved in the evening, so we had to remain for forty-eight hours and then for another night, which made sixty hours altogether, that is to say three nights, partly in the rain and always on the look-out. I enjoy having to do that sort of job and stand such a strain ; I am so proud to think that I am equal to it.

Our object here is to hold the position, to prevent the enemy breaking through, and to wait till the right wing (Calais !) has come into line with us. Then we shall advance. The right wing seems to be going victoriously forward. We have had all sorts of news in the last few days : Dixmuide is said to have fallen ; America to have declared war on England ; 1,000 French deserted, many taken prisoner, etc. The distant thunder of guns never ceases. I shall be glad when things begin to move here and we can start on our march to Paris.

I am always most deeply grateful for all the things you send, and still more for your letters, which fill me with love and reverence for you. Your thoughts and feelings show so clearly and splendidly the wonderful depths of parental love that I cannot read them often enough. They make me feel that when we meet again I shall have to kiss your dear old hands and foreheads and eyes as if they were something sacred. God will be with us—that I firmly believe. Certainly, however, when I reflect how those at home are praying for the safe return of every soldier, especially the Landwehr [1] men and the fathers of families, and how many are already bearing sorrow and suffering, then I feel what an immeasurable, what an undeserved favour, what a miracle it would be if just I myself should be spared in answer to such prayers.

I feel proud when you write of me so proudly and humble when I think of my possible fate. I am proud because I know that through me our family has a share in the destiny of the Fatherland and is able to make a sacrifice for it.

To-day, the 13th of November, at 10 o'clock, we had a Parade Service. A village church, which had already served as a Field Hospital and was strewn with straw, was decorated with greenhouse plants and flowers. The Divisional Protestant Chaplain read a passage from the Bible and we sang a hymn ('Follow me, Christians'). Then came a sermon,

[1] The 2nd Reserve.

followed by the chorale ' Now thank we all our God '. It was a moving ceremony, full of thoughts of home ; our minds turned from outward things and occupied with deep, manly, sorrowful meditation, with religious faith, hope, and gratitude. The men often tell one another how much more religious our people have become owing to this war ; it is touching to hear the men talk confidentially to us too about this ; scoffers either no longer dare to express their views or else they have ceased to exist.

I thank dear Mother for the little text out of the Psalms which she sent me ; it did me a great deal of good. And so good-bye, you dear ones, with whom I am always united at this great, grand, solemn time, and the thought of whom makes me stronger and more religious.

Near Fournes, December 18*th,* 1914.

It is a strange kind of Christmas this year : so really contrary to the Gospel of Love—and yet it will be more productive of love than any other— love for one's own people and love to God. I honestly believe that this year the Feast will make a deeper impression than ever and therefore will bring a blessing to many, in spite of the war.

I have been singing our Christmas hymns with great delight and moved by the most devout feelings. We sing them in two parts in our rest-billet, a big warm cow-house, with, on the one table, a little lit-up Christmas tree which somebody has had sent from home. I realized the whole mystery of the Redemption and the miracle of the Incarnation as I never have during a sermon. On Christmas Day I shall be at home in thought all the time, and I cannot do more than wish you all a devout, holy Christmas Feast, which will bring blessing and joy into the house, and trust in the God of Love who will protect us all. I can have no better support than the thought that you are praying for me. I have perfect confidence in the future. This firm faith in which we all humbly live will give beauty and fortitude to our Christmas.

I am writing this early in the morning, by candle-light, on the table in the cow-house. The comrades are shaking themselves free of the straw and washing themselves. We had to sleep last night in ' Alarm Order '—that means with our packs and all our equipment strapped and buckled on, which is very uncomfortable. All night there was a tremendous noise of gun and rifle-fire ; great flames shooting up into the sky on the horizon ; and in six days it will be Christmas !

Near Fournes, Christmas, 1914.

Christmas at the Front ! We were relieved on the evening of the 23rd about 10 o'clock. The English had been singing hymns, including a fine quartet. On our side too the beautiful old songs resounded, with only now and then a shot in between. The sentry-posts in the trenches were decorated with fir-branches and tinsel from home, also the dug-outs.

Then at 10 o'clock another company arrived and we marched to billets, an hour and a half away.

It was the clearest, most beautiful night we have had for a long time, just as still and pure as Christmas ought to be. It was freezing too, which put an end to the mud and filth. I thought much about home and was sorry you were not having a Christmas tree, because I wasn't able to picture what you were doing.

It was delightful to see the men all standing together while the names were read out and the parcels handed out over their heads. They were all real 'Christmas children' as they knelt before the packages and burrowed into them—by a manger in a cow-house, as on the first 'Holy Night'.

In the evening we had our real Christmas celebration. There were two big trees, standing all lit up on big tables. We got everything we could possibly wish for : knitted comforts, tobacco, cake, chocolate, sausages—all 'Love-Gifts'. [1]—What Germany has done for us ! Then the Colonel and the Divisional Chaplain came in, the Bible story of Christmas was read and the dear old hymns were sung.

January 3rd, 1915.

I have lit a pipe and settled myself at the table in our cow-house in order to write home, where they are certainly looking for news again. The pipe tastes good and the old soldier is also otherwise all right.

New Year's Eve was very queer here. An English officer came across with a white flag and asked for

[1] See *ante*, p. 7.

a truce from 11 o'clock till 3 to bury the dead (just before Christmas there were some fearful enemy attacks here in which the English lost many in killed and prisoners). The truce was granted. It is good not to see the corpses lying out in front of us any more. The truce was moreover extended. The English came out of their trenches into no-man's-land and exchanged cigarettes, tinned-meat and photographs with our men, and said they didn't want to shoot any more. So there is an extraordinary hush, which seems quite uncanny. Our men and theirs are standing up on the parapet above the trenches. . . .

That couldn't go on indefinitely, so we sent across to say that they must get back into their trenches as we were going to start firing. The officers answered that they were sorry, but their men wouldn't obey orders. They didn't want to go on. The soldiers said they had had enough of lying in wet trenches, and that France was done for.

They really are much dirtier than we are, have more water in their trenches and more sick. Of course they are only mercenaries, and so they are simply going on strike. Naturally we didn't shoot either, for our communication trench leading from the village to the firing-line is always full of water, so we are very glad to be able to walk on the top without any risk. Suppose the whole English army strikes, and forces the gentlemen in London to chuck the whole business ! Our lieutenants went over and wrote their names in an album belonging to the English officers.

(35)

Then one day an English officer came across and said that the Higher Command had given orders to fire on our trench and that our men must take cover, and the (French) artillery began to fire, certainly with great violence but without inflicting any casualties.

On New Year's Eve we called across to tell each other the time and agreed to fire a salvo at 12. It was a cold night. We sang songs, and they clapped (we were only 60–70 yards apart) ; we played the mouth-organ and they sang and we clapped. Then I asked if they hadn't got any musical instruments, and they produced some bagpipes (they are the Scots Guards, with the short petticoats and bare legs [1]) and they played some of their beautiful elegies on them, and sang, too. Then at 12 we all fired salvos *into the air* ! Then there were a few shots from our guns (I don't know what they were firing at) and the usually so dangerous Verey lights crackled like fireworks, and we waved torches and cheered. We had brewed some grog and drank the toast of the Kaiser and the New Year. It was a real good ' Silvester ', just like peace-time !

Between Lille and La Bassée, January 10th, 1915.

The trenches are full of mud and water: water from below and rain from above. We slave day and

---

[1] One brigade of the 7th Division, which was holding the British Line at this point, consisted of Grenadier Guards, Scots Guards and Gordon Highlanders, which may have given rise to the mistaken idea that the Scots Guards were a kilted regiment.

night shovelling earth and dipping and pumping out water. And it is all fruitless and in vain : the water remains. And the rain still goes on falling in heavy showers. And in addition there is the depressing effect of pitch darkness, as any light would give us away ! Things are unspeakably gloomy, when perfect darkness gathers, in the pouring rain !

I must admit that I often feel perfectly sick of life in this mud and filth and everlasting, bitterly cold, perfectly futile work. Nobody would ever put up with such hardships for any ordinary cause in time of peace. Only one thing comforts me a little, which is that one's strength seems to increase with the demands on it. I feel conscious of an amount of patience and endurance such as I never knew before and should never have believed myself capable of. And it is splendid how the men put up with it all, how nobody gives in to exhaustion or despair, even when the dug-out has fallen in and one has to work all night making a fresh one. It is a joy to see how fundamentally religious the general frame of mind is and how, if one regards religion as the connecting link, one can feel the respect and awe inspired by perfect serenity. One hardly ever hears frivolous remarks now. They all seem imbued with a new life. This tragically late, awkward development into maturity and calm is delicious ! Some of the old Folk Songs move men to tears, men from whom one would never expect such a thing, who seemed just what one used to call proletarians. They sing songs of the Fatherland, soldier-songs and hymns quite naturally. One nearly always hears hymns

(37)

from the sentries at night.   There was a fellow with whom I was on sentry-duty in the trench only yesterday : he sang a hymn and then one of these old, slow, rather melancholy soldier-songs ; in spite of all he had gone through, he was still just a cheery peasant. A few hours later he lay dead, with his face in the mud.   This chance of coming into direct contact with a rich vein in the life of our people is very valuable to me, especially as it is certainly a new development.

KARL JOSENHANS, Student of Theology, Tübingen

Born October 4th, 1892, at Leonberg.
Killed January 29th, 1915, in the Argonne.

Schloss Hindenburg, November 9th, 1914.

WE moved up into the newly taken position. A few
dead were still lying in front of and behind the
trench. I myself had two French and three Germans
buried and took their letter-cases off them. There
one finds the letters they have had from home.
One Catholic Landwehr's mother had sent him all
sorts of prayers supposed to be specially efficacious,
and she feels sure of seeing him again. Then there
were a lot of French letters. One woman always
ends with : ' Petit-petit est toujours bien sage.'
The sister of another wrote that she was sending
him two pounds of chocolate. She will also send
him some gloves which won't absorb the mist so
much, and a hood to keep out the rain. Everything
just like it is with us, and when one reads such
things it quenches the last spark of hatred towards
the French, even if one still felt one.

 . . . One murderous instrument with which we
have the advantage is the big trench-mortar. They
hurl huge shells about a thousand feet into the air
and they fall almost vertically. I have been able
to observe their effect narrowly this time. Earth
and branches are flung into the air to the height
of a house, and although the shells fell eighty yards
away from us, the ground under us shook. During
the explosions I was looking through a periscope

(39)

into the French trench opposite and could see the terrified men running away to the rear. But somebody was evidently standing behind them with a revolver, for one after another came crawling back again. This war is simply a matter of hounding men to death, and that is a degrading business. We can indeed be thankful that we are not to blame for it, for even as it is one often feels absolutely sickened by it. But one thing I must say—the sight of the dead, even with the most ghastly wounds, has no effect on me at all. The look of these pitiful remains proves to one how little this mortal body has to do with the immortal soul, and one thinks much less about one's body out here than one does in time of peace at home.

. . . I have just been round the sentries, who were all standing behind steel shields. I had hardly passed one of them when he dropped, without a sound. It was pitch-dark, which made it all the more gruesome to hear his life flowing away in a rushing stream. As I did not know whether it was still possible to do anything for him, the first thing was to strike a light, and then I saw at once that it was all over. He had raised his head a little above the top of the shield, where there was a sandbag, and at that very moment a bullet had pierced the sandbag, turned off at an angle and struck the man in the forehead. The French bullets are rather longer than ours, and a so-called ' ricochet ' inflicts a horrible wound.

As regards physical hardships, I really have none. I have blankets at night and always enough to eat and drink. One simply doesn't notice the bullets that whistle by and lodge in the walls of the trench. It is only the responsibility that is a strain. It gives one simply no rest at night ; one is constantly seeing after one's sentries to make sure that they are all on the alert. And this feeling haunts one even after one has been relieved, so that one dreams all night of sentries and trenches. By the second night things are better, so that one even dreams of peace-time. It sounds a mere mockery when a town parson writes, as one did to a friend of mine (a teacher) : ' We must not wish for a speedy end to the war, because it is impossible.' I should like that man to have just one look at things as they are here. A great many letters too that are written from the Front give no true picture ; the people who write fine-sounding letters are mostly running round miles away from the trenches. So we shall calmly continue to pray for a speedy end.

Schloss Hindenburg, November 21st, 1915.

. . . In the last two nights of ' rest ' I have been in the trenches in my dreams, but I hope I shall have peace to-night. It is a mercy that one *can* forget and that things get dim in the memory, otherwise one would break down altogether. You will understand how narrow one's horizon becomes ; one can't think of the general situation and is inclined to judge of it entirely by one's own. During these last days my only prayer has been, ' Lord, it is enough ! ' and I would gladly have repeated the rest of Elijah's words too. But we must stick to our post ; that idea is firmly implanted in our souls in spite of all we have to bear. The band outside has just been playing, ' Praise the Lord, the mighty King of Glory.' We haven't got as far as that yet, but at any rate we have not lost our belief that in spite of everything God is leading us to a good end—otherwise the sooner we are dead the better. . . .

January 12*th*, 1915.

On December 31st our Company had to supply the working-party for cleaning-up. An immense number of things were collected. We also had to bury the dead. The French had twelve inches of water in their trenches. There could not be a more gruesome job than dragging the dead bodies out of there and taking off their identity discs. Nearly all the French wear blessed medals, mostly with the inscription : ' La Vierge Immaculée.' We found photographs too, and notebooks with verses written in them. I should be willing to bet that you would not find such things on a single German soldier. I don't want to make sweeping generalizations about the French, because in letters written to them one constantly finds : ' Dieu te protégera.' But I have never yet seen, what I have often read in German letters : ' If it is the will of God.'

. . . Our Company Commander is the only officer who has three decorations. I am quite sure that in fearlessness and power of endurance he is the equal of any Englishman, for in spite of many bodily infirmities he is always first on the spot, and since September 4th he has not been absent for a single day. For the rest he is a great puzzle to me. The truth of the saying, ' They that be whole need no physician ', has never been more clearly demonstrated than in him. His opinion is that Christianity is only for the weak, who without it would be incapable of rising to the height of despising death and doing their duty faithfully. He possesses both powers in a high degree. In addition he is a man of deep feeling, who takes every loss in the Company very much to heart. He doesn't care in the slightest what other people think of him—what he thinks right is done, even if everybody else is of a different opinion. I don't know much about Nietzsche, but I should think he must have been just like that. I don't wish to set myself up as a judge, but when I am with him it is quite plain to me that I am one of the weaklings, and that even if in this war business I do feel easier and happier than I did at first, it is only because I have been enabled to realize that neither death nor anything else can separate us from the love of God.

I have read just lately that in war one is obliged to choose between absolute indifference and a living faith. I might subscribe to that, but my Company Commander is an exception.

AUGUST HOPP, Student of Theology, Leipzig

Born April 17th, 1891, at Schopflohe-on-Ries, near Öttingen.
Killed March 18th, 1915, on the Heights of Combres.

Frianville, March 1st, 1915.

EVER nearer sounded the thunder of the guns.
Already we could see in the distance the Heights
of Combres, and on them the dark clouds raised
by bursting shells and the white puffs of shrapnel.
At half-past four we arrived at St. Maurice. The
whole place was full of wounded. Along the road
from St. Maurice to Hannonville came car after
car, crammed full of wounded ; other cars return-
ing empty ; the slightly wounded were struggling
along on foot.

Just as we got to Hannonville, which is only a
mile or so from the Combres Heights—as if to try
and scare us away—hell broke loose up there ! It
was no longer a case of single crashes, but a continuous and absolutely staggering thunder. One
could no longer distinguish between the different
explosions, the whole hill looked like a fire-belching
volcano. And into that we had of course to go, in
order to help our comrades whose ranks were already
terribly thinned. In Hannonville we snatched a
hasty meal—for many their last—and a few farewell
words were scribbled.

It was already dark, with a lowering sky, when
at 6.30 the order was given : ' Fall in. Out of
step,[1] march ! ' The thunder up there had not

[1] A regular word of command in the German Army.

diminished, and in addition we could now hear the rattle of rifle-fire. The bursting of the hail of iron lit up the darkness for moments at a time. The nearer we got to Combres the thicker became the stream of wounded ; we saw also a detachment of French prisoners. We marched through Herbenville and from there got to Combres in twenty minutes.

' Halt ! fall out on the right of the road. The battalion will await further orders ! ' And already it had begun ! Boom, boom, *ratch* !—one after another—in front of us, behind us, close to us, crackling into the houses where there was nothing left to destroy and where we were trying to find shelter behind what remained of the walls. So there we lay, in the icy-cold night, in that awful, heavy gun fire (which the French had shifted back, because on the top of the hill, which rises steeply behind the town, the battle was raging), expecting that at any moment one of these monsters would strew death and destruction in our ranks.

At last, after three hours of waiting, came the order : ' Forward ! ' Meanwhile the French had pressed on to the crest of the hill, and had wrested some trenches from the shell-shattered 130th Regiment ; but a Prussian battalion of the 154th Regiment, which was already lying in reserve, had counter-attacked, flung the French back, and re-captured the most important trenches. So we were done out of that attack. The Regiment moved forward to relieve the 130th, the 1st Battalion farthest on the left, the 2nd in the middle, and the 3rd in the most dangerous position on the right,

(45)

where the fiercest fighting for the trenches had taken place and where it had to hold some absolutely blown-in trenches.

It was a pitch-dark night. We marched slowly up the steep incline in bottomless mud. Every second one stumbled into a shell-hole. Thank God the enemy's shells were dropping farther back, the French evidently thinking that they were already in possession of the hill.

Meanwhile our Major had arrived at a gallop, our Captain was absent. The 10th, 9th and 12th Companies took up their positions, and we, the 11th, waited—gradually crawling up the hill—one hour, two hours, three hours; we couldn't sit or lie down, we simply stood, up to our calves in deep, sticky mud. We waited till at last, at 4 a.m., came the order : ' The Company will await instructions from the Battalion Commander.' Then we hunted round for huts, which were pretty well shot to pieces, and a few men found scanty shelter in them, but most of us stayed where we were, for if we moved we only fell over one another in the mud and shell-holes, and waited for the dawn.

Then at last came the order : ' The Company will at once relieve a Company of the 154th in the recaptured trench.' Under the guidance of a Lieutenant of the 154th, who knew the forward terrain thoroughly, we started, through a boyau [1] to a trench half-way down the northern slope of the wooded hill. And there the real tragedy began.

[1] A short connecting trench running at right angles and frequent intervals between the lines of trenches.

Already, while in the reserve position, we had occasionally, in the darkness of the night, stumbled over some of the dead bodies which were scattered all over the side of the hill, but in these trenches one saw death in a hundredfold most frightful forms. Right at the entrance lay one of the 130th, leaning against the breastwork, as if he had dropped asleep as he fell, a little bloody hole in his forehead, cold and stark. And then we forced ourselves along, for we had to get through to the far side of the left flank, one behind the other, through the trench, on the bottom of which were stagnating pools of blood in which lay, in wildest confusion, corpses of Germans and French, almost blocking the way every few steps, so that one had to clamber over the heaped-up bodies, constantly finding one's hands and face in contact with ghastly, bleeding wounds. A mixture of blood and mud was smeared over our boots and clothes and hands. One couldn't walk upright, one *must* not, for down in the gully, 30 yards away, lay the French trenches. As soon as even the spike of a helmet showed above the parapet—bang, bang!—a bullet whistled over our heads. At the same time we saw the terrible effect of the artillery-fire, for not a tree was left standing in the upper part of the wood behind or in front of the trenches. The ground looked as if there had been an earthquake ; the trench was here and there a chaos of earth, stones, tree-trunks and corpses, and the nearer we got to the left wing the more ghastly it became, the thicker and thicker lay the bodies, and the more the bullets whistled.

The Lieutenant of the left flank, whose platoon I was to relieve, came to meet me and give me the most necessary instructions as quickly as possible : ' Cover your left as much as you can, it is badly threatened, and hold the trench ! '

One glance was enough to show one the whole danger of the situation. The trench on the left flank had been so battered by shells that it was a mere trough. At the far end a poor sort of emergency barrier had been erected, for at the other end of the trench lay the French, barely 40 yards away. One could distinctly see their flanking-trenches. Half-left of the barrier ran a boyau. ' What's in there ? ' I asked. The Lieutenant only knew for certain that it was full of corpses—' But it may be occupied by the French.'

I quickly divided up my men, four to the barrier, all the rest to the breastwork : ' The trench will be held to the last man ! ' I ordered six of my snipers and my smartest N.C.O. to protect my left flank. They had to lie absolutely flat, outside the trench, behind little hastily thrown-up mounds of earth, facing the enemy's flanking-trenches. I took them out myself and showed each sniper his position, crawling from one to the other. And just then we got our first greeting ! I had carelessly raised myself up to get a better view across—and how it crackled and hissed and hummed and whistled ! The mud splashed up into my eyes. Bullets were pitching all round me and then a murderous rattle started over there—that meant a machine-gun. They were shooting with their pipes in their mouths.

(48)

My snipers and I did not allow ourselves to get flustered. Nobody was hit. Over there the képis kept bobbing up incautiously, to look across, and each of my men aimed at a képi, fired, and many a képi gave a bounce into the air and disappeared for good. But the machine-gun kept on rattling, especially by the barrier. If only we had more cover ! How will the day end ?

It was 9 a.m., and the so-called trench was full of corpses and all sorts of equipment. We stood and sat on bodies as if they were stones or logs of wood. Nobody worried if one had its head stuck through or torn off, or a third had gory bones sticking out through its torn coat. And outside the trench one could see them lying in every kind of position. There was one quite young little chap, a Frenchman, sitting in a shell-hole, with his rifle on his arm and his head bent forward, but he was holding his hands, as if to protect himself, in front of his chest in which there was a deep bayonet wound. And so they lay, in all their different positions, mostly Frenchmen, with their heads battered in by blows from mallets and even spades, and all around rifles, equipment of all kinds and any number of képis. The 154th had fought like furies in their attack, to revenge themselves for the shell-fire.

A heap of five corpses lay just this side of the barrier ; we were constantly having to tread on them to try and squash them down into the mud, because, in consequence of the gun-fire, we couldn't get them out of the trench. Suddenly I noticed with horror that one of the supposed corpses, lying underneath three others, was beginning to move—he was a big bearded Frenchman—opened his eyes and began to groan hideously. He must have lain insensible all night beneath the corpses. We dragged him out, screaming with pain. I gave him a drink, but we couldn't do anything else for him, and he soon sank back into a deep swoon. Our feelings gradually became quite blunted.

I had received orders from the Company Commander, on behalf of the Battalion, to storm the opposite trench with three parties of volunteers : ' The trench must be taken by 11 o'clock ! ' The necessary dispositions were at once made, the smartest men being chosen. One's heart quaked a little. I was going to begin the attack from the boyau, and at the same moment the 10th Company was to start from the opposite side. The most important thing was to make sure whether the boyau was clear of the enemy, in order to begin the attack from there. I myself climbed over the barrier into the boyau ; enemy shots flickered by, but didn't hit me. The boyau was full of bodies. Holding my revolver in front of me, I advanced— 5, 10, 20 yards. At that point the way was barred by a barbed-wire obstruction, so there was no choice but to scramble over the traverse. I succeeded in doing this unnoticed. I could see that beyond the traverse there were none of the enemy, so that I could bring my attacking party as far as here and get the enemy's trench almost on the flank. If the French had been already in the boyau, it would certainly have been all up with me. So I went back to the barrier and told the men to climb over it, one by one, into the boyau.

That went off splendidly, unnoticed by the enemy ; I had my thirty-two little men safely in the boyau and all ready. ' Fix bayonets ! There will be no shooting, but with one spring we shall be in the enemy's trench and everybody in it will be killed or taken prisoner. Only we must not be seen beforehand, so be careful ! ' Those were my orders. I couldn't see any sign of the 10th Company advancing, which seemed ominous !

We proceeded soundlessly, in single file, along the trench until we reached that damned barbed-wire obstruction, where we had got to climb over the traverse. It wasn't so easy for thirty-two men to do that unobserved as it had been for one, with the French not 30 yards away. I was in front and got safely over ; my rifle was handed to me by the man behind and the next 1, 2, 3, 4, 5, 6, 7, 8 also got over all right. Then, just as the 9th man, who had perhaps humped his back up too high, was in the act of clambering over, all of a sudden a crackling machine-gun and rifle-fire was directed at this very spot. The bullets came rattling against the thin layer of earth. The 9th man got safely over simply by letting himself fall into the trench, and at the same moment the whole front of the trench was struck by a murderous volley. We ducked down as well as we could—there was no question of going farther, and then—what the devil is that ? All at once there was a whistling of bullets over us

(51)

from behind. The shots were being fired from our rear position against the French trench where the boyau which we already occupied ran into the French communication trenches—our men evidently not knowing that we were trying to attack by the boyau. It was a horrible situation, caught between the fire from our own side and the enemy's.

I sent back word at once that the shooting from behind must be stopped or I couldn't possibly advance. But immediately after that there was another awful moment—down below in the gully we heard a murderous yell : ' Allez, allez, en avant ! ' and ' Hurrah ! ' At the same time there was a hellish volley of shots—no doubt a French attack, and there was I, stuck in the boyau !

Just then there came a message from the rest of my platoon : ' The French are advancing towards the trench in a dense crowd ! '—' Sir, we must get back ! ' my men themselves shouted. There was nothing to be done but give the order : ' About turn, back into the trench and defend it to the last man ! '

In a most terrific fire we were over the traverse, through the trench and over the barrier in a moment, myself last. It was a perfect miracle that nobody was hit. The French were firing so furiously that it was high time to be back in the trench. Then we saw that they were already advancing out of the gully and from the left flank, leaping forward, in a stooping position, from behind every bush and mound of earth.

Now was the time for coolness and determination !

In front of me every one of my men was on the alert, especially my six snipers on the flank ; it was like shooting driven birds : just as a Frenchman was on the leap from one bit of cover to another, the well-aimed German bullet struck him. I was lying in the open beside the snipers and firing with a French rifle until the barrel was red-hot. The sweat was running down us. The French were soon back in their trenches.

Two paces half-left of me I heard a soft exclamation : ' They've got me ! ' His right arm was hanging limp, smashed by a bullet. One of my best snipers had to crawl back ! And as I was looking after him, something buzzed by my left ear, deafening me for a moment, and at the same instant I felt a burning pain in my left thumb. I looked down—thank God, nothing serious ! Only a slight cut ! A bullet had struck a small stone in front of me, the stone had hit me on the thumb, while the bullet slanted off past my ear. Almost at the same moment the sniper beside me caught it in the right little finger ; I tied up the wound and he calmly went on firing and had done for a lot more Frenchmen before a shell finished him in the afternoon.

My Corporal Seckinger yelled with every shot he fired, sitting like an Indian—most of them were sitting ; he caught it in the afternoon too, just in the same place. I had to get down into the trench ; those on the flank had already had their lesson. Just as I am crawling down, one of my men, in the very act of aiming, gives a leap into the air, and

(53)

falls as if struck by lightning, as limp as a sack—dead. Shot in the head. Steaming blood ran over the bottom of the trench where he lay. Some of the French had got as near as 10 yards, and had even thrown bombs, but not one of those got back alive.

The attack was brought to a standstill, and I breathed again! Suddenly there was a shout from below: "'urrah!' Furious firing again! But what's that? Field-Greys below there! My Lance-Corporal shouted to me: 'Herr Fähnrich,[1] it's the 10th Company!' Heavens, we were firing on our own men who had attacked! 'Cease fire, cease fire!' I bellowed as loud as ever I could. German discipline caused an instantaneous lull!

Yes, they really are Field-Greys down there; one could see their helmets. With one spring I was out of the trench and down towards the 10th Company. But hardly was I out of the trench than it began to whistle and clatter all round me, so that I could neither see nor hear, and even as I dropped to the ground I perceived quite close to me six fellows in helmets, hidden behind tree-trunks. The devil! what a dirty trick! One bullet hit the iron on the heel of my boot. With one single movement I was up, stumbled and fell back into the trench. Lance-Corporal Rössle, with two shots, killed two of the rascals dead as mutton. It is to be hoped that the other four didn't get away either; they had German helmets and overcoats on to deceive us. My men

[1] Fähnrich = Ensign. A youth of good family, qualifying for a commission.

shot simply as fast as the bullets could quit the rifle, and down in the gully we heard cries and great confusion.

All at once there was silence. Not a Frenchman stirred. And we too could stop and puff a bit. We were black with gunpowder-smoke and dripping with sweat. The men too were quite out of breath in consequence of having accompanied all their shots with a continual stream of abuse and curses in real ' Bavarian dialect ! Everybody thought that I was wounded ; Lieutenant Schmidt was all ready to relieve me, but I stuck to my platoon, for there was nothing the matter with me. Also one's nerves were quieted down by a cigarette and a bit of bread. The French had evidently had enough. Out in front one could hear wounded whimpering pitifully.

The time had passed without our realizing it and it was now 11 o'clock. One couldn't, however, think of getting any rest, for swift vengeance was taken in the form of a perfectly frantic artillery-fire. The first shot burst only a yard from me in the flank position. Three of us were half covered with earth ; otherwise, wonderful to say, nothing happened to us. Then they went on coming, one after the other, with awful crashes, immediately before, behind and in front of the second platoon, one wounding a man, who died immediately after, while Lieutenant Hohmüller, who was not a yard and a half away, wasn't touched. We ducked down and took cover as best we could, lying on corpses. The firing went on till half-past twelve, not causing many casualties but getting on our nerves. One thanked God for the nth time when at last the guns were silent.

At 2 o'clock we had orders to take the trench. I begged Lieutenant Hohmüller to let me at least take my whole platoon with me this time, as the trench was so strongly occupied. I also said : 'Anyhow, I am going straight on, but I won't answer for it that a single man comes back.'

We talked it over and decided that Hohmüller should first speak to the Major and explain the situation, which made success practically impossible, to him. This was done ; all the Company Commanders took part in the discussion, and as a member of the General Staff told the Major straight out that not one platoon but a whole regiment would be necessary in order to take this labyrinth of trenches, he was at last persuaded to abandon the idea. At the same time his mistake was explained—he had meant the *boyau*, which he thought was in the hands of the French, but through which we had already advanced. My platoon and I would simply have gone west. It was quite difficult enough to hold the trench, but at least we were saved, thank God, from that useless attack !

But the worst was still to come ! The bombardment ! It was just like the one we had seen yesterday, only this time we were in the middle of it. It started at 3 o'clock, and at the same time they poured in a terrific flanking fire on our left. One after another of my brave men met his fate, either from artillery or infantry fire. It was ghastly ;

I had to keep urging the men to stick it out, not to lose courage, knowing all the time that I might be hit myself at any moment.

I crawled out again to the flank position, where there was no cover at all, and encouraged the men who were lying there—Corporal Seckinger and Privates Platzr and Plemmer—to keep a good look out, so that the enemy should not suddenly fall upon our flank in case the awful artillery fire should be too much for us. I had to shout into their ears, such a thunder was going on all round. Then, just as I had crawled down again into the trench, I was thrown over by a fearful concussion. Up above, where the three were lying, a soft, gurgling sound was heard ; the legs of the one nearest me jerked convulsively once ; then all was deathly still ! Platzr, who had been lying between Seckinger and Plemmer, came creeping down into the trench, his face deathly pale and streaming with blood. ' Seckinger and Plemmer don't move ! ' was all he said. Three men hit by one shell !

And so came the turn of one after another. In front, by the barrier, one man got a bullet through the chest. I gave him a drink and he died directly after. Yet another got a shell-splinter in the heart ; he remained, sitting on the breastwork, as if he were asleep ; once or twice in the night I was just going to wake him up. I told another to fire, because Frenchmen were showing themselves down below. Tearfully he answered, ' Sir, I can't,' and held out the shattered stump of his right hand. The cry burst from my lips : ' O God, help us ! '

5

But we didn't budge from the trench, while it thundered and rattled unceasingly.

There was a panic on the right : the men imagining that the whole left wing was smashed up. ' The French are coming ! ' one of the wounded had shouted in his bewildered excitement. For one moment the ranks were shaken, they all made a rush to the right, with the one idea of escaping from this horrible, agonizing hell in the trench. I sprang to the right. My platoon was alone, isolated. Then I snatched my revolver out of my pocket, leapt as far as possible to the right and drove them all back again to the left. They went of their own accord when they saw that I was still alive. If the French had attacked at that moment it might have gone badly with us. Nerves had given way for a moment, but we quickly pulled ourselves together again. This will give you some idea of the intensity of the fire.

About 9 o'clock I heard that the Company on our right had been withdrawn. Firing continued till half-past five. After that we all lay with our nerves strung up, waiting for the attack for which we supposed the artillery fire had been preparing. But it didn't come. In spite of it all they would have found us at our posts, although they were still firing on our flank and killing and wounding many. But one gets by degrees so callous about death that one hardly looks round when anybody falls. The thing one minds most is the lamentations of the badly wounded when one can't do anything for them. The afternoon cost us thirty men, eleven being dead and the rest mostly severely wounded, the greater number being of my platoon. I was reinforced, at my request, from another platoon.

I have never in my life so longed for nightfall as on this 21st of February ; but it brought us no rest, not to mention sleep. The rifle-fire went on rattling too, but the gracious darkness protected us from the frightful gun-fire. My platoon was relieved by the 2nd for the night. My men were allowed to shift along to the right flank of the Company where it was less dangerous. I remained to hand over. The stretcher-bearers also came at last to fetch the wounded. Some of them died on the difficult, painful journey through the narrow trench. Seckinger and Plemmer were not dead but frightfully wounded. Seckinger had a shell-splinter right through his eyes. It had torn out both eyes and injured the brain. And the poor chap was still alive and even conscious as I pressed his hand in a last farewell, saying : ' You were faithful unto death. I commend you into God's hands.' ' Goodbye,' he answered. He died four hours later. Plemmer had a shell-splinter in the head, was insensible, and died in a quarter of an hour. It was a bloody, ghastly business. I never thought at all about my own slight wound. . . .

The night passed. We sat on corpses without worrying—as long as one didn't have to sit in the mud ! . . .

(59)

ALBIN MÜLLER, Student of Theology, Bamberg Lyceum

Born December 16th, 1892, at Tiefenstockheim, Unterfranken.
Died March 28th, 1915, in the Military Hospital at Tourcoing.

Comines, January 19th, 1915.

HERE with us it pours with rain every day. You can't possibly imagine how filthy we get, wet to the skin. To-day we had to lie down in such filth that at first it made me shudder. But then I said to myself : ' Into it, in the name of God ! ' And while the others were cursing I thought of the story of our Holy Father St. Francis, how he said to one of the Brothers : ' When we get home, soaked with rain and besmirched with mud as we are, and knock at the door of the Convent, and the porter strikes us and calls us thieves and rogues, therein is perfect joy.'

LOTHAR DIETZ, Student of Philosophy, Leipzig

Born December 12th, 1889, in Pegau.
Killed April 15th, 1915, near Ypres.

*November, 1914. Dug-out in the Trenches on Hill 59 ;
3 km. south-east of Ypres.*

You at home can't have the faintest idea of what
it means to us when in the newspaper it simply
and blandly says : ' In Flanders to-day again only
artillery activity '. Far better go over the top in
the most foolhardy attack, cost what it may, than
stick it out all day long under shell-fire, wondering
all the time whether the next one will maim one
or blow one to bits. For the last three hours a
corporal has been lying groaning on my right,
here in the dug-out, with one arm and both legs
shattered by a shell. The boyau runs down so
steeply that it is impossible to carry him that way
on a ground-sheet, and the other communication
trench is under water. So ' good advice is dear '.
Anyone who is badly wounded generally dies while
he is being got out of here. To-day has cost us four
killed, two dangerously and three slightly wounded.

Only 60 yards away from us are the English, and
they are very much on the alert as they would be
only too glad to get back our hill. We have a
fairly decent trench up here, because we drain all
the water into the English trenches lower down, but
our neighbours on the left, the 143rd, have to keep
two electric pumps going night and day, otherwise
they couldn't escape the wet.

Six hundred yards behind here is our reserve position, a little wooded valley in which the most frightful hand-to-hand fighting has taken place. Trees and bushes are torn to pieces by shells and larded with rifle-bullets. All about in the shell-holes are still lying bodies, though we have already buried many. Any number of dud shells of every calibre have burrowed into the ground in the wood. There is a quantity of French equipment lying about. In the slope on one side of the valley we have constructed our dug-outs : holes in the earth, with plank floors, ceilings of tarred felt, and provided with small stoves which are certainly not enough to heat the place, but at least serve for warming up food, and even for cooking.

As one can't possibly feel happy in a place where all nature has been devasted, we have done our best to improve things. First we built quite a neat causeway of logs, with a railing to it, along the bottom of the valley. Then from a pinewood close by, which had also been destroyed by shells, we dragged all the best tree-tops and stuck them upright in the ground ; certainly they have no roots, but we don't expect to be here more than a month and they are sure to stay green that long. Out of the gardens of the ruined chateaux of Hollebecke and Camp we fetched rhododendrons, box, snowdrops and primroses and made quite nice little flower-beds. We have cleaned out the little brook which flows through the valley, and some clever comrades have built little dams and constructed pretty little water-mills, so called 'parole-clocks', which, by their revolutions, are supposed to count how many minutes more the war is going to last. We have planted whole bushes of willow and hazel with pretty catkins on them and little firs *with* their roots, so that a melancholy desert is transformed into an idyllic grove. Every dug-out has its board carved with a name suited to the situation : ' Villa Woodland-Peace ', ' Heart of the Rhine ', ' Eagle's Nest ', etc. Luckily there is no lack of birds, especially thrushes, which have now got used to the whistling of bullets and falling of shells, and wake us in the morning with their cheerful twittering.

Zwickau, November 13th, 1914.

Nine hundred men are just off from here to reinforce 105 at the Front, with bands playing and church-bells ringing, and the tears are running down my face because I have to sit here doing nothing while my comrades out there are fighting so gallantly. I should be in absolute despair if I were not sure of being back in the line in a few weeks' time. I have been persuading the doctor to pronounce me fit for active service as soon as it is anyway possible. He is quite pleased with the way my wound is healing. It is discharging a lot now, but that is a good thing as it gets rid of the poison. As clinical treatment is not necessary, I am entered as an out-patient, which means I only have to go to the hospital every day to have the wound dressed.

I was wounded in the attack on that louse's-nest Gheluveld, which had been fortified and was defended by 18,000 picked English troops, after we had captured two lines of trenches protected by the most awful barbed-wire entanglements and contact-mines. Out of the seventeen Deputy Officers who went to the Front with me, five have been killed and seven wounded.

WILHELM WOLTER, Student of Philosophy, Munich

Born May 28th, 1895, at Kladow, Mecklenburg.
Killed April 16th, 1915, near Vouziers.

Near Vouziers, April, 1915.

OUTSIDE, the rifle-fire has been rattling all night; from what we have observed, they seem to be getting ready for another attack. I have been long since prepared for anything that may happen. People are always saying that it is easier for the young men to face death than for the older ones, the fathers of families and others. I hardly think so, for such a man knows—at least, if he has been conscious of any mission in life—that he has at any rate partially fulfilled it, and that he will survive in his works, of whatever kind they are, and in his children. It can't be so hard for *him* to die in a just cause. But I too feel that I have a mission in life. I believe that I have a message to deliver and I long to give back to mankind some of that rich treasure which God has put into my heart and before which I have sometimes trembled with joy. But I have not yet had time for any harvest; and am I to be allowed no reaping? Forgive such words. It will not be so, and even if it were, God in His goodness will always provide some compensation, some means of perfecting and fulfilling one's desires, and it must be one's consolation that such sublime beauty is certainly eternal, a foretaste of immortality which gives a faint presage of the reality and cannot end with death.

ERNST HIEBER, Student of Theology, Tübingen

Born June 24th, 1892, at Stuttgart.
Killed April 19th, 1915, south of Binarville.

April 14th, 1915.

I HAVE now been back at the Front for three months —a quarter of a year—every day watching the fire of rifles and guns and seeing many men killed, and this soon makes one feel rather lonely. It sometimes seems to me as if the dead were reproaching me : ' Why should I have been killed and not you ? Why I, who had just ordered my life so nicely, and not you, who have perhaps something beautiful to look back on, but nothing definite to look forward to ? ' I think anybody who has been out here a long time has such feelings.

Where we are it is very quiet just for the moment and we are settling down as if we meant to stop here till peace is declared. Peace ! All the longing felt by one who has been long separated from his dear ones ; all the wishes he cherishes for himself ; all the dreams of the future that he has in his dug-out ; all are comprised in that one lovely word—Peace.

PAUL ROHWEDER, Student of Theology, Kiel

Born December 18th, 1890, at Zarpen (Holstein).
Killed April 23rd, 1915, near Het Sas.

October 29th, 1914.

UNDER a golden poplar lies a dead comrade. In the peasants' farmyards lie dead cattle. The windows are broken by shell-fire. Not a bird is to be seen. All nature holds its breath with fear. The air is heavy with the reek of gunpowder. The sun is setting, blood-red. Yet I cannot say that things are going ill with me. A man feels himself really free and independent only when he has learned to be ready to give up his life at any moment.

I have already fired many a shot and the bullets may have gone home. I can now only think with disgust of the battle-pictures which one sees in books. They show a repulsive levity. One never takes a real battle lightly. When one is in the midst of it and fully conscious of its reality, one can speak of it only in the most deeply earnest spirit. How many a quite young married man have I seen lying dead ! One must not attempt to sweeten or beautify such a thing as that.

I dream so often of you. Then I see our house in the moonlight. In the sitting-room a light is burning. Round the table I see your dear heads : Uncle Lau is reading ; Mum is knitting stockings ; Dad is smoking his long pipe and holding forth about the war. I know that you are all thinking of me.

If only our warfare achieves the right kind of

success ; if it brings blessing upon the Fatherland and eventually on the whole of mankind ; if we were sure of that, we should bear our sufferings and privations gladly. How I thank God that I am naturally endowed with such powers of endurance ! I never felt so strong as I do now.

WALTER ROY, Student of Medicine, Jena

Born June 1st, 1894, at Hamburg.
Killed April 24th, 1915, in the attack on the Heights of
    Combres, near Les Eparges.

Döberitz, November 14th, 1914.

. . . Oh how suddenly everything has changed !
First the free, sunshiny, enchanting summer, golden
happiness, a life of liberty, enthusiasm for Nature,
poetry, music, brightness and joy, all the efferves-
cence of youth : oh, what a lovely summer it was !
And now cold, cruel, bitter earnest, stormy winter,
death and misery ! And everything vanished so
suddenly. How I lived and loved is now like a
dream, a passing mood, the sweet remembrance of a
passing mood. Only one thing is real now—the war !
And the only thing that now inspires and uplifts
one is love for the German Fatherland and the desire
to fight and risk all for Emperor and Empire. All
else is thrust into the background and is like a dream,
like a distant rosy cloud in the evening sky.

When, on the march, I observed the autumn
beauties of Nature, then indeed I thought sadly and
yearningly : I should like to dream about you, to
love you, to sing of you, to be rapt and meditative,
but I have no time for you now : I am entirely
occupied with thoughts of war and suffering and with
enthusiasm for our holiest duty. Lenau, Goethe,
Eichendorff, Schwind and Feuerbach, Beethoven,
Wagner, Puccini, and Mozart—how I long for them !
But I could not really enjoy them now, I could not

live in their spirit. Thoughts press in upon me, so many, so urgent, but I can't think them. I lack the needful repose and quiet.

I sometimes think that I have become rather strange. But when at last, at long last, I get to the Front—it should be about December—then if only I might give my life for our Germany, for my Kaiser, for my Fatherland ! I have had a life, short indeed, but so beautiful, so golden, so full of light and warmth, that I should be happy to die if I had only myself to consider. And this life full of light and sunshine I owe to the dear people whose thoughts accompany me and of whom you too are one.

Before the attack on April 24th, 1915.

YOU, MY DEAR ONES,—

I hope that a trusty comrade will not have to send this letter to you, for it is a farewell letter. If it comes into your hands, you will know that I have died for my Kaiser, for my Fatherland and for you all.

There is going to be a terrible battle and it is radiant, enchanting springtime !

I have nothing more to tell you, for I have had no secrets. You know how I thank you all three for all your goodness to me, how I thank you for all the sunshine and happiness in my life. If I am to die, I shall do so joyfully, gratefully and happily ! This is just another message of purest love to you all and to all who love me. I shall carry this last greeting with me till the last. Then it will be sent to you by my faithful comrades and I shall be with you in spirit. May the great and gracious God protect and bless you and my German Fatherland !

In tenderest love,

Your devoted

WALTER.

ALFONS ANKENBRAND, Student of Theology
Freiburg i. Baden

Born October 31st, 1893, at Vöhrenbach, Baden.
Killed April 25th, 1915, before Souchez.

Souchez, March 11th, 1915.

' So fare you well, for we must now be parting,' so run the first lines of a soldier-song which we often sang through the streets of the capital. These words are truer than ever now, and these lines are to bid farewell to you, to all my nearest and dearest, to all who wish me well or ill, and to all that I value and prize.

Our regiment has been transferred to this dangerous spot, Souchez. No end of blood has already flowed down this hill. A week ago the 142nd attacked and took four trenches from the French. It is to hold these trenches that we have been brought here. There is something uncanny about this hill-position. Already, times without number, other battalions of our regiment have been ordered here in support, and each time the company came back with a loss of twenty, thirty or more men. In the days when we had to stick it out here before, we had 22 killed and 27 wounded. Shells roar, bullets whistle ; no dug-outs, or very bad ones ; mud, clay, filth, shell-holes so deep that one could bathe in them.

This letter has been interrupted no end of times. Shells began to pitch close to us—great English 12-inch ones—and we had to take refuge in a cellar.

One such shell struck the next house and buried four men, who were got out from under the ruins horribly mutilated. I saw them and it was ghastly !

Everybody must be prepared now for death in some form or other. Two cemeteries have been made up here, the losses have been so great. I ought not to write that to you, but I do so all the same, because the newspapers have probably given you quite a different impression. They tell only of our gains and say nothing about the blood that has been shed, of the cries of agony that never cease. The newspaper doesn't give any description either of *how* the ' heroes ' are laid to rest, though it talks about ' heroes' graves ' and writes poems and such-like about them. Certainly in Lens I have attended funeral-parades where a number of dead were buried in one large grave with pomp and circumstance. But up here it is pitiful the way one throws the dead bodies out of the trench and lets them lie there, or scatters dirt over the remains of those which have been torn to pieces by shells.

I look upon death and call upon life. I have not accomplished much in my short life, which has been chiefly occupied with study. I have commended my soul to the Lord God. It bears His seal and is altogether His. Now I am free to dare anything. My future life belongs to God, my present one to the Fatherland, and I myself still possess happiness and strength.

Fatherland ! Home ! How often have I rejoiced in your woods and mountains ! Now you have need of your sons, and I too have heard the

6 (73)

call and have come, stepped into the ranks, and will be true to the last.

> ' So fare you well, my parents and belov'd ones,
>   For the last time we press each other's hand.
> If here on earth it is the final parting,
>   We hope to meet in yonder Better Land.'

It is painful to die far away from home, without a loving eye to look down upon one. A grave at home surrounded with love, to which loved ones come to weep and pray, is granted to few soldiers. But hush ! The Heavenly Father has commanded the Guardian Angel to console the dying ; he bends lovingly over him and shows him already the crown, the unfading crown, which awaits him above.

> ' And now will I boldly fight,
>   Even should I die to-night.'

JOHANNES IWER, Doctor of Philosophy, Berlin

Born May 30th, 1892, in Berlin.
Killed April 28th, 1915, near Het Sas in Flanders.

You can form absolutely no idea of our incredible privations. But all the same my health is, thank God, quite satisfactory. When at night I have to crouch, in the bitter cold, with rain streaming unceasingly down on us poor ' Field-Greys ', keeping a sharp look-out on the enemy trenches, I just roll myself in a blanket and am thankful for my warm underclothing.

I am quite cheerful too in spite of everything. Certainly when, on one of the endless marches, the pack begins to press heavily and one's aching feet can hardly drag one's exhausted body along, then I do sigh occasionally, and when the shells burst uncomfortably near, I tremble just a little bit. But my war experiences up till now and my unquenchable optimism give me always fresh strength, and above all the faith which has helped me so far and will continue to help me.

You know me and are aware that it is not easy to me to speak of such things, but so much I can tell you, that in the very worst times it has never seemed to me a paradox that ' My yoke is easy and my burden is light '. And in all the hate by which I am surrounded, I feel more and more strongly the power of love. And I believe in it more and more, and it becomes ever clearer to me that the aim of my future life must be to plunge ever deeper into

(75)

the ocean of love. Real love is the only thing that transcends this world of outward appearance ; it alone is everlasting, and when one has grasped this, one is lifted above all the so-called horror.

ROBERT OTTO MARCUS, Medical Candidate,[1]
Munich

Born July 9th, 1890, at Kamen, Westphalia.
Killed April 30th, 1915, in the Argonne.

In the middle of the Argonne, March 27th, 1915.

THIS war *must* come to an end soon. I have come
to this conclusion during the last two days, for before
that I had no idea, from personal experience, of
what war was really like. Judging from my impressions of the last two days, the people of Znor
must take a back seat. Of course I saw a great deal
of suffering there too, but after all it is just the same
at home. Typhoid, para-typhoid and dysentery
were our daily lot. Cases of smallpox were reported
but did not appear, and we had one case of scarlet-
fever. Of the war itself I really saw very little at
Znor. Of course one could hear the thunder of the
Argonne guns quite plainly. Also there were burnt
villages, mass-burial graves and battle-fields in the
neighbourhood, which spoke in some ways more
plainly than the thunder of guns and the rattle of
rifles. But the ruined villages and the graves dated
from the earliest days of the war.

Last Thursday week, the Chief sent for me into
his room : ' I only wanted to tell you that you are
going to be transferred to the 67th or 98th Infantry.
I don't myself know exactly, as the order has not
come through yet. I have only just heard about
it, but I thought I'd just warn you.' It gave me

[1] A not yet fully-qualified doctor.

rather a creepy feeling under my hide just for a moment, to find myself suddenly whipped off into the Argonne, but in another instant I realized that I had escaped a great danger—that of being sent farther back and having to accompany ambulance trains.

On Wednesday morning I started off on the box of a ration-wagon serving the troops at the Front, into the forest, and towards noon I reached my destination, the ' Mill of the Dead Man ', the much-envied quarters of all the six doctors of the regiment.

We are on blood-stained, hotly-contested ground which has been mentioned in almost every dispatch, between Binarville and Bagatelle. Here one does not have to prick one's ears in order to hear the thunder of guns and rifle-fire. The Argonne is a beautiful forest—in summer it must be unique—but the everlasting crashes, the howling of shells over our heads, the whistling of stray bullets all around us and the noise they make striking the tree-trunks, after a time quite spoil one's enjoyment.

The wounded, carried out of our trenches to the Mill or arriving on their own feet, sometimes only two or three, sometimes half a dozen at a time, give us unfortunately plenty to do. There are dead too every day. That which is going on here, only a few hundred yards from the Mill, can't really be called ' war '. And that brings me back to the wish which I expressed at the beginning of this letter, that *this war* may soon have an end—not this *war*, but this abominable, cruel, wholesale assassination. If it were just a cheery ' Up and at 'em ! '—but here we fight with trench-mortars which contain hundreds of pounds of explosives, with bombs, with weapons out of the Dark Ages, with boiling oil which is squirted into the enemy trenches. Is not such a way of waging war unworthy of human beings?

One cannot sufficiently admire the courage of the men in the trenches, who are literally looking death in the face every moment, and who for five days on end have their nerves strained to breaking-point. At one instant they must have the presence of mind to snatch up an enemy bomb before it has time to explode and fling it back into the enemy trench. At another they see a 'Minnie' approaching and have only the fraction of a second in which to escape destruction.

Forest of the Argonne, April 15th, 1915.

. . . Naturally, dear Father, I was greatly interested in your enclosure—the letter and newspaper cutting about the granting of leave to Medical Candidates—and I was not long in making up my mind about it. Of course I should be glad to get through my exam. Then I should have all that stuff behind me, and have finished my work at the University for the time being. But I won't do it just now. My chief reason is that I could not bear the thought of being stuck for six months in Munich, far away from the war and all danger, while my comrades out here were ready to give their lives for the Fatherland at any moment. Of course I should work hard and make sure of passing, but it is equally certain that I should try to make amends to myself

(79)

for all the privations here by indulging in all sorts of amusements. I should be able to make excuses to myself for the craving for amusement.

And then I couldn't stand the thought that other people were letting themselves be all smashed up for my benefit, while I was enjoying myself going to afternoon concerts and promenading about Partenkirchen. I am sure you won't think it is due to any slackness on my part if, as things are now, I don't go in for the exam. I simply could not be answerable to myself for pursuing my own interests at such a time, even if my conduct was sanctioned by the Government. Certainly there is not very much to do here, but even when I am bored I have at least the consciousness that it is for the Fatherland, and if I were not here somebody else would have to take my place. I am also aware that I form at least a small part of the great army machine, and that will be enough for me till the end of the war ; after that my own rights will again step into the foreground ; then, and not before, will I pursue any ' egotistical object '.

WALTER HORWITZ, Student of Philosophy, Heidelberg

Born October 20th, 1893, at Hamburg.
Died May 1st, 1915, in the Military Hospital at Roulers, of wounds received April 24th, near Kerselaere.

Poelcapelle Station, January 12th, 1915.

AT last I can find time and self-command to thank you for the brave letter in which you told me the very sad news of the death of our dear Hans.

I had already heard it, just before Christmas, from Gotthilf, when we were in billets at Westroosebeke. He came in, looking very much upset, and whispered to me that he had had bad news from home, and then out it came : ' Hans is killed.' We went outside and I tried in vain to find words to comfort him ; it was impossible for me to express my own sympathy with him either : I felt too plainly how much he, you, and I and all of us have lost. And so too to-day I don't know what to say to you when at last I at least try to tell you how much I grieve with you for the loss of this splendid comrade. Only one text comes into my mind, the one I quoted to my own family, telling them to comfort themselves with it if God should also call me—it must and will help us in the death and loss of our dear ones : ' Death is swallowed up in victory ! O death, where is thy sting ? O grave, where is thy victory ? ' When Brahms wrote his glorious ' German Requiem ' to comfort himself for the death of his beloved mother, he made this Bible text its climax,

(81)

because it seemed to him to comprise all that was necessary for the acceptance of the inevitable. In the same way in which I quoted it to my family, so I now send it to you, dear friend, although I know that your brave German heart possesses in itself enough strength to support this heavy loss. It will comfort you, all the same, when you see that all the people who stood nearest to your fallen hero understand and share your suffering.

Dear friend, we are all looking death in the face almost daily, and that makes the soul quite calm in the presence of eternity. All the best of us are ready to tread the same path along which Hans has gone before as a shining example. We are ready with our whole hearts, because we are ripe for the great harvest and will greet the reaper worthily and willingly when he reaches out his sickle towards us.

FRITZ PHILIPPS, Student of Agriculture, Jena

Born November 21st, 1889.
Killed May 2nd, 1915, near Ciezkowice, Galicia.

October 1st, 1914.

FAREWELL Letter, only to be opened if I am killed.

I am going with all my heart, freely and willingly, into the war, never doubting but that Germany will bring it to a favourable and victorious end. I wish that there may be no laying down of arms until we have won a real world-victory. I need scarcely say that I hate war in itself, but for that very reason I will fight and take part in this great affair and willingly die, if I can thereby contribute to the transformation of World War into World Peace. . . . Do not have my body brought home even if that is possible ; let me lie there where I have fought and fallen. Do not put on any mourning for me ; let nobody feel any constraint; but rejoice that you too have been allowed to offer a sacrifice on the altar of the Fatherland.

November 24th, 1914.

I went through a very bad time yesterday afternoon. I was sent forward with a topping, stout-hearted Volunteer, to occupy an observation-post. That I am still alive and totally unhurt is a marvel.

We marched up the main-road towards Ypres as far as the northern entrance to Gheluwe. Every afternoon at dusk that road is under very heavy enemy fire. Several shells of light and heavy calibre plunged into the muck before and behind us. All of a sudden—s—sh—crash !—a shell landed not six yards ahead of us. For a moment I thought, ' It's all up ! ' But the whole shower of fragments went right beyond us—we were between the explosion and its effect. S—sh—crash !—a second shell, just behind us ! We looked at each other, very red in the face. Then we marched straight on, without looking to the right or the left, dumbly, with clenched teeth, to the observation-post. All the trees along the road were torn to bits by bullets—left and right dead men and dead horses—the houses in the street, ruins.

Down in the cellar of the observation-post were several officers and N.C.O.'s of the —th Regiment. I borrowed their periscope and one of the N.C.O.'s fixed it up in a gable of the roof which was entirely shot to pieces, and vanished as quickly as he had come. The officers called out to me : ' Don't move, whatever you do, the enemy have registered this place and they have already scored several direct hits to-day.' That was very promising, but it was no use to worry. I could observe excellently.

Suddenly the fun began. S—sh—crash !—and a whole rain of shells landed on the house. My plucky Volunteer was nearly brained by a brick, but it just missed him. The officers down below shouted : ' Come down, come down ! ' For one moment I quailed. ' What do you think ? Shall we stop ? ' He : ' Yes.' I : ' Right.' I shut my eyes again for a moment, gave myself a shake, and then went on observing quite calmly.

An hour later I brought a good report back to the battery. Out here one becomes a different man, willy-

nilly. . . . At every moment of danger I thought :
' I wonder if Mother is praying for me now ? '

December 8th, 1914.

Don't get a shock ! Early this morning (9.30), in
the gun-line, I got an urgent message to say that I was
ordered to the 2nd Kaiser Franz Grenadier Guards ;
so behold me transformed into an Infantry officer !

With the bullets whistling round me, I moved
with my few rags down here, and reported to the
C.O., whom I found very pleasant. . . . The
Infantry have no officers left—all killed. Already
the only Company Commanders are officers of the
Reserve, and Lieutenants at that. I am quite
pleased and proud to help to fill the gaps and shall
continue to do my utmost to serve the Fatherland in
the Infantry. Don't lose courage. I have plenty,
and when they blow,[1] ' Potato-soup, potato-soup ! '
I shall charge like the devil !

I belong to the Pioneer Battalion, which lost all its
officers in the attack of December 11th, here at Ypres.
Now we gunners have to spring into the breach. I
am quite willing. I don't want to be any better
off than the rest. I should like, just as much as
anybody else, to come safely home as a conquering
hero, but I don't ask for that. I am as ready as any
of my fellow-soldiers to give up my life. Only one
wish I have, and that is for Mother's sake—that my
body may be found and that you may get certain
news of my death so that you won't go on being
anxious : that is the only thing I ask.

[1] The German signal to attack was given by whistle.

LUDWIG FRANZ MEYER, Student of Law, Freiburg i. Br.

Born December 9th, 1894.
Killed May 3rd, 1915, at Sochajew.

Krolowa Wola, February, 1915.

TO MY MOTHER.

Not we who fight, attack, and win or die,
　Bear the most tragic wounds in this our fight,
　For us full many an hour is gay and bright,
But from the mothers comes a bitter cry.

For if our life is hard, early and late,
　Custom soon blunts us, and we little care.
　It is the Mother who has most to bear,
Trembling and thinking always of our fate.

Sadly she turns away from dainty fare,
　(To us dry bread is a delicious thing,
　When all else fails 'tis food fit for a king !)
' Perhaps my son is hungry over there ! '

' Where lies my son upon this bitter night ? '
　The pale dawn shines upon her sleepless head.
　Cold 'neath the fleecy coverings of her bed,
She cannot rest for thinking of his plight.

We do not heed the noise of war and strife,
　We do not heed the passing shells' shrill scream ;
　Each night she hears them whistle in a dream
And thinks each one has robbed her son of life.

Swiftly will peace our present ills repair ;
　Suffering and wounds will swiftly lose their powers.
　She still will bear the trace of those sad hours
In sorrow's silvery sheen on her soft hair.

(86)

I think that if some day we meet again,
   Upon my knees I must fall humbly down
   And kiss those silvered strands that form her crown,
' Oh, Mother, see the fruit of all your pain !

Let me now kiss your dear white hands and say :
   " Oh my sweet Mother, dearest of my heart,
   In all this combat you have borne a part.
You are the greatest heroine of this day ! "

LUDWIG FINKE, Student of Law, Freiburg

Born July 20th, 1893, at Münster i. W.
Killed May 9th, 1915, before Nieuport.

December 19th, 1914.

A WARM wind from the sea rustles softly through the leafless treetops and almost drives the breath back into one's lungs. How long have we already been marching in the still moonlight ? There are riders on the country road. A troop of refugees passes almost without a sound ; the children whimper softly, their elders creep by hollow-eyed, with faces of dumb misery. We are getting near the Front. Smashed-up carts, ammunition-wagons. Here and there a dead horse which lies with its legs stretched out and its neck sunk into the boggy ditch which separates meadow from road. Then the dead warriors.

In the distance glows a burning farm. Beside a building ruined by shell-fire begins a long mound of earth which runs far out into the plain, fading into the distance.

Now we have arrived. In half an hour our cover is prepared. All rest after the march. Only an occasional sentry, rifle on shoulder, peers watchfully into the palely flickering lights upon the plain. Not a movement anywhere. The dead cattle in the pasture are not more lifeless than the ruined farm. A quiet night in the trenches.

Morning dawns in glowing colours over the distant forest. Dark rain-clouds, edged by the sun with purple and gold, drive before the morning wind. Into the cold, stiff limbs creeps gradually the warmth of the coming day. I yawn and stretch myself a little, but a bullet promptly aimed at the spike of my helmet throws sand up into my face and warns me to remain seated.

Meanwhile the choir of artillery strikes up on both sides. Louder and louder come the crashes and between them the humming and whistling in the air. There !—a crash and a splintering among the roof-tiles of the house ten yards away from us. That was the first greeting. Then follows the slow seeking of the enemy guns for us ; that calm, sure eating of their way nearer and nearer which affects one's nerves till one trembles like a thoroughbred horse which hears the crack of a whip close by. But keep cool, keep cool ! Let earth and stones roll down the ground-sheet and the shrapnel-bullets drum on the mound of earth and make a racket among the slates of the roof !

I peep cautiously out. The atmosphere is thick with gas. There are little white clouds in the air and at intervals the resonant sound of falling shells. Hark ! that wasn't far off. The earth of our protecting cover crumbles and splinters whiz past. One soon gets used to the whole business and lights a pipe. That tastes all right, *ergo* everything is all right. Let them whiz if they want to. The crashes are already diminishing, the duel is over.

Evening. A rain-storm is rustling and heavy drops are pattering in the forest. We are hastening along between the tree-trunks. The officers are urging us on. Why on earth ?

Suddenly the column is held up. There is a soft whisper in front—water! It came suddenly. It gushed out of the ground. The sea has broken through again. We wade through water, first knee-deep, then up to our waists, then again up to our knees. One's coat gets heavy. One man has lost his boots.—On again.—Squalls of rain veil the evening gold. One man suddenly stumbles and plunges into the water. Curses and low laughter, for at a first glance the effect is comic. Comrades help him out. Then the way lies through the deep slough of a ploughed field. One's legs nearly stick fast in it, but they have to be dragged out however much they seem disposed to stop where they are. Behind us the slough closes up again. The sheet of water is rippled by the wind. The pestilent smell of salt-water mud oppresses one's lungs.

In a stable, its roof full of holes through which the moonlight falls pale and silvery, we get a few hours' rest. One lies anyhow, not knowing whether one's neighbours are horses or men. Not knowing either how long one lies there. One's feet have long since lost all feeling.

When we go on again, the moon is high in the heavens. The thunder of guns rumbles on through the night. Nobody knows whether we are marching towards the enemy or retreating. We merely march. Gradually the rumbling becomes fainter, and when the sun rises it is only heard far away in the distance.

Roulers, December 26th, 1914.

Two awful days came to an end on Christmas

Eve. We had forty-eight hours of horror behind us. Many a time, with my hands folded round my rifle, I sent a prayer up to the starry sky. Nobody believed that we should ever get home again. But I was not frightened. I only thought : ' God's will be done ! ' And then came the feeling : ' If one could only do something oneself ! '

I was sent off on the 23rd to fetch rations. When I got back I found that a direct-hit had struck my dug-out. Henn, the man with whom I shared it, was dead, lying up to the waist in rain-water, his skull smashed and a splinter in his back. He was sitting just as he was when I left him a quarter of an hour before, his rifle on his arm. My dear neighbour, Friend F., had two bad wounds. Altogether we lost eight killed and 37 wounded out of 85 !

As I was without cover, owing to this direct-hit, the Sergeant, my Corporal, four men and I did the only possible thing—we started to dig. We got out of the trench and dragged some planks together. None of us took any notice of the rifle-fire ; one gets used to that. So we worked in the moonlight like niggers, shovel to shovel, planks between. And thereby the certainty that if a direct hit lands on the top it is all in vain. But at least it was something to do, and it gives one a feeling of security. Then the wire which the Pioneers had left was fixed up. Now get your rifles ready and take the identity-discs off the dead. Then dawned Christmas Eve.

The whole of the 24th we lay in the dug-out, the Sergeant-Platoon-Commander next to me. We smoked unceasingly and counted the shots. The

Sergeant had been in the south-west and had been through everything since the 8th of August. He was in the deadly attack on Dixmuide and in the hail of shells in the Yser. But up till now he had never experienced forty-eight hours in the trenches under direct shell-fire with only a short respite at night. As I was passing on the report that our Company-Commander had been killed, at a spot where everybody had been killed or wounded, a small splinter struck my helmet. My rifle was smashed to bits. I fetched the rifle of a dead comrade.

Then came the star-lit 'Holy Night', and our Christmas music was a horrible blending of the screams of the wounded, the whistling of rifle-bullets and the bursting of shells. At last, at 2 o'clock, we were relieved. The new lot had not been up before and were upset by the awful rifle-fire, so that everything got in a muddle. Thank God the scoundrels over there did not attack. We trotted across the frozen meadow. In the ruined village I found the Acting-Company-Commander, who was quite upset by the death of his predecessor. We collected a few men, and as I was the only one who knew the way, I guided them from the battle-field.

I won't describe the blissful feeling with which, on Christmas Day, after a good seven hours' sleep, I looked out upon the glistening winter landscape and the golden-red sun. One must own that it is a fine thing to be alive! And the Christmas memories . . . I have spent delightful hours since that ghastly Christmas Eve. We have been having a concentrated Feast—' Oh thou joyful, oh thou sacred '. And it is snowing outside ! Now grog is being fetched and we are going to drink your health, and to-morrow we go up the line again. Good-bye and thank you for everything.

Wilskerke, near Middelkerke, February 22nd, 1915.

DEAR COMRADE,—

I am sitting at the High Altar of a beautiful, big, village church. In a choir-stall lie the remains of my evening meal. My writing-desk is the altar, at the foot of which I lie, rolled up in my blanket on a heap of straw, and sleep dreamlessly as we travel-worn soldiers do sleep—as long as we can. We are billeted in the J. Church. The pictures and statues look down with strangely sad faces upon us. Up here in my corner I don't allow any coarse, army jokes. If we are compelled to use the churches, we can at least behave decently in them. All the valuable things that were lying about, and which I have learned from childhood to honour and regard as sacred, I carefully preserved, folded and laid together, and asked the Battalion-Commander to keep an eye on them. We don't want to be Vandals. . . . The sunlight falls in warm, velvety tints through the stained-glass windows. The soldiers are never tired of looking at them.

The village is small and within the range of heavy enemy guns, so that we can't have any light at night. Half the inhabitants are boxed up, as being under suspicion, from 6 o'clock in the evening, under guard.

In the meadow behind the church lies a dud-shell, fenced round like a dangerously savage dog. There

is a strange fascination about the monster, one has
to keep looking at him ! Such a great, lumping
thing ! Otherwise it is very peaceful here. In the
garden of the shell-wrecked presbytery there are
snowdrops in bloom. I am putting some into this
letter. Birds are singing ; there are ploughs at work
in a field ; hens peck about in the sheds. The field-
kitchen stands among the crosses in the graveyard ;
the musketeers are lounging against the grassy
mounds and singing their songs—a queer mixture
of joy in life and proximity to death. . . .

Comrade, I am looking forward so enormously to
being at home again. Shall I ever get there safe
and sound ? It will certainly be a long time yet,
but some day ? If only everything at home is not
too much changed before then, and one's comrades
are all just what they were ! Otherwise I shan't go !

It is getting dusk in the church. And I am always
tired, so tired ! When one is asleep one is not
homesick, is one ? Go on praying that all may
remain well !

Ostende, March 19*th,* 1915.

Through the elegantly simple colonnade of the
Palace Hotel an icy wind from the sea sweeps white
clouds of snowflakes. Across the race-course it
roars and whirls, grey into grey ; through the pillars
it whistles and echoes ; a winter storm is raging over
the City of the Dunes, short and sharp, not lasting
so long or snowing so heavily as it does with us in the
mountains. And when, after having a bath, we
come back to the colonnade, the sun is again smiling

(94)

on the little white roofs of the bathing-machines, which have been hauled up on to the race-course and are standing there—a whole dead city of little white roofs—patiently waiting for the return of the gay, care-free life of other days. Just such a rough, sharp, winter storm has passed over that life too.

In the gardens near the Head Post Office there are daisies in flower ; little green leaves on the bushes are anticipating the spring ; the sun weaves a web of bright rays round the mossy boughs, and the birds sing overhead. There is a scent of spring in the mild air. On the lake the swans pursue their calm course, stretch out their white necks and observe the children who are playing on the bank under the supervision of a little dame of sixty. The sun shines warmly down and the old woman listens to the children's gay laughter and watches the swans. Might one not well forget the times we are living in and all about the sufferings of the winter ? But already one can hear the distant thunder of the guns, and little white clouds in the spring sky show that they are firing again at an airman. Shrapnel after shrapnel follows its course with a sharp, malignant, hissing sound. . . .

There is only one part of the ' Digue ' where people other than officers are allowed to come and enjoy a view of the broad Channel. The slender, white lighthouses rear themselves dazzlingly into the blue sky. The Mole of the harbour lies still and deserted, as does the whole stretch of shore as far as Blankenburg and Zeebrugge. One has a wide, clear view to-day. The tide is coming in ; wave after wave rolls over the sand, breaks and ebbs away—they chase each other and frolic like children. Steel-grey, then a strange warm brown, then gleaming in the sunlight, then flecked with white, lies the broad surface before our eyes. And far away on the horizon the softly shimmering fringe made by the breakers on the dunes fades away into the velvety lilac of the midday haze. . . .

We wander home. Most of the hotels are shut up. The ordinary life of the seaside resort is dead, yet Ostende is not such a completely dead town as its wealthy rival Westende Bains. Certainly it is chiefly soldiers—Field-Grey troops from the Front, blue Landsturm, sailors in their becoming uniform— who crowd the streets, look in at the shop-windows, stroll on the boulevards and fill the restaurants and cafés which have all donned as it were a little German cloak in order to have the attraction of being ' homelike '.

But look ! there on the Place, where the military band is playing, one can see, promenading in the Kursaal gardens, an elegant, well-born lady, with her peculiarly imperious, haughty air ; the grand-mother, with her sweet little grandchild—oh, what pretty fair curls she has !—and many a walking fashion-plate who, with her high-heeled shoes, trans-parent (hardly visible) stockings, daring little hat and costly fur, seems to have stepped straight out of a mannequin-parade. Her tiny pet dog she is forced, by ' barbarous German regulations ', to have on a lead. This accounts for the hostile glance she bestows upon a coarse infantry-man who clicks his tongue at her as encouragingly as if he were in a dancing-saloon at home. . . .

Reserve Position, Village of Westende, April 21st, 1915.

I much enjoy my expeditions among the dunes. Armed with a walking-stick I set off, always straight ahead till I reach the dunes, for in the meadows there is danger of shrapnel.

The way lies through the old positions ; there are shell-smashed rifles, empty Belgian haversacks, behind every mound of earth, from which the fellows were chased by our marine battalions. Here and there, among the heather and scrub, a lonely grave, the weather-beaten wooden cross adorned by a marine-helmet or a bullet-perforated sailor's cap. Every now and then a peasant's dwelling in the midst of its well-tilled patch of ground, the house a ruin, empty, with ragged scraps of clothing, broken crockery and rubbish in the living-room, and the cellars still full of potatoes. The cupboards torn open, pictures and photographs blowing about in the breeze—an old Flemish prayer-book the only thing intact. A shell has overturned the cooking-stove, the pump is battered out of shape, and the wind is dashing bits of slate from the roof into the parlour.

Then we reach a large, lonely house beside the causeway leading to the dunes. That is the ' Villa Scolaire '. The fighting just at this spot must have been terrific, both on the French and German side. Shell-holes and fragments of metal, rifles, dud shells and fuses, helmets and képis, knapsacks and belts.

But also many graves, which the marines have adorned according to their own taste with patterns of shell-cases and duds, flowers and bits of glass, arabesques of shrapnel bullets between, or bits of stuff and ornaments.

' Villa Scolaire ' stands above the gateway on the road to Westende Bains, and fragments of glass-plates still show the names of founders and benefactors who have contributed to its establishment. I take it to have been some sort of institution, perhaps a holiday-home or a school such as convents have. A gymnasium is still standing in which a partially destroyed poster exhibits the names of Titlis, Engelberg and Stanserhorn. Next to it is a big light room in which a quantity of medium-sized iron bedsteads are piled one on top of another in the dust —I suppose it was a children's dormitory. Shells from the French side have made some large breaches in the wall. Rhubarb is growing among the ruins.

From the Villa Scolaire I stroll in among the dunes. . . . The fine sand blows over the hillocks whose outlines stand out against the blue sky like the snow-crowned crests of the Alps. Here and there is a bush of dune-catkins with their yellow flowers, otherwise only the fine, white, soft sand. It is like wandering in the clefts of one of the great Bernese glaciers, up and down, the sand sings as it blows and the waves splash. . . .

Soon one wanders down the sandy slope to the shore. There the foamy crests of the steel-blue billows roll to one's feet ; the cloudless spring sky stretches above the wide sheet of water ; the waves splash and prattle ; the shifting sand sings and hums ; the sun shines in midday splendour over the silent and solitary dunes. And the stormy-petrel shoots up into the air above the white, softly undulating crests, and away out into the distance over the sea. If one could but fly with him ! . . .

ERNST GÜNTER SCHALLERT, Student of Philosophy, Berlin

Born November 12th, 1892, in Berlin.
Killed May 24th, 1915, near Jaroslau.

Sechy, near Douai, January 10th, 1915.

MY DEAR PARENTS,—

Yesterday I wrote to you that Helmut was a little better. To-day you have only two sons left ! I went to Douai again to-day, to No. 1 Field Hospital. My first glance was towards his bed : it was empty and freshly made. This gave me a terrible shock. I looked round for the Sister, but she was not in the ward. I then asked a comrade who is there after Helmut. ' Yes, well, he'll be lying in one of the cemeteries here, but I don't know which.' That is how I learnt the sad news. . . .

We must all do our duty to the Fatherland. And we offer our sacrifice willingly and gladly. Out here we do not place a very high value on life, for every day we see a comrade bravely treading the same path. You, dear Parents, lose more, for you have cared for us for twenty years, but you offered us up gladly when we left you. Our struggle is for the Fatherland. Only if we devote our whole strength to the very last can we be victorious. So, dear Parents, do not grieve for your son. Think of the words : ' Greater love hath no man than this, that he lay down his life for his friends.' And of those other words of St. John : ' Be thou faithful unto death and I will give thee the crown of life.'

(100)

Plarona on the Biala, Galicia, April 27th, 1915.

When I laughingly called out to you as I was leaving that I was off to the Carpathians, I little thought how soon I should really be standing on a spur of those mountains !

On Sunday, April 18th, we had sudden orders : ' The Companies will entrain this afternoon.' Nobody knew where we were going, whether east or west ! We travelled right through Germany. When we reached Cassel, we thought we might be sure that we were bound for the eastern front. How the men rejoiced to find themselves in Germany again, and people greeted us with the greatest enthusiasm ! During the journey we still did not find out where we were going. Every few hours the engine-driver and guard were changed. So at last we got to Posen. Then we thought : now we are going straight to the east ! But the train turned and went south via Lissa to Breslau-Beuten. On Wednesday we were in Austria. Everybody who saw us waved violently and shouted : ' Hoch Deutschland ! Hoch Kaiser Wilhelm ! ' At noon we detrained at Hotwina Brzesco—we were in Galicia !

The day was hot ; the weather beautiful and as warm as it is with us in May or June. We marched on to the mountains. It was country like our German Mittel-Gebirge : woods of mixed pines, firs and deciduous trees ; well-cultivated fields on the slopes. But the inhabitants ! The houses ! Nothing but wooden hovels in which people and animals live all together with the lice and fleas. The Jews, who still go about here in their peculiar costume and with long beards, are distinguished from the real natives by being slightly more human. For the rest, their one idea is to get money out of our soldiers, who have come to protect them, as long as there is any to be got.

From the evening of the 22nd to early on the 26th we rested. The officers joined some Austrian gentlemen and had a very pleasant time ; the men bivouacked. The war has some delightful moments ; I enjoyed the march just as if it had been a walking-tour for pleasure. We marched right over the mountains. Down below us flowed the rushing stream of the Dunajec to join the Vistula, and in the far distance we could see, peeping over the wooded heights, the snow-crowned summit of the Tatra. In the evenings I enjoyed seeing the troops bivouacking. They lit great fires and lay round them singing. The moon was shining too. An Austrian doctor, who is also a total-abstainer, an officer of our battalion, and I used to go for delightful evening walks while the other gentlemen were paying their devotions to Bacchus. As the sunshine was so topping and a jolly little stream flowed through the district, I took the opportunity of having air and water baths, in which the doctor joined me. I made great friends with him and was sorry to part from him on the Monday.

Of course we are not here for fun, but in order to chuck the Russians out of Galicia. It won't be an easy job because of the mountains and rivers. All the same our chaps are as cheery as possible. We mean to get the Russians on the run and then to finish off the business. To-day we are moving up into the trenches. Then we shall get orders to attack, and we *shall* attack ! I have got myself a carbine and shall carry that. If I don't come back, think of what Pastor Rodatz said : ' If I am not in the triumphal entry, then sorrow not.' On the contrary, rejoice that you have been permitted to give two sons for the Fatherland ! But don't go imagining things from my letters. I have no pre-monition of death, am perfectly jolly and hope to survive to work for my ideals. But still I am not *over* keen on living. My life has been so beautiful that it may just as well end now.

HERBERT WEISSER, Student of Architecture, Technical High School, Charlottenburg

Born May 6th, 1894, at Lissa.
Killed May 25th, 1915, before Ypres.

5th Day of Mobilization.

CAN you believe that now I sometimes cannot get away from the thought that I shall be killed ? Then come quite close to me ! I lay my hand upon your curly head and speak to you. Then I feel as if a God-given strength went out from me and as if all my wishes for you must be realized. Come, let me look deep into your eyes ! I can see something burning there, but not for me ; that is not necessary, really not. That fire must develop into a constant, steady flame, and that flame shall guide your children along the road that we have conquered together. . . .

Do you know, I have always longed to be to the German people a true German Master-Builder ; I have always fought uncompromisingly against every form of sham, both in actual building and also in all that concerns our special German style. I wished to help to restore the art of German architecture such as it was in the time of the Ottos, and in the brickmaking-industry of the Mark.

I had hoped too to give to the German Fatherland a few boys and girls who would not be forced to waste their gifts in struggling vainly against their own instincts, as you and I have done, or in fighting against the overwhelming false prejudices of their time.

(104)

I stroke your hair gently, gently as one strokes the hair of the girl one loves, and I beg you not to forget all this ; to remember all your life what we have been through together and to see that our efforts bear fruit. . . . I wish, I most heartily wish, that your future may be as full of sunshine as you yourself can picture it ; that you may some day have a son, with blue far-seeing eyes, firmly fixed on a distant goal, who will grow tall and slim, with a noble brow and finely-cut nostrils—can you guess where he will get all that from ? And then, you know, it is not impossible that he may become an architect. Then you will tell him all about our German cathedrals and show him what real German master-builders have created ; how German architecture demonstrates an appreciation of what is grand and at the same time simple ; of all that is honest, logical and strong ; how it sends rays of light all over the world and how these rays are reflected back into the heavens in aspirations after the ideal. And then show him that man's whole interior life can also be full of beauty and sunshine if, instead of suppressing his own gifts, he perfects and ennobles them.

See, those are the things that I am thinking about before I go to the Front. And I am convinced that I could accomplish far more for the Fatherland along the lines in which I have already begun, and later on could produce much as the result of what I have absorbed during my youth. But we must not think of that now. Our present task is to defend all that German culture has built up through a thousand years of work, in toil and sweat and blood. But

8 (105)

one would be glad to leave some trace behind one when one disappears from this world. You are the one who, during all our professional studies and also otherwise in life, has stood closest to me and on whom my personality has had most influence, even if you were not perhaps the one whom I loved best—that you know—and if I am killed you must carry on my life with your own. We can no longer believe in a life beyond the grave, but we can survive in our works, which are chiefly preserved in our friends . . . perhaps you will find a life's companion who will help you in this.

6th Day of Mobilization.

My thoughts give me no peace, they carry me again and again to you. But you must not imagine, because I say that, that I am sitting here with my knees quaking at the thought of French or Russian bullets. On the contrary, I am not in the least afraid of *bullets*, but I am filled with bitterness and sorrow because so much youth and latent talent must be sacrificed by people simply because they cannot rise above their own contemptible envy and ill-will. It is a just retribution for not having conquered these weaknesses in themselves. But there are also people who have no such petty feelings, who have conquered them, and who could and so gladly would help others to do the same—they also are sacrificed. . . .

And then I am thinking about having to leave a widowed mother here. I have talked much with her lately about all these things, and I wish so much that you could make friends with her for my sake. My mother brought me up herself and has watched over me for twenty years. Besides, on account of her greater age and experience, she would be able to advise you in many ways, and you would be a joy to her as you are to me. Perhaps you could be a little comfort to her too if anything bad happens to me. All that could not be accomplished by letters —you would have to come and spend some time here, and you may be sure that that would be a great pleasure to my mother. She already guesses that we have been a great deal to one another, so she would give you a cordial welcome. And if you are fond of me, you would be fond of her, for although I have accomplished much by myself, still everything, or at any rate all my ideals, had their origin in her.

September 27th, 1914.

This longing for productivity after having been for twenty years merely receptive, makes it hard for me to think that my life is no longer my own. Whatever I may do in the war cannot be called production. . . . But, on the other hand, one cannot stand by and see the German people and all that they have created during hundreds of years destroyed by other nations. The only lightning-conductor is burning hatred and contempt for those few men— if they can still possibly be described by that name —who have brought the war about. Those people are lucky who can hold the enemy's whole nation responsible and believe that they are aiming their rifles at the actual culprits. I personally cannot feel any hatred against individual Frenchmen—on the contrary, I regret every young life which will be cut off through my instrumentality. Also I cannot rejoice unreservedly in our victories ; but do you know what I do thoroughly and boundlessly rejoice in ? In the German character, which now has an opportunity of exhibiting itself in shining splendour ; in the faultless functioning of the gigantic machine to which each individual can and does contribute ; in the discipline shown by our troops in their treatment of the inhabitants of enemy country ; in the eagerness with which each one works for the general good ; and in the firm, un-shakable sense of justice which is displayed on the German side on every occasion. The great strength of our noble people does not lie in wielding the sword, but in its sense of the high responsibility of making the best use of its gifts, and in its inner worth as the people of culture. Other nations can tear down and destroy in war, but we understand, better than any other, how to build up, and of this I have been certain only since the beginning of the war. Therefore I do not trouble much as to whether the war has a positive or negative end for us.

March 7th, 1915.

. . . Soon after our meeting at M. station, you wrote me a postcard in which you said that you tried to remove my ' pessimistic view ' of the war. At the end you added that you had perhaps mis-understood the reason of my low spirits. And really

—I will make an attempt to explain at least one thing : in 1870 the soldiers went into battle saying to themselves : ' If we don't get home we get heaven ' (I have to express myself briefly). Very few take that view now ; a great many don't consider the question at all ; others do, and then it depends on what sort of a religion they have worked out for themselves whether it is easier or harder for them to give up their young lives. Many abandon all claim on a future life after death—I am too young for that, and I did hope to survive in what I had created, and above all in the influence which I had exercised on the younger generation, in whom I should see realized all the results of my experience. Some men say : ' I am married and the father of five children, therefore I make a particularly great sacrifice for the Fatherland.' In their place I I should say : ' Thank God that I have a wife who has loved me and whom I have loved, and still more that I have five children who will continue to develop in accordance with my ideas and will justify my existence. Otherwise my position would have been merely receptive and would only have influenced my own and perhaps the previous generation—even the former very imperfectly.' That was what depressed me, personally.

Then came the objective view : our nation was, as I believe, on the right road towards self-regeneration from within, though the powers which were to bring about this regeneration were very limited, Now comes the war, tears everything out of the process of being and developing, and deprives us of just what we most needed—the youth of the present generation, who were growing up with progressive ideas.

I also imagined beforehand, what I now find abundantly confirmed : that the notions which our parents, our books and our history lessons had given us of war are either entirely false, or at least incomplete and therefore misleading. We were given to understand that heroic deeds were of the essence and the most frequent result of war. But is that so ? How many such actions are in any case simply brought about by the impulse of the moment, perhaps by the bloodthirstiness and unjust hatred which a nation's political views spread among all its members and for which they have to suffer ? Of course there are many quiet, unobserved acts of heroism, but are these really so much rarer in time of peace ? And what of the drunkenness, the brutality both in the æsthetic and ethical sense ; the spiritual and physical slothfulness, when does one ever hear of them in accounts of war ? And the slack ideas with regard to morality and marriage, what about them ? All this was going through my mind at that time. It was no slack disinclination that I felt, but a profound sadness which nevertheless was just as productive of determined action as the enthusiasm of other (better ?) men.

April 6th, 1915.

Yesterday I was in the trenches. There I have at last been able to see what war is really like. The whole business is enacted on one narrow, though certainly endless, strip of ground, which seems much, much too narrow for its gigantic significance. And this strip of ground bears grass, many coloured flowers, trees, and pretty little houses. The ground rises and falls gently, the green fields are intersected by hedges and streams. But do you know what else is in these meadows ? The Marburg Jaegers, students and professors, the hope and impetus towards progress of the German people. One beside the other they lie, stretched out upon the grass.

Yes—among them I saw one quite young fellow, right in front, perhaps the foremost in the attack. Forgetting everything around him he dashed forward, charging amid a hail of bullets : ' One more spring and I shall be in the enemy trench ! ' But he was not able to complete the thought, for three yards from the trench he fell, and perhaps had time to see that it was all in vain, that the attack had failed ; perhaps he lived for another day and slowly died of hunger, because there, in ' no-man's-land ', nobody could come to his assistance.

You ask if I am happy ? I can't honestly answer that I am. But I believe that in three to five years I shall be able to realize the grandeur of this time, and then I shall be glad about it. My imagination is overpowered at present, almost like that of a child to whom its nurse is telling gruesome fairy-tales.

That does not of course prevent me in any way from doing my duty, and even doing it with a kind of enjoyment—as, for instance, yesterday when, during an attack from our side, I was close behind the trench, mending the telephone-wire, under gun- and rifle-fire, with two others. We were without any means of communicating with our troops, and did not know how the battle was going and whether we might not at any moment be cut off by the French. Unarmed ! And when, in a hail of bullets, one has to climb up into a tree instead of hiding underground, then one feels that one is young, laughs a little in one's sleeve, and almost fancies oneself invulnerable !

Those are fine moments and I have often experienced them just lately. You have of course read in the newspapers about our advance here. We are just in the most frantic corner and are the first who have broken through, away from that tedious sticking in one position. But then one sees the long, long processions of wounded ; the dead bodies on the battle-fields ; one sees the spiritual and moral effects of war ; the burning villages and everything ; so it is easier for you at home to go on feeling happy than for us.

Flanders, May, 1915. [*On hearing of the death of a comrade.*]

DEAR MOTHER,—

Everybody who goes to the front is prepared for a lonely death. There is nothing so very horrible in that. Death is no longer horrible when it comes close to one. The only thing that makes it hard to die is the knowledge that one's relations are tormenting themselves by imagining the most ghastly situations, of which the one that seems to them the worst is in reality the most splendid, even though it may be the last hour of our life. What is there so very dreadful in lying alone on the field of battle and knowing that the end is near? It is not dreadful at all. One can feel calm and peaceful as one has never been since childhood. In thinking of the death of a son, you should regard it as calmly and without horrible details as the son himself will. By not doing so, you pour a drop of bitterness into the last hour of his life.

ARTHUR, COUNT von der GROEBEN, Doctor of Philosophy, Freiburg i. B.

Born April 26th, 1882, at Frankfurt-on-the-Oder.
Killed May 26th, 1915, near Jaroslau, Galicia.

Château Boncourt, near Douai, March 19th, 1915.

I AM living here in what the owner calls a ' Château '. It is a not-bad rococo building of 1765. A well-laid-out park, with what, for France, are fine trees, lies before me when I look out of the window. In the park are some quite interesting things. A stone obelisk is said to mark the spot where the gallows used to stand, for the Barons Bequet de Mégille had the right of inflicting capital punishment. This right they evidently valued so highly that they wished to have the symbol of it always before their eyes, for they could not escape seeing the gallows every time they walked in the park. Not far off, a rococo Diana testifies to the apparently not exacting artistic tastes of the original owners. Perhaps she stands in direct relation to the gallows, for in pre-Revolutionary France the game-laws were somewhat Draconic—whoever shot a rabbit belonging to the Seigneur may have risked his neck, and rabbits abound in the park to this day.

The Baron Bequet also laid out his Petit-Trianon in the form of an artificially ruined summer-house. I can imagine that about 1780 the people here led just such a life as that of M. Brotteaux des Islettes in Anatole France's *Les dieux ont soif.* Later generations have most culpably spoiled the outside of the house by tasteless additions. Altogether one gets the impression here that good taste in France, at least in the provinces, is a thing of the past. The old buildings, old furniture, and old bric-à-brac are often beautiful, pretty, charming—but everything new is abominable.

Sadowa, Galicia, April 25th, 1915.

DEAR FATHER,—

. . . I really am looking forward to an encounter with the enemy. I can really say that without exaggeration. And it surpasses all my expectations that I am to be allowed to lead a troop. God grant that I may do it to the benefit of the Fatherland. I hope to meet you again with the glad consciousness of having at last been of some use ; but if I do not see you, you and Mother, again, then I hope you will be able to think of me as a member of the family who, at any rate at the last, kept up its traditions. I have never in all my life been so happy as I am now, and I thank you, dear Father, and I thank Mother too, for it, because it is the example which you have given me and your training which have made me, finally at least, capable of becoming a Prussian soldier and officer. Please greet all the family for me in case I am not able to do it myself.

Galicia, May 8th, 1915.

That was a wonderful picture upon which I looked on the evening of May 1st. The sun had set behind the wonderful, glittering, pink-tinged peaks of the

Tatra, and I thought I had never seen a wood so flooded with gold and colour as the one where I sat upon a slope carpeted with violets, buttercups and daisies ; but everything was perhaps transfigured by the idea that it might not impossibly be my last evening on earth. For I was not alone. Five of us were sitting there, and one, the Battalion-Commander, was just dictating words which immediately concerned me : ' Punctually at 10 a.m., precisely according to time to be previously synchronized, the 8th Company will storm Hill 382, Hill 376, and so on. Hill 382 and its obstructions are sufficiently known to you.' That certainly was quite true, because for a number of days in succession the 8th Company, which I command, had been taking turns with another in a strip of trench which had been first Russian and then Austrian and which ended 80 yards from Hill 382, where there were three Russian trenches, one behind the other.

I stayed awake the whole night, because the Russians, made nervous by the constant firing of our guns, were shooting so continuously at my trench that I almost feared a Russian attack during the night—or I might say *hoped for*, because it would not have had any luck.

Punctually at 6 in the morning began the hellish concert. The German and Austrian artillery had got the range exactly during the previous days, and shells and shrapnel came roaring over, each with its own peculiar sound—howling, singing, whistling, booming, ear-splittingly crashing—into the Russian position. The particularly loathsome grey-black smoke of bursting shells below, white puffs of German shrapnel above, white and red clouds of Austrian explosive, smothered the Russian trenches, from which came a continuous rattle of rifle-fire and the regular ticking of machine-guns.

The quarter of an hour from 9.45 till 10 seemed endless to me as I lay in one of the attack-openings of my trench, with my watch in my hand and my leader's whistle in my mouth. Every now and then a grenadier whispered in an unusually confidential manner : ' Isn't it nearly time, Herr Graf ? ' ' No, still five—still two—still one and a half minutes.' Then—three piercing whistles and I remember nothing more but a mad rush forward, wild cheering, screams of fear from the absolutely overwhelmed Russians, while I yelled my orders—till I found myself sitting in a wood and writing, yes, writing, the correct official report : ' To Captain von B., commanding the 2nd Company, 4th Foot Guards. Have just taken Hill 382. Casualties slight. Am now advancing farther. Count Groeben, Lieut. and Company-Commander.'

On again. Suddenly, just in front of Hill 376, there is an explosion. I fall on my face ; so does the Platoon-Commander beside me ; thick tree-trunks snap like reeds ; the horrible grey-black smoke from two bursting shells smothers everything ; either our own artillery or the Austrian don't know that we have already advanced so far and we are in our own barrage ! Thank God, it was only the force of the explosion that knocked us down. The bayonet of one of the carbineers was shattered and a small splinter from it got me in the face. Sent a man flying back with another report. On again. Hill 376 is taken !

Whom have I still got with me ? Some soldiers of the Augusta Regiment and a stray Lieutenant from another Company. I bawl : ' Every one takes orders from me ! Half-right of the opening in the wood, Range 1200/1100, fire !—Too far !—Range 1000/1100, fire quicker, quicker ! ! ' My voice cracks, I make a whistling noise—try to shout again —to fire—to storm farther—everything now is a confused memory. Machine-guns arrive—the Lieutenant in command begs me to cover him as we have the Russian front, now broken, on both sides of us. He sends a few more sharp greetings after the wildly retreating grey-green mass. Then we gradually reorganize, actually far beyond what was fixed as the furthest point of attack. My first feeling was not one of triumph but a fear of getting ' told off '. But all the same—600 prisoners, three machine-guns, etc.

Just received orders to move to Hill 357 and attack northward from there, so must end and say—perhaps —good-bye.

FRITZ MEESE, Medical Candidate,[1] Berlin

Born September 11th, 1891, at Coblentz.
Killed May 26th, 1915, near the Loretto Hill.

November, 1914.

. . . For the last week in a trench which is a mere
ruin through which water flows in wet weather—
stiff with clay and filth, and thereby supposed to
protect us from the awful shell-fire. A feeble
human defence against powerful forces. I am still
alive and unwounded though my pack and my
clothes are torn to rags by bullets. I can't say that
I am enjoying myself, but I have not lost my sense
of humour. Pray for fine weather and food for me,
for wet and hunger are the worst enemies. You
simply can have no idea what it is like, to be in the
trenches for days and weeks on end under enemy
fire. Never again shall I be able to shout a thought-
less ' hurrah ' in a café at the news of a victory—oh
the poor patriots !

I have been on sentry-duty for five hours and shall
probably be awake all night, but, anyhow, to sleep
standing up or half sitting on the wet clay is a very
doubtful pleasure. My letter has of course been
written like this : five words and then a long look
at the enemy, now and then up with the ' cannon '
and a shot.

Boys, you don't realize how well off we were in
Berlin ! Truly and honestly, if I ever felt inclined
to moralize about my past life, every such thought

[1] See p. 77.

has vanished now. I am quite convinced that everybody who gets home safe and sound will be a totally different fellow in every way. He will certainly be more considerate towards other people, especially in the matter of exploiting them for his own ends. The habit of comradeship necessitated by the war will have that result.

Life here isn't worth a damn, one thinks nothing of losing it. To-day, for instance, I walked for half an hour through violent rifle-fire just to have a wash and because I hoped to get one or two cigarettes. . . .

December, 1914.

. . . Had a few pleasant hours in billets to-day at coffee-time. Some comrades got a big parcel. There was singing. Thoughts of home. One becomes a child again here in the war. At one moment under the most terrific fire, at the next innocently gay. Happy the man who knows how to live in the mood of the present moment, paying no heed to the next. One learns to do that. Outside the enemy thunder growls, and inside it is like home—almost !

Boys, how one gets to love one's home when one has learnt to bear what one would otherwise never have imagined possible ! One can never tell what are the little things that weigh most upon different individuals, nor can one, on the other hand, explain what are the things which are shaping us and chiselling such deep impressions on our characters. Anybody who can send home high-flown accounts of life

(120)

at the Front has had no real experience of it. If one could describe actual facts ! But one can never write about things as they really are, and, and, thank God, the next minute brings relief. One would have to write at the actual moment, and that's not possible, thank God. Therefore nobody will ever know how despairing one sometimes feels and yet how, in the midst of that depression, one is revived by a mixture of duty, necessity and ambition. So it must go on. . . .

My dear friend Ernst is missing. There it stands, short and plain, and yet I felt a lump in my throat when I read it. Poor dear chap—Missing ! that is a terrible word to anybody who understands what it means. It brings old pictures to my mind. I am lying before Dixmuide, in the evening of October 21st. We have been repulsed, nobody knows how. In front of us is a farm and on the right the road, as far as which we had advanced as gaily confident of victory as if on the parade-ground. Forward we went, step by step, upright too, too proud to duck before the continuous whistle of bullets. Then suddenly we were lying in the front line with our machine-gun. Our Corporal was killed beside me. On my right J. was shot in the arm and I got a bullet through my mess-tin. So we lay, behind a hedge ; were supposed to fire, but could see no enemy. Then came the order : ' Up, march, march into the farm ! ' There a metallic song was whistling and singing among the branches, the house was burning, and behind what was left of the wall where Jaegers and the 201st, while

9   (121)

machine-gun fire was crumbling the wall, stone by stone. I tied up first N. and then R. with the Field Service dressing which could only with difficulty be compressed (he is running round Berlin to-day hardly realizing that I saved his life with that bandage). We went farther on, getting into complete disorder, no officers left and comrades falling in rows. Still we went on (for nobody dreamt in those days that we could possibly not be winning), till suddenly—tick—tack—our own machine-guns firing at our backs, and that finished us. Back, bitterly disappointed, grinding our teeth. And then, from behind the last straw-stack, we heard the cries of badly wounded comrades lying still under heavy fire. Two comrades and I crawled out in spite of the fire but couldn't get them in. Then we went back a bit farther and dug ourselves in where we were, still waiting for the enemy to be repulsed. And between us and the enemy, under fire from both, lay the wounded. . . . Weeks later, when we had advanced again, I came upon them, on patrol, and had to crawl over them—rows of dead bodies.

FRITZ FRANKE, Student of Medicine, Berlin

Born December 31st, 1892, at Munich.
Killed May 29th, 1915, near Kelmy on the Dubissa.

Louve, November 5th, 1914.

YESTERDAY we didn't feel sure that a single one of us would come through alive. You can't possibly picture to yourselves what such a battle-field looks like. It is impossible to describe it, and even now, when it is a day behind us, I myself can hardly believe that such bestial barbarity and unspeakable suffering are possible. Every foot of ground contested ; every hundred yards another trench ; and everywhere bodies—rows of them ! All the trees shot to pieces ; the whole ground churned up a yard deep by the heaviest shells ; dead animals ; houses and churches so utterly destroyed by shell-fire that they can never be of the least use again. And every troop that advances in support must pass through a mile of this chaos, through this gigantic burial-ground and the reek of corpses.

In this way we advanced on Tuesday, marching for three hours, a silent column, in the moonlight, towards the Front and into a trench as Reserve, two to three hundred yards from the English, close behind our own infantry.

There we lay the whole day, a yard and a half to two yards below the level of the ground, crouching in the narrow trench on a thin layer of straw, in an overpowering din which never ceased all day or the greater part of the night—the whole ground tremb-

(123)

ling and shaking ! There is every variety of sound —whistling, whining, ringing, crashing, rolling . . . the beastly things pitch right above one and burst and the fragments buzz in all directions, and the only question one asks is : ' Why doesn't one get me ? ' Often the things land within a hand's breadth and one just looks on. One gets so hardened to it that at the most one ducks one's head a little if a great, big naval-gun shell comes a bit too near and its grey-green stink is a bit too thick. Otherwise one soon just lies there and thinks of other things. And then one pulls out the Field Regulations or an old letter from home, and all at once one has fallen asleep in spite of the row.

Then suddenly comes the order : ' Back to the horses. You are relieved ! ' And one runs for a mile or so, mounts, and is a gay trooper once more ; hola, away, through night and mist, in gallop and in trot !

One just lives from one hour to the next. For instance, if one starts to prepare some food, one never knows if one mayn't have to leave it behind within an hour. If you lie down to sleep, you must always be ' in Alarm Order '. On the road, you have just to ride behind the man in front of you without knowing where you are going, or at the most only the direction for half a day.

All the same, there is a lot that is pleasant in it all. We often go careering through lovely country in beautiful weather. And above all one acquires a knowledge of human nature ! We all live so naturally and unconventionally here, every one according to his own instincts. That brings much that is good and much that is ugly to the surface, but in every one there is a large amount of truth, and above all strength—strength developed almost to a mania !

Gorze, March 26th, 1915.

. . . It will be a big undertaking for our whole nation—and especially for our Parliamentary Parties —after peace is restored to draw practical results from our spiritual experience, and success will be only partial.

GEORG STILLER, Commercial High School, Berlin

Born September 20th, 1895.
Killed May 29th, 1915, near the Heights of Combres.

Sunday, May 16th, 1915.

TO-DAY I am sitting in the worst position on the Hill of Combres. It is Sunday ; elsewhere there is rest and peace ; here the murdering goes on—everlasting shells, shrapnel and rifle-fire. Nature wears its most beautiful spring dress, the sun laughs from the blue tent of heaven, but through blossoming, green-growing Nature fly the shells, destroying trees and fresh bushes, tearing deep holes in the earth, and annihilating young, blossoming human lives.

I have performed my Sunday devotions to-day, a thing I very seldom did in. time of peace. One learns to pray again here and to cling to one's dear God. Here one first discovers what a support in time of need and danger is a real, fervent faith, and how comforting and soothing a hymn or a psalm can be. If the good God spares my life, if He brings me safely through the war, then I will always be His faithful, devoted disciple. It is a strange thing about the human heart—when danger is nearest, God is greatest—which I should express less bluntly by saying that so long as all goes well with a man he does not think of asking God to guide his actions and ways, but if he is in danger he suddenly remembers that he has a support to which he can cling. I don't want to make myself out better than I am, but that is how it has been with me. Since leaving school I had arranged a religion for myself, just what happened to suit me, without reference to my conscience or my deepest convictions. Danger has brought me near to my God again. I believe that this has been the experience of many others who also had thoughtlessly forgotten God and their religion, but who now, through death and danger, have regained their faith. And this will be not least among the advantages gained through the gigantic World War—it has deprived us of so much that we held dear, but it will also be productive of much good. After the war there will be a deepening of religious feeling and people will be simpler and more devout.

ADOLF WITTE, Student of Philosophy, Berlin

Born July 2nd, 1890, in Berlin.
Killed June 13th, 1915, near Chaplupki, Galicia.

Lewarde, January 6th, 1915.

AT midnight the fun begins. ' All out ! Leave
packs ! Fall in ! ' We scramble out. ' Across the
road at the double ! ' That tells us that we have
got to take the trench on the right of the shell-
wrecked road, which the French had occupied
during the absence of our men. A break-through
had to be prevented and the red-legs driven back
to their hole.

January 7th, 1915, 5 *p.m.*

On the right of the Menin-Ypres road. ' Fall in !
In file ; right turn ; march ! Avoid all noise !
Keep touch ! ' So off we go, in the pitch-black,
cold night. Where to ? Orientation gone to pot !
I stump valiantly along behind the man in front of
me through all the shell-holes and slush.

' Halt ! Fix bayonets ! ' Softly the order is
passed along from man to man ; back from the
wing comes the response : ' *Order received.*' ' Left
turn ! Take touch ! [1] ' As far as I can see on
both sides of me the bayonets are bristling from the
rifles. [1] ' Cloth-touching, slowly forward ! ' Humph,
I say to myself, that's evidently so that no bullet

[1] Orders which have no exact equivalent in the British
Army have been translated literally.

(128)

from over there shall have a chance to get past us ;
but the soldier does as he is told. Half upright, half
stooping, the line goes on a little way.

'Halt! Lie down!' It is whispered down the
file. Now we are all lying close to one another.
Behind us are the reserves. A few arrangements
are made ; to the left and right further sections
are added.

'What on earth are we at?' I whisper to my
neighbours. 'How should I know?' one answers ;
the other is asleep. Well, I settle myself down as
comfortably as I can. It just happens not to have
rained that day, and we are lying in a fairly dry
spot.

'The troops will advance, cloth-touching! Pass
it along!' '*The troops will advance, cloth-touching!
Pass it along!*' 'Order received! Order received!'
(All in a whisper.) ('If only one knew, Neighbour,
what we are to do when we get to the enemy—are
we to hop into the trench and whack around, or
stand on the edge and bang at him, or what?')
'If flares go up, lie still!' '*If flares go up, lie still!*'
'Order received! Order received!' 'Up! Up!
Up!' The file crawls slowly forward under cover.
'Don't lose touch on the right!' 'Give way on
the left!' 'By the right!' ('*Cursed squash!*'
'*Shut your jaw!*') 'Lie down! Lie down! Lie
down!' . . .

For a good two hours we lay there on the bare
ground. I kept shivering and trying to pull the
skirts of my coat over my knees. The man next to
me was of course asleep again. . . . 'Here, you!'

(129)

. . . The first flare goes up opposite ! Heads down ! Of course a few fools must needs look up and watch the damned thing. It slowly dies out. Everything quiet over there. (Are we still so far away that they haven't seen us, or are we under cover ?) . . . Pscht ! . . . Another one ! All dark again. I try, as best I can, to do physical jerks on the ground so as not to get stiff—kick out my legs and so on.

' Hi, when the Pioneers throw bombs, everybody up and off ! ' ' Here you, wake up and pass it along : *when the Pioneers throw bombs . . .*' ' All right, *when the Pioneers throw bombs . . .*' (If one did but know how much farther it is ! Everything is so still, and yet we can't be far away—one doesn't charge for hundreds of yards !) . . . Pscht ! . . . another flare ! I squint up at it too. It really looks very pretty ; a thing like that makes everything as light as day for quite a long way. Well, anyhow we must be still quite a long way off or the red-legs would be bound to see us and then they'd fire. . . .

The jostling and pushing and cursing start again. As far as possible direction is preserved. Stop, there's a trench slanting across in front of us ! The left wing is already over. One behind the other, we hop after them. Our centre is barely over when—ping, ping !—the first shots from opposite ! It is all dark. . . . ' Up ! ' Pscht ! . . . another flare ! And then hell breaks loose ! Whole salvos crash and the air seems full of hailstones. Everybody starts to run. . . . Pscht ! . . . a light ! . . . In

(130)

long files to my right are the attacking comrades. The left wing was somewhat delayed by the trench. I run a few steps. . . . Flare ! . . . (You must lie down !) Here and there others are already down on their bellies and crawling forward. . . . So am I. . . . On the right : ' Hurrah, hurrah ! ' . . . I'm up. Hurrah ! . . . A Verey light. Down again and crawl ! . . . Ssst ! . . . Krrrch ! . . . Shells right into the middle of the files. Damn ! . . . Ssst ! . . . Krrrch ! . . . They are getting nearer. No matter, crawl on ! The enemy fire makes a fearful noise. It's all dark. No more cheering to be heard, only the sound of firing. I remain lying down. Ssst ! . . . ssst ! . . . the bullets keep coming, thicker and lower. What's to be done ? . . . Pscht ! . . . Verey light. I press close against the ground and look about me.

Close by a good many men are lying motionless. There is one writhing and groaning. Well, now ? Am I to go on attacking ? I have no idea of the direction. The bullets are coming from several sides. No orders are to be heard. Not a living comrade anywhere near. Thirty to fifty yards from the enemy's rifle-barrels. . . . I choose the better part of valour, discretion, and for the time being remain quietly where I am. Some day the gentlemen over there will lame their fingers with firing. They can't see anything, anyhow.

All this time it is whistling unpleasantly all round me. Psst ! Dash it all, the dirty beast, right in front of my nose into the muck ! I try to flatten myself out if possible yet a little more, and feel for

(131)

my spade. It's gone. Well, anyhow I seem to be fairly safe as I lie, perhaps there's a little lump in the ground, however small ; or else I am so close to the enemy that they are shooting over me !

Just think—a Volunteer, with twelve weeks' training, accustomed to do nothing without orders, lying among dead and wounded, thirty yards from the enemy . . . there are Volunteers here the ' silly asses, damned fools '—what is anyone like that to do ? Naturally he tries if possible to get out of the mess. That was the way my thoughts ran on, and I was already smothering the noble impulses which urged me to stop, to get up, to look for a superior officer. Not much ! . . . But this was disgraceful ! I, a Prussian, with a rifle in my hand—that only lasted a moment ; discretion got the upper hand again. So it went on, first one way and then the other. Have I really decided right ? . . . Yes, they ought to have told me what I was supposed to be doing. No distance given— darkness—the others all throwing themselves down —well, anyhow there was nothing to be done now. I was certainly puzzled as to what had become of my comrade. I had heard nothing of any order to close up again. . . .

I don't know how long I lay there motionless. The firing seemed to be gradually dying down. Slowly, very slowly, I wriggled along sideways, more or less in the direction of the trench that we had had to cross while attacking. From there I should be able to get on, or at least to get a certain amount of cover. Strange, now I begin to feel a little nervous about being seen. After all, it's a beastly thing to funk. . . . I get as far as the trench—roll myself up on to the parapet and fall full length, plump, into the water and on top of several others who are already there! Slightly and badly wounded are lying and sitting about, and some unwounded too. Just the right place for me! No N.C.O.; nobody knows what's happening. The bullets are whistling from right and left into the parapet. Everybody makes himself as small as possible. The wounded groan and implore us not to leave them there. Then somebody asks whether we oughtn't to try and get back to the rest from here, where we are nearest to the road, into which the trench leads. I don't feel better until I have helped a comrade to carry a wounded Corporal in, right across the French field of rifle- and shell-fire. Then I can persuade myself that I have done something, anyhow. The first man I tried to bring in was shot dead in my arms. . . .

The next morning the survivors gradually collect in billets. The Captain is wounded, the Sergeant-Major and goodness knows how many men are missing—I think thirty of our company, not counting wounded. Repulsed! Shall we advance again? Two days later the trench was taken after a sufficient preparation by artillery and trench-mortars, etc.

June 11th, 1915. *Laszky, in Galicia.*

This morning, inspection of the position, sleeping, eating, writing. To-night the 11th and 12th

Companies are to cross the Sklo, dig themselves in and attack to-morrow at 10. a.m.

I am again troubled with anxious forebodings. I can't believe that this show is going to be a success. I am always getting into this state. Is it the instinct of self-preservation ? Fear is, after all, nothing but the anticipation of an approaching evil which one can hardly hope to avoid by caution. I look at my sound limbs, hear the crashing of shrapnel, the whizzing of the fragments of metal, and can't help imagining the way such a thing could injure me too. I have seen the sort of wounds that such things can inflict. Metal against human flesh ! And with the feeling of fear is the shudderingly sweet premonition of death which one doesn't want to believe in but which one can't escape. The best way to get over these feelings is to express them all in writing as I am doing now. Then one gradually feels better. The dissection of melancholy sensations seems to cure them. I feel better already and hope I shall get rid of them altogether. I want to go on living ! If that does not sound too presumptuous !

WALTER LANGE, Student of Philosophy, Berlin

Born January 5th, 1895, at Charlottenburg.
Died August 13th, 1915, in the Field Hospital at Zaglemboki,
of wounds received August 11th, near Orrechow Nowy.

June 18th, 1915.

MANY thanks for the beautiful page out of your art-calendar. It reminds me of a dream I had last night. I was at home, and everything was just as it used to be, we were all so merry, and even my art-calendar exhibited the same leaf as on the last day. Then I went up to it and, with the greatest curiosity, pulled off all the pages that I had missed during the war, an occupation to which I devoted myself with much enjoyment for a long time. Then we had coffee and cakes.

I am always dreaming such strange things now. A little while ago, I thought I was sitting having coffee with Christel Strohman, as I so often did in time of peace. We were in a very remarkable room, small but quite up-to-date in its appointments. There was no paper on the walls, but they were covered with some sort of stuff, fixed on by strips of beading, and hung with a few small pictures. On both sides were doorways, or rather openings in the walls. I describe it all so exactly because every detail impressed itself so strangely on my mind. Well, I was sitting there with Christel and talking. I could not get rid of an uncomfortable feeling for which I could not account. At last the question escaped me : ' But how is this possible ?

(**135**)

You were killed long ago !' 'Yes, of course I was,' he answered, smiling, 'and so were you. All the people you see here have been killed, and the man and woman who have just gone by were God and his wife.'

What do you think of such a curious dream ? Is it a premonition ?

ULRICH TIMM, Student of Theology, Rostock

Born June 19th, 1897, at Pritzier, Mecklenburg.
Killed June 20th, 1915, near Zurawno, Galicia.

October 23rd, 1914.

OF our battalion 125 men—that is, an eighth part —have already been killed, and the same thing may happen to any of us. Oh, my Parents, whom I love more than everything, last night, when I couldn't sleep because of the violent fighting going on outside, my thoughts flew to you both at home. Who knows, perhaps I shall never see you again, and so I want to thank you, from the bottom of my heart, for all the love and devotion you have shown me all my life. I realize more and more what a beautiful youth I have had in my parents' house and that nobody ever had such dear parents as mine.

Flanders, end of October, 1914.

The bullet came from the right front, went first through my right leg, then through the left leg, and finally through my pocket, which was stuffed with fifty field-postcards, my New Testament, your last letter, my pay-book, and a lot of other small books. Through all this the bullet went, so it must have been travelling with considerable velocity ! The wounds only hurt badly during the first few hours ; after that, and now, very little.

The whole of October 23rd we had been lying as Artillery Cover by the village of Merkem, not far from Dixmuide. In the evening, a little before 7, came a request from the infantry in front of us for support, as they wanted to storm the enemy position. Immediately we swarmed out of our trench, fixed bayonets and doubled to the attack, ' Hurrah, Hurrah ! '

It was a complete failure, for, in the first place, there were more of our own men in front of us, being constantly fired at not only by the enemy opposite but by their own comrades in the rear. Not a few were killed by German bullets during those days. In the second place we were still a mile or more away from the enemy position when we began storming, so that we were tired before the attack really started.

After we had stormed through a thicket and some fields of roots and crossed a broad, deep trench (not without risking our lives, for the bullets were whistling past our ears), we were supposed to capture a wide, exposed hill. I was quite prepared to stick my bayonet into the body of the first Englishman I could see, when suddenly I was seized by some irresistible force and hurled to the ground. For a moment I didn't know where I was, but I soon pulled myself together. Hallo ! what's happened ? Aha, you've caught it, there's blood running out of your trousers ! Just try and see if you can stand up. Quite all right. It can't be so bad then, but get down again quickly or you may catch it again. So, now what shall I do ? Aha, there's a straw-stack ten yards away ! I'll crawl under there ! It's not so easy. Quite a lot of men there already, wounded and unwounded Jaegers. ' Hi, Comrade, just tie a rag round my legs ! So, thank you.' But now to groan a bit, for it really hurts confoundedly. ' Hallo, Schliemann, are you wounded too ? ' ' Yes, can't see out of one eye. I'm going to the dressing-station.' ' Then send help to me and my comrades, we can't walk.'

The unwounded continued the attack. It grew quieter round us. I look at the time : nearly 8 o'clock. Will help come ? No—we waited in vain till next morning.

When it got light we saw stretcher-bearers collecting wounded a few hundred yards away. We shouted. ' Coming to you directly.' But they did not return. We waited in vain till the evening : it was horrible. One who could still walk a little, started off. He had hardly gone a hundred yards when I saw him fall. Those damned snipers !

Another long, anxious night. At midnight I woke suddenly out of a doze. Now what's happening ? We were lying in the middle of shell- and rifle-fire. ' Comrades, get closer to the stack ! Don't anybody raise himself up ! ' An appalling uproar all round us—terrible ! I shall never forget it as long as I live. It is gruesome when a shell bursts right over you like that. And then the fear that the stack would be set on fire. I have never prayed as I did that night. And so it passed. . . . So did the next battle at 4 o'clock.

The weather next day was beautiful. But it was our second day between the English and German lines. We were in the greatest danger ! The man next to me got a shell-splinter added to his body-wound during the night. The others were also badly wounded. Then I thought I'd try if I could stand, and lo ! I succeeded. Well then, I'll try my luck ! And I got safely as far as the trench which was strewn with bodies. Opposite, a little way off, I could see Germans in their trench. ' Don't fire ! I'm wounded, help ! ' And they came and brought me to the dressing-station and then fetched the others too. I thanked God that I was saved. I had lain out there from Friday evening to Sunday morning.

HANS MARTENS, Technical Student, Charlottenburg

Born September 23rd, 1892.
Killed July 14th, 1915, near Rudnicki, on the Szlota Lipa.

February 4th, 1915.

IT won't be long now before I am at the Front again, thank God ! I'd rather be in the filthiest trench than here—one doesn't notice all the suffering so much out there. My one and only wish is that I may at last really *do* something in a battle ! For when you simply stand in a trench and mayn't move, while shells and trench-mortars keep coming over, well, that may be fighting but far from *doing anything* : it is the exact and horrible opposite. And that is the disgusting part of this war : it's all so mechanical ; one might call it the trade of systematic manslaughter. One takes part in it out of enthusiasm for the object, while hating and despising the means one is forced to employ to attain that object.

The trench-mortars which both sides have recently introduced are the most abominable things of all. They fire noiselessly and a single one often kills as many as 30 men. One stands in the trench, and at any moment a thing like that may burst. The only consolation when one sees the awful explosion made by ours, which is so terrific that sometimes fragments fly back as far as our own parapet, is that in this case too our productions are more effective than those of the French.

Very few people have the chance of doing any-

(141)

thing active out here, and I regret that so far I have not been one of them.

Döberitz, May 12th, 1915.

. . . To-morrow is Ascension Day ! And I imagine you lying in a meadow beside the brook, letting the May wind play about your brow and gazing into the blue, spring sky, while ranunculus and foam-weed have nothing better to do than to form the gaily coloured frame for this charming picture.

Hey, presto ! there I am on the grass beside you ! And now you must put up with my company for an hour of blissful idleness. If you want pleasant conversation, however, in addition to sunshine, shade and meadow flowers, you will have to provide it yourself, for the fellow beside you is in a state of too great inward disorder and confusion—sparkling fancies ; crumbling, cobwebby hopes ; dreary, harsh principles ; wistful memories ; vain dreams —all these things are heaped up anyhow in the lumber-room of his soul, and as the said poor soul has only this one small storage-place, there is not much room for peace, confidence, and the like.

Perhaps you have sometimes stood before the entrance to the grounds of some beautiful castle, and as the gate was open you have innocently stepped in and admired the shady walks, the gay flower-beds and the gleaming marble statues ; and then suddenly an extremely dignified porter appeared and said morosely : ' No admittance.

Kindly move on ! ' And, bang ! he shuts the gate and stands in front of it with his legs well apart so that you may see as little as possible of the forbidden ground ; and feeling much mortified you go on your way, while gay voices from inside the garden ring out behind you.

That is like what has happened to me this year with the spring. I have always gone away some-where at this season of the year and the most delight-ful hours have been those when, like you, I could lie in a meadow and enjoy life in retrospect, in actual consciousness and in anticipation. And this year ? I have walked in the beech-woods of the town, I have lain upon the green grass, and the sky was as blue as in any other year, but I could not enjoy it —everything seemed different and sober thoughts soon arose in my mind and drove me away.

When I went to the war I said to myself quite simply : I have finished with everything, I don't hope to come back, I regard my future life as leave granted me by death ; but if after all I do come back, I will begin a new, a nobler life. Yes, I thought in those days, in a few weeks you will either be no longer here or the war will be over, and now ? Leave granted by death ? Yes, one can take a few days or weeks, but what about a year or longer ? To go on in the world in perfect in-difference, enjoying nothing, complaining about nothing, to loosen all old ties and make no new ones, and to think of nothing but war, and always war. Good heavens, it's impossible, nobody could ever stand it. I still have warm blood in my veins and

(143)

the sun still shines so brightly ; and I get up and
wander out into the spring-time :

> ' For May is here,
>> The trees are bursting into leaf,
>>> Who knows but in the distance
>>> Happiness dawns for me——'

But then from the mountains comes the echo,
the words sound differently as they are borne back
to my ears, and from the dark pines the message
comes : ' Yesterday still upon noble steeds . . .'
And I go in again and drearily study my Handbook
of Machine-gun-Company Drill.

Rudnicki, July 13th, 1915. [*The eve of his death.*]

To-day I have had a very snug dug-out made
for me, and at last some straw has arrived. Now
I am lying in it, thinking over my destiny, and
waiting impatiently, like everybody else, for things
to begin to move.

I certainly am quite safe from bullets here, for
I am with the staff, nearly a mile behind the Line,
and it is only when I go up at night on inspection
duty, walking through the cornfields in the rain,
that a few stray bullets whistle past my ears. Stray
bullets—and supposing one should hit me ? Why,
let it ! No, that's not quite honest ; I don't feel
like that ; I do not want to be hit, at any rate not
like that, by accident, and I always duck very
promptly when such a greeting whizzes by. In a
battle, of course, one doesn't think about it ; one's
nerves are already overstrained in other directions,

and one just does one's duty regardless of whether one is hit or not ; but here, as I walk along all alone, then it suddenly comes over me : no, you shan't, you mayn't be killed ! You have still a whole life before you ; you have hardly begun, and nobody could expect you to make an end so soon ! A soldier's life has made me so strong and fit. A little harder perhaps, a little rougher than formerly, but for that very reason I feel all the more full of vitality and able to realize how very much there is in the world to achieve, to perfect, and to enjoy.

> ' I feel the power to launch out into life,
>   To wrestle with the storm,
> To brave the wreck, nor heed the billows' strife.'

And this capacity for strength and enjoyment, is it to be wasted ? All my life long till now I have had to sit on a school-bench and learn all sorts of stupid as well as interesting things, and done nothing but go on learning ; and am I never to have a chance to *do* anything, to create anything ? Is this to be the end of it all ? Were those comrades right after all who used to say : ' Make the most of the last few weeks you've got left ; enjoy at least the surface pleasures of life, if death won't allow you time to go deeper ' ? No, I feel certain that there is still something for me to say and do in life ; there will be peace and a new life for me too, with young, vigorous powers, unblunted senses, with trials, difficulties and cares.

Is it wrong of me, is it unpatriotic, to think like

this ? Has a soldier no right to want to live ? Perhaps, but I can't help it ! The desire to live, the courage to live, increase every day. I know too little of life in general to throw it carelessly away, without a thought of regret. But as for contempt of death, heroism—I own, with shame, that I should only be capable of either in the intoxication of over-excited, bewildered senses, in the delirium of battle. Ah me, I thought it would be so easy to sacrifice one's life ; I talked so glibly about it at first ; but now : ' O Königin, das Leben ist doch schön ! ' [1]

[1] Nevertheless, Life is beautiful, O Queen !

ARTHUR MEESS, Engineering Diploma, Charlottenburg

Born March 28th, 1889, at Kaiserslautern.
Killed July 24th, 1915, near Nieuport.

October 18th, 1914.

YOUR silence of the last few days and the absence of news from Walter made me anxious. To-day I heard that the 23rd Infantry had been practically wiped out. I was just sitting down to prepare you for the worst, when I got the Express Letter in your writing, dear Else, and I knew at once what had happened.

At that same moment I realized how the dear, faithful fellow had grown into my heart. Oh how I wish that I could press his hand once more ! Those hours with him in Berlin are now doubly precious to me. But as for mourning for him— good heavens, yes, my heart aches, of course, but at this time, when our dear Fatherland is in danger greater even than that of a hundred years ago, is not every drop of blood that is shed hallowed, and has not Walter died the most splendid, the most glorious death that one can imagine ? Good Lord, how I envy him, how proud I feel of him, how I long—forgive me—to shed my blood too for the dearly loved Fatherland, for Kaiser and King ! To him that joy has been granted ; his last thought was of us ; and we will bear him in our hearts as our hero and our pride !

But to you I cry : ' Lift up your heads ; look

around you ; all that we hold most sacred is at stake, and our best is not too good to sacrifice in such a cause ; therefore show pride in your faces in spite of the sorrow in your hearts ! ' For one thing only we must hope, as I said to Walter at parting : ' Nothing else matters—only victory ! '

KURT PETERSON, Student of Philosophy, Berlin

Born February 2nd, 1894, at Magdeburg.
Killed August 3rd, 1915, near Cykow, in Russian Poland.

October 25th, 1914, near Dixmuide.

IT is Sunday. We are blessed with glorious sunshine. How glad I am to greet it once more after
all the horrors ! I thought never to see it again !
Terrible were the days which now lie behind us.
Dixmuide brought us a baptism of fire such as
scarcely any troops on active service can have
experienced before : out of 180 men, only 110
unwounded ; the 9th and 10th Companies had to
be reorganized as one ; several Captains killed and
wounded ; one Major dangerously wounded, the
other missing ; the Colonel wounded. Our
Regiment suffered horribly. It was complimented
by the Division.

What experiences one goes through during such
an attack ! It makes one years older ! Death
roars around one ; a hail of machine-gun and
rifle bullets ; every moment one expects to be hit ;
one is certain of it. One's memory is in perfect
working order ; one sees and feels quite clearly.
One thinks of one's parents. Then there rise in
every man thoughts of defiance and of rage and
finally a cry for help : away with war ! Away
with this vile abortion brought forth by human
wickedness ! Human-beings are slaughtering
thousands of other human-beings whom they
neither know, nor hate, nor love. Cursed be those

who, while not themselves obliged to face the horrors of war, bring it to pass ! May they all be utterly destroyed, for they are brutes and beasts of prey !

How one gossips with the sun after such a night of battle ! With what different eyes one looks upon Nature ! One becomes once more a loving, sensitive human-being after such soul-racking pain and struggle. One's eyes are opened to the importance of man and his achievements in the realm of culture. To war against war ; to fight against it with every possible weapon : that will be the work which I shall undertake with the greatest eagerness if the Almighty grants me a safe and happy return ! Here one becomes another man. My parents will receive me as a new-born child, maturer, simpler. And in this respect these horrors are justified : they are the despicable offspring of the lowest abysses of hell, yet they provide a stern, thorough training for the human soul. Good God !——

My beloved Parents, keep well and pray for me ! It makes me giddy with happiness to think that we may be permitted to meet again ; and to what do I owe this hopeful frame of mind ? To the sun, the dear sun, on Sunday, the 25th October. It shines down upon the earth, pouring a mild warmth and a blessing into the despairing human heart. The thunder of the guns no longer sounds so awful. As the night flees before the dawn, so must the foul dragon of war flee before the sunshine of culture !

October 27th, 1914.

In the night of the 25th, we were overtaken by rain in the trench. I don't know how many nights we have not lain out in the cold and wet without proper food or shelter, and so it has been till to-day. That same night we came out of the trench towards 2 o'clock. I was attached to the 2nd Company. Where my own Company is, I don't know. There was an attack on Dixmuide. Ghastly ! A repetition of the first attack. Again frustrated by the awful machine-gun fire. The half-uttered ' hurrah ' was choked. We all lay like logs on the ground and all about us death hissed and howled. Such a night is enough to make an old man of one. Strangely enough I kept perfectly calm. I can't describe my frame of mind, but it was quite simple. My brain was clear and bright ; only the thought of the Mother of Mercy predominated and on her I concentrated all my pain and torment. Otherwise I was quite cool and calm ; not resigned, but prepared for death. Oh, terrible moments ! One dreads death and yet one could almost long for it through horror at this kind of death. One thinks : ' I have been in two attacks, may I never see another ! ' This is one's most earnest desire, together with that of getting home safe and sound. What has become of all one's courage ? We have had enough of war. One is not necessarily a coward because one's whole nature revolts against this barbarity, this gruesome slaughter. Away, away with this war ! Put an end to it as speedily as possible !

We were lying quite close to the French line. I could hear the French words of command, while death whizzed over us. With several comrades I managed to creep away, and by crawling and leaping through the ever-pursuing rifle-fire, to reach a comparatively safe spot. We joined a machine-gun section, to which I am still attached to-day as Infantry Cover. I can learn nothing of my Company. It is supposed to be about six miles away. When shall I see it again? Soon, I hope.

To-night there is to be another attack. Whether it will succeed or not, nobody knows. I don't scruple to admit that from this standpoint I am glad not to be with my own troop and have to take part in this horrible dying. It is mean of me, but the cur in man is too strong. Put an end, O Lord, Thou Guide of the Universe, to this horror! Give us peace soon, very soon. Or rather grant us a joyous home-coming and time to put into practice the terrible lessons we have learnt here—for we have all been learning. Beloved Parents, I don't think you will be disappointed in your son. God strengthen, bless and comfort you and preserve you so that I may once more enjoy a life of love and blessedness together with you. Adieu!

October 29th, 1914.

One thinks that one will never be able to learn to laugh again after one has been through such an experience! Melancholy, deep melancholy, takes possession of one. I know that nothing in my whole life can awake such a feeling of happiness as will be mine if I am again united, safe and sound, to my dear parents. What they were to me, and in how many ways I was wanting in my behaviour to them, is now so bitterly clear to me. My Parents, you shall have a changed son restored to you !

The last three wounded from the first attack were still lying out in the open. Only one more could be fetched in. The enemy has no consideration for efforts at succour. He redoubles his fire. On the second trip the bearers deserted me. Two wounded were still lying there. 'I can only take one. Who will wait?' 'Take him,' said the younger of the two, as if it were a matter of course, pointing to his older and badly wounded comrade, a Landsturm[1] man and the father of a family. 'But you won't leave me in the lurch, will you, Comrade?' Impulsively I held out my hand to him. That was a promise. I had sworn to myself that nothing should force me under fire for a third time, but the magnanimity of this wounded man was sufficient to upset this resolution. Thank God I have not become a scoundrel and a breaker of my word. The Lieutenant would not let me go. In the evening he gave in. He went through the whole Company till at last he found volunteers. The wounded man was carried in on a ground-sheet. 'I have been looking forward all day to your coming back!' That was how he greeted us. If one could only do as much for everybody !

[1] The 3rd Reserve, composed of elderly and ' C3 ' men.

PETER FRENZEL, Student of Law, Berlin

Born May 11th, 1892, at Rössel, East Prussia.
Killed August 13th, 1915, near Luniew.

WHEN we were on our way from Kielce to the Front, it seemed to me that the world ended at the rail-head—far away lay the war, but the space between was empty. The same pictures kept recurring. Simple wooden crosses beside the road and shell-shattered, still smouldering dwellings. One tragic feature was strikingly repeated : the tall, lonely chimney, standing beside the hearth, like a pathetic, forsaken member of the family, patiently awaiting the return of his dear ones.

Every evening there is a repetition of another scene. In their flight the Russians set fire to the villages, and especially the bridges. After sunset the glare lights up the sky in two or three different places, and the most remarkable cloud-formations drift across the heavens. For instance, a few days ago I saw a maiden rising out of the smoke and lifting imploring hands towards the setting sun. Another time I saw a picture from an old French tapestry—a husband and wife in flight, carrying a gaily shouting child.

It is very extraordinary how I seem to have ceased to feel anything here ; only my imagination is more lively and full of fantasy than ever, and the longing for home, for quiet tranquil work and a mature enjoyment of life, grows daily greater.

(154)

EDUARD BRUHN, Student of Theology, Kiel

Born October 18th, 1890, at Schlamersdorf.
Killed September 17th, 1915, in Russia.

September 17th, 1915.

DEAR PARENTS,—

I am lying on the battle-field badly wounded. Whether I recover is in God's hands. If I die, do not weep. I am going blissfully home. A hearty greeting to you all once more. May God soon send you peace and grant me a blessed home-coming. Jesus is with me, so it is easy to die. In heartfelt love,

EDUARD.

GOTTHOLD von ROHDEN, Student of Theology, Marburg

Born February 4th, 1895, at Bielefeld.
Killed September 26th, 1915, in Champagne.

Beaurains, before Arras, December 26th, 1914.

. . . On Christmas Eve we were more than usually on the alert, as it seemed likely that the French would attack. The half-moon was shining in full glory—most unsuitable weather for going on patrol ! Six War-Volunteers put themselves under my guidance and soon after it got dark we crawled out, the enemy being barely 400 yards away.

A slight natural hollow in the ground ran down towards the enemy, and in its shelter we managed to get fairly close. While you were sitting happily round the glittering Christmas tree and the children were excitedly awaiting the removal of the snow-white coverings from the present-tables, after which every one had adequately to admire the wonderful things which the others had received ; and while, later on, you were perhaps sitting cosily and contentedly side by side, enjoying the mere being together, I was creeping, step by step, with every nerve strained to the utmost in order to detect the slightest rustle or sign of a dark form, towards the enemy's trench.

At last I got so far that I thought only one more ' lap ' would be necessary, but meanwhile the Frenchies had at last become conscious of our approach, and the sound of the first sharp shots

rang through the ' Holy Night '. We four manni-
kins—I had already left two behind for fear of our
being cut off—crouched behind a small bit of
cover. I had at once made up my mind what to
do : to defend ourselves would certainly be fatal,
for they were advancing upon us from the right
and from straight in front, so that we could not
prevent ourselves from being surrounded—we must
get back. I had seen and observed quite enough.

Thirty yards behind us was another little bit of
cover, but before we could reach it, one of the
many bullets brought down my comrade K. W.
One of the other men, who had one bullet through
the sleeve of his tunic and overcoat, and another
through his coat between his legs, wanted to stay
with me, and only when I sternly ordered him to
go did he make his escape into the darkness. The
fourth man had lost his head, rushed back and
upset the whole Company, including the Captain,
by informing them that W. and I had been taken
prisoner.

The French came nearer, and my fate seemed
sealed : Adieu, you over there and you at home.
If the French have any humanity we may meet
again after the war ! In any case I couldn't, of
course, leave W. alone. Every second I expected
to see the French come round the edge of my
cover, but God had other designs for us : at the
very spot where we had been just before they
paused and stood audibly talking, evidently dis-
cussing this nocturnal disturbance.

So there I lay with the wounded man ; made a

pillow for his head ; whispered words of comfort and encouragement to him ; tried to bind up his wound, which was in the upper part of the thigh ; and thought about Christmas—and about many other things.

And no doubt it was just the fact of its being Christmas that saved us, for the Frenchies had evidently been seeking to celebrate the Feast with alcohol and were now loudly singing the Marseillaise, ' God save the King ', a Christmas hymn, and soldier-songs. One bellowed across : ' You want come to Paris ; you not come ! '

Our own men sang Christmas hymns in parts and the songs of the Fatherland. When one gave a solo, those opposite clapped in applause. The Frenchmen kept as quiet as mice while they listened to the Christmas hymns which no doubt you were singing at the same time.

The enemy close in front of us has moved away, and does not trouble to send out a patrol to see whether anything is happening in ' no-man's-land '. Only once does he take any notice of the wounded man's movements and groans, and then the bullets pass over us.

When I saw how much blood W. was losing I did think of giving myself up, lest he should bleed to death. The Captain laughed at me when I told him that, and said I was indeed a sweet innocent if I imagined that the enemy would be magnanimous enough to bother about a wounded German ! Luckily W. himself quickly dissuaded me : ' Anything rather than be taken prisoner ! ' he whispered ;

then he added, more loudly : ' Won't they ever come and fetch us ! '

As I gradually became convinced that the French would not discover us for the present, I began to think about how we could escape, though that had seemed so hopeless at first. With impatient longing I watched the shadow of the bank lengthen as the moon sank. It would be impossible for me to relate in a few sentences all that I thought and felt during those two hours before it really grew darker and a plucky stretcher-bearer did manage to crawl out to us, although he did not know where we were lying, how far away we might be, or even whether we were still there, and might well have turned back ten yards sooner. One thing only I must tell you—I was perfectly calm and never felt a moment's fear of what might happen, knowing myself to be in a Higher Hand. Also just the consciousness of being the only hope and protection of another is in itself a help and support.

Boiry, February 19*th,* 1915.

A few days ago I came upon a bit of trench which was decorated in a highly original manner : the bays and breastwork were adorned with pots of flowers, the most noticeable being some Howitzer cartridge-cases full of snowdrops, the first flowers of the coming spring. Their frail delicacy seems particularly out of keeping with the surrounding shambles. No careful hand will tend them. Shells will tear up the ground, and crush and smother them. When I saw the first I picked and kept

(159)

them. It wasn't easy to get them, I had to crawl out on my tummy, for the Frenchie keeps a good look-out !

One part of the trench runs through the middle of a beautiful park. When the trees are green it must be an idyllic spot, in striking contrast to the shattered dwellings. It is miserable to clamber over the ruins and see that not a single house has been spared. Even the church has been shot to bits by the French ; against the exposed wall leans a whitewashed pedestal on which is a gaily painted, bare-headed saint, letting the rain pour down on him and the sun dry him, while he gazes down from morning till night on the devastation at his feet, with only a look of silent reproach visible in his eyes. In the churchyard the crosses and tomb-stones are broken ; even the dead have no rest beneath the earth, for the shells plunge deep into the ground and blow up the graves ; at such spots one realizes to the full the misery of war.

Salency, July 8th, 1915.

. . . I can quite understand your wishing us to tell you as much as possible, but I can't myself place as much value on the written word as you do —I mean on the use of writing at all—I only do it to please you. It seems to me as if we who are face to face with the enemy are loosed from every bond that used to hold us ; we stand quite detached, so that death may not find any ties to cut painfully through. All our thoughts and feelings are trans-formed, and if I were not afraid of being misunder-

(160)

stood I might almost say that we are *alienated* from all the people and things connected with our former life.

From your 'neutral' standpoint you reproach me for being *too* ready to sacrifice myself. Oh, you dear things ! Harald is quite right when he speaks enthusiastically of the work we shall have to do after the war. I should be surprised if it were otherwise. But we who are *in* the war—and compared with those of others my experiences are almost nothing—feel that we are confronting powers and influences where every normal, sensible, logical force, or what is generally considered as such, is utterly useless. The mind is no longer capable of Harald's 'right way of thinking'. We can only say, ' Death, here you have me ! ' feeling at the same time, ' but you shall not take me lying down, or too easily ! ' One man regains his balance more quickly, thanks to a naturally optimistic temperament ; another is hampered by his tendency to be always seeking after truth, and owing to his more thoughtful nature, takes a darker view. But such waverings aren't of much account.

All attempts, however, to put such things into words seem banal and almost sacrilegious ; such immense effects cannot be compressed into the tiny compass of human understanding. I have had to live through the experience of seeing my old regiment fight and die, and I cannot talk about it. All we can do is to be silent and hold up our heads. ' After the war ' expresses an idea which seems miles away from us.

(161)

July 23rd, 1915.

Many thanks for your letter of July 16th. I return the Casualty List at once. I hadn't seen any details before about what happened to the 2nd Battalion of the 26th or the 2nd and 3rd Companies, and that interests me particularly. Now I know all about what occurred during the battle. The 3rd and 4th Companies were wiped out—*one* patrol only fought its way through. They were surrounded and attempts on the part of the 2nd and 3rd Battalion to rescue them failed, the 3rd being blown up, while the 4th, under their heroic wounded Commander, held out for six days without succour, until they had fired their last cartridge. One of the Platoon-Commanders—the 17-year-old youngest Lieutenant in the regiment—was killed, and his elder brother, commanding the 9th Company of the 26th, was wounded. Four officers were taken prisoner—we have had good news of them ; my Fähnrich comrade H. H. is said by an eye-witness to have been killed. Only three Regular officers of the old regiment are left. The Machine-gun Corps had few casualties.

These are mere bald statements of events, but what terrible memories do they not hold for the human soul ! All the books in the world could not contain them ! It is enough to haunt a man for the rest of his life to have seen *one* man die ; the soldier is doomed to appear unfeeling, hard and brutal. And during an attack ? you ask. ' Then a man is no longer a man,' as once said a Jaeger officer who had been in the Argonne since September and taken part in storm after storm, including the last. Each of these experiences stands alone, incomprehensible, inexplicable, irrational.

Many a fine poem, enthusiastically composed perhaps in a snug sitting-room, about the hero's end and the glory of such a death, will now be read with a bitter smile.

August 2nd, 1915.

. . . Your question, the old, old question about the Redemption, has found a strange answer here. Even those who call themselves Christians, Christians of the old believing kind, have, in moments of the most intense physical, and perhaps also spiritual, suffering, found themselves unable to accept the idea of Redemption through the death of Christ ; others have gone to their death with a consciousness of the sacred call of duty, content to leave all question of a life after death to a Higher Power, for one's own ego, with its realization of sin and despair, steps quite into the background. I myself cast all care with regard to my physical and spiritual well-being upon the Power above me, and leave it at that !

That is all very well during the war. Afterwards ? Well, then your questions will again become more and more important, weightier, and more pressing.

ALFRED E. VAETH, Student of Philosophy, Heidelberg

Born December 25th, 1889, at Krozingen, Baden.
Killed October 16th, 1915, near Leintrey.

In the Trenches near Beaumont, November 4th, 1914.

WHAT you want most to know is whether I am still just the same as ever ? I don't think, my Friend, that I have changed in the least. I have experienced one great joy : that of seeing my conceptions of life and the world put to the test and finding that they have not failed me. Many are now crying out and taking ignominious refuge in all sorts of things ; I have found comfort in my old ideas, even now when death is always close to us.

You know that I was one of the first to join up, of my own free will. We have been through some bad times since then and have endured many hardships, but I can honestly say that I should volunteer again all the same. Life here is hard ; nearly everybody would be glad to go home ; but there is much in it that is fine and valuable, and it is only the weather, the cold and wet, that often forces me to say : ' I wish we could have peace and be at home again ! ' But it will last a long, long time yet. If only the winter is not too severe !

There is straw in the dug-outs, but it is very cold all the same, and directly it rains it is horrible. When we are not obliged to dig communication trenches, etc., we just lie about in the dug-outs and clean our rifles and equipment—we can't clean ourselves, as there is scarcely enough water even

(164)

for drinking purposes—or stew apples (fetched under enemy rifle-fire), write letters, make notes, or—which is what I like best—just dream and think about all sorts of things. Now and then the firing gets a little more intense ; then one looks for something to aim at and goes man-shooting.

At night, however, stern duty holds sway. One has to go on guard again and again. For we are a very thin line—one regiment against three French ones. If they had more pluck, we should soon be done for—tired-out, grimy little crowd that we are !

The worst thing is lying still under enemy shell-fire. Nothing else is to be compared with that. It is a frightful strain on the nerves. Anyhow, waiting and not being allowed to do anything is much worse than fighting. The French have withdrawn a bit to-day. Before that we were only about 100 yards away from each other. The unpleasant part of that was that one was always expecting to be blown up by a mine. I shouldn't like to die that way. I should prefer a fine, sunny day, when the barrage has cleared the way and the inspiriting order comes : ' Fix bayonets ! Up ! March ! March ! Hurrah ! '

In Miraumont, January 26th, 1915.

Relieved at last, after seven weeks in the line ! A wash at last ! Rest at last ! Only in the far distance the thunder of the guns, and though the Heavy Batteries can carry as far as here, still here death would be an accident, whereas during all this last time it has stood almost hourly close to us.

I am making immediate use of the opportunity

to work off all my debts in the way of correspondence, and as I have just received your nice letter telling about things one would otherwise never hear of nowadays, however much one may long for them, you shall get the first reply.

Much in your letter surprised me, you show such wonderful insight into our feelings. In the first place, many of us do wish to come home safe and sound simply in order to prevent our falling back into our former state. To bring about a new life —vain dream ! I feel sure that it is only a dream. But all the same we will attempt to realize it, if only because it is our duty to do so. Also we want to be able to tell the truth about many things which would otherwise be hushed up, for everything is not as it should be. We true patriots, who in peace-time derided Jingoism—the so-called ' Hurrah Patriotism ' (this reminds me of Byron's lines : ' And when I laugh at any mortal thing, 'tis that I may not weep ')—hoped that this community of sacrifice, this facing of a death common to all, would bring about an end of all class-distinctions. This is not the case. You do not believe it ? I will give you an example : in the trench three privates are fighting over a loaf ; inside the dug-out the officers have more wine than they can drink. It makes one's heart bleed. All honour to our Regular officers, who as a rule take more care of their men than, for instance, the officers of the Reserve. Honour to all who deserve it. But of that concern for the well-being of the soldier of which you read so much in the newspapers, we see but little.

Then with regard to the awarding of the Iron Cross : there will be a row about it before long, if some calm voice is not soon raised in protest. And there are plenty of other things : for instance, one-year men who shirk any duty they can, regardless of the fact that others may suffer for it.

Oh Lord ! One joined up with all sorts of hopes, and one experiences disappointment after disappointment ! I can't understand some people at all. It is a joy to me that my comrades love me ; that one of my best friends is a stonemason and another a worker in an iron-foundry. It is no pleasure to me that I have been recommended for the Iron Cross, but what does please me is that when men of other sections, and even of other platoons, have a dangerous job on they come and ask me to go with them. I am delighted when I hear them say : ' That bloke's a student, but he's a good sort.' And yet that ' but ' has something humiliating in it. At any rate here is the point where the real work of peace begins with all its brutal truth. For truth is always brutal. It is said that the young men of the present day are degenerates, but they are doing greater things than their fathers in 1870. Many of us have vowed that if (yes, *if*) we come back, the songs of triumph shall not be allowed to drown the notes of sorrow. But everything depends on that ' if '. . . .

You ask how things are going. Well, we don't know. Whether we are winning or not we don't know. We only know that we have got to win, and that however war-weary we may be, we shall go on doing our duty. We shall not be beaten anyhow, but we may bleed to death. . . .

As you see, I am still at Zabern. The latest is that the Course at Döberitz is to begin on the 12th. I'm sure I hope it does; I can't stand much more of this hanging about doing nothing. To-day I heard by express of Helfert's death and of Altschuler's being dangerously wounded. I have seldom before realized so clearly and mournfully how terrible our losses are. One after another goes, in such regular succession that it is sometimes quite terrifying. Helfert was the last of the old lot. With Altschuler the second batch starts. But all the same the sooner I get back the better I shall be pleased, especially as there is heavy fighting again on the Western Front. One feels almost like a deserter—perfectly fit and strong and doing nothing. My conscience gives me real pain when I think that I, who am young, strong and unmarried, am lurking about here, while many an old Landwehr man is shedding his blood out there. I am bad-tempered and discontented. How often I have wished the whole Officers' Training Course at the devil, you can imagine! I only hope it will soon start. You'll go out again too then, won't you, even if it costs you your other eye?

Sennelager, near Paderborn, Officers' Training Course, July 12*th,* 1915.

. . . What impressions did I get in Germany?

I did not get the impression that the German people have grown, nor did I get the impression that they have grasped the seriousness of the war, and I did get the impression that it will be just as I expected while I was at the Front : things will go on just in the same bad old way as ever.

I am now here, doing a Course which is to finish (at last) on the 7th of August. Then I return to the Front. Before this I was training recruits at Dettweiler, the youngest lot. I must say that I much enjoyed converting those young spirits to a realization of the seriousness and at the same time the grandeur of the present times ; in showing them the gravity of the task set before them, and in making it easier for them.

Now we are stuck here, very much bored, indignant at much that goes on behind the line, and with only *one* pleasure and *one* satisfaction, that of having found comrades. One makes friends very rapidly and firmly in war-time, for one's power of discrimination has grown even more rapidly. An account of one experience is enough to show one whether the teller is a humbug or a decent chap. So we have made some good friends ; one has to do it quickly because death may soon be again calling for many of us.

The fine thing about it is that at last one has acquaintances who really take a lively interest in the needs of the times, and that we again have any quantity of good books to choose from. Comrades from all parts have been blown together here : some from Ypres ; some who fought with us at

Arras and Albert ; and also genuine Volunteers, who in October and November sang as they attacked Dixmuide ; men of the 208th, of whom only 300 are left out of the whole Regiment ; and chaps who have fought in Russia, Poland, and Galicia. Thus we have at last a chance of getting an accurate general view of this gigantic war and learning how it affects the souls of our warriors.

September 12*th*, 1915.

Here I sit, deep underground, in French Lorraine. Outside there is a glorious blue sky and brilliant sunshine, just such as we used so often to have in Heidelberg when we lay in our slender boats on the Neckar. I so often think of that time. There is something inexpressibly sad and full of renunciation in this stationary warfare. Life would be so easy if we could march, as they do in Russia, march along into the blue distance in the morning light. It is easy too to see people being killed when you pass quickly by. But here—we burrow deep into the earth. There is a candle burning even now in our dug-out, though it is bright daylight outside. Close by the lads are filling sandbags with which to-night they will stop up the holes made last night by shells in our parapets. Everything is quiet just now. The enemy is waiting for nightfall, because he knows that then we shall be working at our farthest-forward position. So there is no real activity except in the dark.

Compared with some of the places I was in before, this is not so bad. We are 400 yards apart here, compared with 80 in those days. That state of secret nervous tension which then extended from trench to trench is now absent. Sometimes when I am censoring the men's letters, I am obliged to smile at the way they write about how bad things are here, knowing myself what it was like at Arras.

Also we haven't got any of the old servile type of fellow here, such as we already had then in the 99th. These are quite young chaps : decent fellows, but not hardened to their job yet, and I can't help feeling a little anxious as to how they would behave in a bad attack. Well, one can exercise a lot of influence over them by setting an example of coolness. Luckily I am still perfectly fit and don't feel the least sign of that nerve-strain which so many experience when they come out for the second time. On the contrary, I feel that things aren't likely to be worse than they were the first time. And if after all they are, well—then they will be ! One must be prepared for anything. The only thing that really troubles me is the utter weariness of the troops. It is terrible how they are longing for peace. They seem to have lost all their spring. There is hardly a man who still seems able to stiffen his backbone, hold up his head and accept things just because they have to be. What particularly scares them is the thought of the winter. That is the most important part of the work we have to set ourselves to do here : to try and keep up the men's spirits in this depressing stationary warfare. We also hear from time to time discordant notes, from home of course. They

(171)

are again busy there abusing everybody who doesn't agree with them. If there is to be a New Germany, the troops will have to take it home with them—it is not to be found there.

October 11th, 1915.

I had your letter the day before yesterday and hasten to reply to it, as it may be the last time that I shall have a chance to write. We are about to undertake a serious attack against a position which has already been assaulted three times in vain, in spite of heavy losses.

I will begin by referring to a passage in your letter . . . ' My ideal for the future has been expressed in the words of Goethe's " Evensong " : " Blessed he who, without hate, withdraws himself from the world." ' But that, you see, is the very ideal that I myself am always opposing, just because it does appeal to me. It is egoism ; it may also be renunciation, or perhaps resignation. Life is a struggle. A struggle on behalf of the nation, you will say. Allow me to reply : A struggle on behalf of the human race. It is hard ; we are often weary of the struggle ; we long for rest ; but we do not give in. It is our duty to be ever under arms— soldiers fighting for the common weal.

I have always believed, and still believe, that on our nation depends the development of peace and world-citizenship. If we are conquered it means the destruction of these fruits of culture. That is why I joined up of my own free will. I came from conviction, not in the excitement of mobilization which made such a powerful impression on all of you. It certainly was a fine sight—the young Reservists singing as they marched to join the colours. You saw that too, but you did not see, as I did, the weeping women running along the pavements beside them. Why did some of the War Volunteers back out after all ? Because they had only joined up in the excitement of mobilization and not from deliberate conviction. Therefore, because *I* did join out of conviction, I am likewise not yet one of those who say : ' If it were only finished, no matter how.'

We have just got our marching orders. We move to-night, but I don't know where we are going. I think we are going to attack. Day and night we hear the thunder from Champagne. Yesterday and to-day we have been practising the ' storm ', and I think we know enough about it now. I think it is to be an attack to give our hard-pressed comrades time to breathe.

The candle burns so flickeringly and one thinks of all sorts of things. One has had luck so many times. But one thing *shall be* : when there is a shout of ' Volunteers, forward ! ' then volunteers *will be there* ! Can one make the chaps go with one? In that connection a poem I once read comes into my mind :

> ' We advance to the attack
> And the clock upon the tower
> Timidly strikes the midnight hour ! . . .'

My dear Friend, once more an honest, straight-forward greeting, one can now say a truly German greeting !

October 12th, 1915.

The attack was terribly beautiful ! The most beautiful and at the same time the most terrible thing I have ever experienced. Our Artillery shot magnificently, and after two hours (the French take seventy) the position was sufficiently prepared for German Infantry. The storm came, as only German Infantry can storm ! It was magnificent the way our men, especially the youngest, advanced, magnificent ! Officers belonging to other regiments, who were looking on, have since admitted they had never seen anything like it ! In the face of appalling machine-gun fire they went on with a confidence which nobody could ever attempt to equal. And so the hill, which had been stormed in vain three times, was taken in an hour. The booty was greater than was stated in the Order of the Day.

But now comes the worst part—to hold the hill ! Bad, very bad days are in front of us. One can scarcely hope to get through safe and sound. The French guns are shooting appallingly, and every night there are counter-attacks and bombing raids. Where I am we are only about 20 yards apart. Now, when one has again got through the easiest part of the attack, one shudders at the thought that one may be torn to bits by a shell in a trench, covered with dirt, and so end—in the mud and filth ! We should all like so much to live a few months longer until an advance towards final victory has been made here.

The attack was glorious !

(174)

WALTER BÖHM, Student of Philosophy, Berlin

Born March 26th, 1894, in Berlin.
Killed October 25th, 1915, near Bol Miedwiece, Volhynia.

Ponarth, January 31st, 1915.

. . . One thing more, dear Parents, and especially you, Mum : I asked you to spare me ' snowball ' prayers, amulets, and so on. Don't be angry with me, please don't, because I quite understand your point of view. But I have received from God, in whom, in my own way, I believe more firmly than ever, two good weapons : my body, which is well trained ; and an iron determination to do my duty to my country, my Commander-in-Chief, and my comrades on the one hand, and to myself and my family on the other. Supernatural means of protection I reject. Do you really think, dear Mother, that the Law of Nature with regard to a bullet is going to be reversed in favour of such an unimportant member of the universe as I am ? I am content if I can die in the consciousness that I have not lived to the disadvantage of anyone, that I have done my duty as a member of human society, and that I have never knowingly injured anybody.

HERBERT JAHN, Student of Mining and Chemistry, Technical High-School, Breslau

Born February 3rd, 1895.
Died April 10th, 1916, in the Military Hospital at Stenay.

North of Verdun, May 1st, 1915.

YESTERDAY evening I was sitting in the ivy-arbour outside our dug-out. The moon shone brightly into my mug. Beside me was a full bottle of wine. From a distance came the muffled sound of a mouth-organ. Only now and then a bullet whistled through the trees. It was the first time that I had noticed that there can be some beauty in war— that it has its poetic side ; I had thought that that only existed in books. Since then I have felt happy ; I have realized that the world is just as beautiful as ever ; that not even this war can rob us of Nature, and as long as I still have that I cannot be altogether unhappy !

May 4th, 1915.

To-day I have again had a delightful spring walk through the budding woods of the hill-side. It had been raining in the night, and I was greeted with another douche as I was starting. I crossed the rich meadow-land, passed through the vine-yards, and mounted ever higher till I reached the woods. From the edge of them I had a last beauti-ful view back over the valley, across the river to the heights on the farther bank where our and the French trenches are. If from that direction one

(176)

had not now and then heard the thunder of guns or the sound of rifle-fire, one could have forgotten all about the war, the landscape looked so peaceful.

Soon I plunge into the green sea : wonderful old beeches and oaks ; beneath them impenetrable undergrowth, over the height of a man—wild-roses, brambles, elder, and all sorts of bushes which one only knows at home as ornamental shrubs in park and garden ; and on the ground a gaily variegated carpet of flowers. One can only penetrate into this wilderness by narrow, slippery paths. Wild-boars and wild-cats are still to be found there, and even mountain-eagles. There is an intoxicating scent and a hot-house atmosphere everywhere. One often has to make detours to avoid tree-trunks which have fallen across the path.

Suddenly, in the midst of the wilderness, a grave, with a simple wooden cross ! And over there another ! The inscription is obliterated ; nobody can tell whether it is friend or foe who rests here ; and his relations do not know either where he is buried, he who set forth to guard his Fatherland. How long will it be before the last traces of the grave have vanished—disappeared like the name !

The path leads me on, ever deeper into the primeval forest. A great bird-of-prey, alarmed by my step, soars into the sky. What thoughts come and go as one wanders along ! There seems no end to the wood ; I go deeper and deeper into the thicket. The green walls stretch themselves on every side and in the distance glimmer further ranges of hills. . . .

July 5th, 1915.

It is strange that for a long time I have been constantly thinking of being killed, though I have really no belief in premonitions. All the same this crazy idea has so far influenced me that I have written a farewell-letter and made my will. Both documents lie, well concealed, in my breast-pocket. I have had amazing luck all my life so far, but I think the best thing of all has been the chance of taking part in this war—even if I am killed, for otherwise I should never have discovered the things I have learnt during the last ten months ; and every day one goes on learning, every day one's horizon widens.

OSKAR MEYER, Student of Philosophy, Kiel

Born March 12th, 1892, at Gliesmarode.
Killed April 18th, 1916, before Verdun.

At the Front, March 14th, 1915.

I THINK I last wrote to you from C., near Laon. On the 17th of February we had orders to prepare to move, and in the evening we started off by train.

When we got to our destination, we sat for a whole hour on the railway-line in the rain. Meanwhile a search was being made for billets. The whole battalion was first crowded into a tent, which had been used as a stable, but as the rain continued we soon left it and found emergency quarters in a church. We did not get a chance of a real rest even there, however, for after a short interval we continued our march, in the rain, along rutty, very wet, muddy roads, in which one's boots stuck fast. It is very trying to march for hours with one's stuffed-full pack, through hilly country.

In the afternoon we reached the position of another regiment and there we halted. Meanwhile our field-kitchen had come up and had just begun serving out food and drink—we had been sweating as if it were midsummer and had a fearful thirst—when the order came : ' The battalion will march at once ! ' So on we went for hours, till long after nightfall.

Fresh orders : ' Back to the village and look for billets ! ' The only houses left were smashed up by shells and already occupied. All we could find

(179)

was a barn with its roof full of holes and part of one side-wall gone, but with a little straw in it. I fell asleep from utter weariness, but the cold soon woke me again, and I was thankful when the night was over.

The next morning we went on again. No sign of the field-kitchen. We had got to get still more used to thirst. In the afternoon we arrived at our destination in Champagne. You are sure to have seen the place often mentioned in the papers.

In the evening came the order : ' The battalion will be ready to march to the trenches at —— o'clock.' In the meantime we were allowed to house ourselves in a cave in the mountain-side.

The battalion fell in punctually, and, after an hour's march through a deep communication-trench sodden with rain, we reached the actual line. Our 6th Company had to occupy a communication-trench. We knew nothing, of course, of the terrain. We saw French flares going up in front of us, behind us and on our left, and were confronted by a puzzle : in case of an enemy attack, in which direction were we to fire ? We couldn't solve the riddle, so we kept quiet all night. Every man possessed himself of a spade, and dug himself a hole, so that he might not freeze. One could hardly think of sleep. So the night passed.

Suddenly, in the morning (it was the 20th of February), we came under heavy shell-fire ; I should reckon the number of shells—they were American ones, which burst with a fearful noise— at several hundred. We crawled into our holes to escape from the flying fragments. Meantime, however, the French made an attack, and penetrated into our trench unobserved by us. My neighbour, a Lance-Corporal, said to me : ' I'll just have a look over the parapet. Generally when there is such violent artillery-fire, the French attack.' He got a fearful shock, and shouted : ' The French are already in our trench ! ' We all crawled out and seized our rifles. In a moment the fight had begun. We drove the French back with heavy loss ; but they returned, reinforced, and succeeded in occupying the shell-shattered wood in our rear. From there they could inflict heavy casualties on us. My dear friend, Willy Kloss, who had fought in the front rank, here met a hero's death, struck by a rifle-bullet. He was not the only one—our dear, good Willy whom all good comrades prized —all my other friends in the Company and many acquaintances were also killed.

Our little band, after being hastily reinforced, succeeded, but only after great efforts, in cleaning up both the wood and the trench. The French went on attacking every day. They took the trench and managed to hold it for some time, then we got it back. Now we have filled it up, as our losses were too great in proportion to the importance of this trench.

Till the 4th of March we remained in the so-called ' Witch's Cauldron ', taking turns in |the trench and in the cave on the hill-side, ' the Rabbit Hutch '. We were thankful when we were relieved. Since the 6th of March we have been in rest.

In the Vosges, August 29th, 1915.

Fourteen days in the Line ! Much has happened during that time. Many times our trench was under heavy French shell-fire, and our battalion has had heavy losses, though the 6th Company has come off comparatively lightly. We lay on a very steep hill-side, which was difficult to shoot at, and many of the boomers intended for us fell into the valley below, where there is still plenty of room !

The French attacked several times, and are still holding some small sections of our line. Some of our saps are less than ten yards apart. At first we threw bombs at each other, but then we agreed not to throw any more, and not to go on firing. Latterly we exchanged cigars, cigarettes, money, letters, etc. We looked out over the parapet in broad daylight and gazed innocently at one another. The French gave our men some photographs of their big guns. One of them photographed our most advanced post, after having shaken him warmly by the hand ! We had several quiet days in that spot. If a Frenchman had orders to throw bombs several times during the night, he agreed with his ' German comrade ' to throw them to the left and right of the trench. At night the French perched themselves on the parapet and smoked cigarettes, which are visible for a long distance.

While we were on such good terms, our Pioneers were able to do a lot of useful work, and constructed a new advance-post without being fired at. Naturally the French Pioneers were not idle either.

The whole incident shows that the French soldiers have a great longing for peace, just as we have, and that if it depended on them, peace would have been made long ago. We too hope that the time may not be very long now.

Yesterday we were relieved and are now lying about half a mile behind the line, on a mountain which has not yet been shelled. I am living in what is, under the circumstances, a very superior hut, with my batman, War-Volunteer David.

I was yesterday elected Officer by the regiment, but until this is confirmed am only promoted Deputy Officer.

Physically I am now in increasingly better condition, and I shall be glad if I can keep up the same rate of improvement spiritually. Well, that can't be forced, it must grow. Every good thought advances one a step, and I am fortunate in having spiritual comfort, namely the recognition of God's place in human life.

EDUARD SCHMIEDER, Student of Administration, Freiburg i. B.

Born October 10th, 1890, at Freiburg i. B.
Killed before Liévin, May 8th, 1916.

Framonville, August 23rd, 1914.

I HAVE been smoking cigars while we lay as Artillery Cover under enemy shrapnel-fire. And in those very moments I have once again vividly realized the beauty of the world and all the happiness which has been mine in life.

In war-time one learns how beautiful, how rich our life is, in spite of small and great drawbacks. Each new day brings gladness even when one knows that it will also bring fresh toil. After each battle one thanks God that one still has life, one values it so much. But we would all sacrifice it gladly for our beautiful Fatherland.

La Bassée, November 2nd, 1914.

I should like to take a peep into my dear home-land at the moment when they are celebrating a victory—my joy would compensate me for a few days in the trenches. I can imagine how lovely it is, when the sun struggles through the thick autumn mist, a blue tent stretches above our dear mountains, and the whole of Nature glows once more in colour and beauty before it dies. There is blissful joy in every victory won for the sake of this beautiful German country.

(184)

Loos, December 17th, 1914.

My Christmas letters—whatever way I begin them—all bear the stamp of a softened, wistful frame of mind. I am thinking too so much about the days of preparation for Christmas Eve, which were among those I loved best. I specially remember a Sunday during that time a few years ago. I went tramping about the festive town, first alone and then with you, and a sudden strange longing came over me, which was realized afterwards in beautiful dreams.

Such dreams and the thunder of guns, which is now disquieting me, do not go well together. It is an unprecedented, continuous thunder to-day, an unceasing crashing and growling and hissing and whistling.

But I must tell you about my last night's dream, which I can't stop thinking of and which would fill me with superstitious fear if it could : I was in the war, but strangely enough with the Russians. I was lying in an advance-post in a castle. I came into a room and as I entered a beautiful, ravishing woman advanced to meet me. I wanted to kiss her, but as I approached her I found a skull grinning at me. For one moment I was paralysed with horror, but then I kissed the skull, kissed it so eagerly and violently that a fragment of its under-jaw remained between my lips. At the same moment this figure of death changed to that of my Anna— and then I must have woken up.

That is the dream of how I embraced death. . . .

WALTER AMBROSELLI, Student of Philosophy, Leipzig

Born August 15th, 1894, at Schwiebus, Brandenburg.
Killed May 12th, 1916, near Douaumont.

At the Front, January 19th, 1915.

ONLY to-day can I manage to keep my promise of telling you something about the battle of Soissons, which lasted from January 12th to the 14th. I can and will only give you a few details now. When the war is over and I am happily with you once more, I will willingly relate all my experiences, but just now I can't bear to recall, even to myself, all the sickening horror of such wholesale murder. We all do our best to forget about it, at least for the present.

At the beginning of January we were lying, as you know, in Fort Condé. It was a quiet life we led there. Every day, just as in garrison at home, the barrack-guard went on duty for 24 hours. On January 11th I was on guard, and doing sentry-duty at night, when suddenly an orderly brought the message : 'Wake the Company at once. March at 2 o'clock. Fighting equipment.'

Within half an hour we were off into the darkness, and marched till about 6 along the sodden roads in the pouring rain. At last we reached a communication-trench which led to the line held by the 48th. It took us two and a half hours to wade through the thick mud of the trench. Step by step we struggled along, working our way through that awful French clay. Those who had gum-boots on kept catching hold of the loops on each side of the boot that had to make a step forward and hauling it out of the mud. In spite of this, somebody got stuck every moment, and then the whole file was held up. Generally the front and rear man of the one who had got stuck seized his foot and dragged it out. We often sank over our knees in the morass. Some men had their boots pulled right off and stood in their stockings, or even bare-foot, pressing themselves against the wall to let the others pass, before trying to retrieve them.

We were dog-tired when at last we reached the 48th's trench. In the hurry of departure, I had not been able to take anything to drink with me. The few slices I had in my bread-sack were soon devoured. The 48th, being no longer able to get back through the communication-trench, had also nothing to eat. We also began to suffer from thirst. So we were all hungry and thirsty together. The dug-outs were bad. The rain came trickling through the roof. To protect themselves from it, our comrades had stretched ground-sheets over the ceiling. As it had been raining constantly for a long time, these had got full of water. We poked holes in them, put our mess-tins underneath, and so got a drink. That was the only one we had.

Early next morning we moved farther up, into the trench of the 52nd. We were dead-tired and hungry when we got there. The artillery-fire was awful. Our trench-mortars were working without a pause. They are projecting machines, which hurl into the enemy-trench shells so powerful that they smash everything up and scatter death and destruction on all sides. The firing of them makes scarcely any noise, but the explosion is terrific.

The enemy gun-fire on our trench was frightful and many a comrade lost his life even before the attack. We had a few hours of anxious waiting under violent shell-fire. Then we moved up through the boyau into the front line. We were all in a state of feverish excitement.

Then—at 12 o'clock—a signal, followed by a deafening ' Hurrah ', and we were off, each man running as hard as he could with bayonet lowered, through the French wire-entanglements and into the first French trench.

There we found only one or two scared Frenchmen in the few dug-outs which had not been destroyed by our shells and trench-mortars. They instantly threw down their arms. Meanwhile, however, the French machine-guns were mowing down our ranks appallingly. They had nearly all been moved back into the second line and were firing on us from there. However, they didn't stop us. After our Corporal and his section had taken five Frenchmen with a machine-gun prisoner, we proceeded to storm the second line, which was the enemy's strongest position. It was a hard fight. Everywhere barbed-wire entanglements and undergrowth, and a stiff hill to climb.

Our Pioneers, who are more feared than anybody because of their bombs, worked with axes and wire-cutters in front of and among us, and just then

I witnessed, with admiration, a heroic deed. A Pioneer caught sight of a Frenchman in the trench who was just about to fire. The Pioneer quickly pulled the stopper out of the fuse, raised his bomb, and was just going to throw it. At that very moment some German comrades came between him and his objective. He could not throw the bomb without hitting them ; so he kept it in his hand, and in a few seconds it exploded, blowing him to pieces.

From the second trench we went on across a field. All about dead and wounded were lying. The clay stuck to our bodies, especially our hands and feet, so that we could hardly get along. I saw some men running bare-foot, their boots having got stuck in the mud. Our ranks kept getting thinner. At this point the Company lost the Commanders of the 1st and 2nd Platoon.

Many of the ghastly things that happened during this attack I couldn't possibly tell you. It makes me sick to think of them. One was ready to weep over the misery of it all, as when, for instance, comrades close to us fell, with a last pathetic look at us.

Then, as we forced our way through the deep, narrow trench, what a horrible sight met our eyes ! In a place where a trench-mortar shell had burst, there lay, torn to pieces, about eight of the Alpine Chasseurs—some of the finest French troops—in a great, bloody heap of mangled human bodies ; dead and wounded ; on the top a corpse without a head or torso ; and underneath some who were still alive, though with limbs torn off or horribly mutilated.

They looked at us with bleeding, mournful eyes. The crying and moaning of these poor, doomed, enemy soldiers went to our hearts. We couldn't get out of the trench to avoid this pile of bodies. However much our hearts shrank from trampling over them with our hob-nailed boots, we were forced to do it !

We became more and more covered with the filthy clay-soil ; face and hands, and even rifles, were plastered with it. The rifle of a Corporal close to me burst while he was firing, because mud had got into the barrel. Then my own rifle wouldn't go off. I had to stop and clean it with my handkerchief in the midst of a hail of bullets, for we were then being violently shot at from the enemy's third line. The French put up a resolute defence at this point, and it was only after the fiercest bayonet-fighting that we succeeded in taking it. In the trench I also came upon a young War Volunteer lying dead, still clutching his rifle. Facing him lay a French Corporal. They had run each other through simultaneously, and their bayonets were still sticking in each other's bodies.

Our Corporal and a few men of our section were still together, but we had got separated from the rest of the platoon. That often happens in hand-to-hand fighting, as companies have to spread out, and individual sections, platoons, companies, and even regiments, get all mixed up. We were now, with the 12th and 8th, under the command of a Captain of the 52nd, attacking a hill from which a French gun was still firing. We swarmed up it from every side. There we finally discovered a French Artillery Major, alone with his gun—fetching the ammunition himself, loading and firing. When we got there, he was just trying to shoot the first one of our men—Corporal Finder of the 2nd Company—with his revolver. The Corporal was too quick for him, however, and sent a bullet through the Major's head. The shot was not immediately fatal. Exerting all his remaining strength the brave enemy officer dragged himself to the telephone in order to send warning to the enemy rear-line. We were just in time to stop him. Then he collapsed. I fetched two French stretcher-bearers out of a hole which we had already captured, so that they might carry the Major out of the line of fire. Without a groan, but also without vouchsafing a glance in my direction, he let himself be carried down into a quarry where there were already a lot of wounded.

Two days later I read in the printed Order-of-the-Day issued by the Army Corps that, in accordance with the personal instructions of the Kaiser, who had been present at the battle, this hero had been buried with full military honours, escorted by officers of even higher rank, behind the line.

CHRISTIAN BRAUTLECHT, Student of Political Economy

Born October 23rd, 1893, at Wyk-on-Föhr.
Killed May 23rd, 1916, near Givenchy.

December, 1914.

. . . To-day, as I begin my letter, it doesn't look at all Christmasy with us. Every one in the trench is in very low spirits because there has been no post, and the clouds in the sky have mingled their moisture with the clay of our trench so that we are filthy from top to toe. But my spirit takes flight and transfers itself to your midst, where for the first time I am absent at Christmas.

> ' I hasten to join you from out of the wood,
> It was Christmassing there just as hard as it could,'

writes Storm. There is a slight frost and a sprinkling of snow in the street. You have already been to church, early, and I think that ' Peace on earth ' must have had a strange sound. I can hear quite clearly the rather hoarse tone of our church bells. We love them just because they have that queer tone—quite different from bells abroad. You hurry home as fast as you can as if by so doing you could shorten the time before the wonderful evening. And then—then everything happens just as it always does. You all dine together, and this time the gathering is rather larger than usual, and the Christmas tree casts its pale light into the room and reminds you, Parents, of the time when we children were all quite small and stood singing round the tree. And then, then you will have received my letter and read it aloud and your thoughts will fly to me in France where the custom of decorating a Christmas tree is unknown. And you will talk about me and try to imagine where I am and how I am getting on, whether, indeed, I am still among the number of those who greet the sunlight and rejoice in the beauty of the world.

See, the twilight comes an hour later here than with you, and then we too, in far-away Gaul, are preparing to celebrate the Christmas Feast. The first night-watch has to stand from 5 to 7 listening for the enemy and imagining how things are looking at home. From 7 to 9 is rest. At that time the kitchen generally serves rations and a short sleep refreshes one's tired limbs. But to-day the dug-out has quite a different appearance. Instead of economizing light, there is quite an illumination with us two or three men who are sitting together. Why sleep to-night ? We have had to be awake so many nights. Why not make some use of the time to-night ? Who knows how long we shall have the chance ! And so there we sit, my good comrade Hans Wohlers and I—and keep Christmas. Thoughts arise in our minds and put themselves into words as they would not at any other time. And we think of the other member of our trio who joined up with us, our Hans Adolf Bartram, and don't know where he is or where he lies. We carried him in that time mortally wounded and have never had any news since. And then we talk of Germany and our homes and the relations who are no doubt thinking of us too at this time, and those friends from whom we have had presents and candles.

' Nine o'clock relief ! ' calls the round. And then we go out again for two hours and listen through the Christmas night for the possibly approaching Frenchie.

HEINZ POHLMANN, Student of Philosophy, Berlin

Born February 14th, 1896, in Berlin.
Killed June 1st, 1916, on the ' Dead Man '.

At the Front, May 25th, 1916.

MOST TENDERLY LOVED PARENTS,—

When you get this letter I am afraid you will be in great sorrow, because then I shall be no longer in the world.

I can understand that, but one thing I beg you : do not lament, do not grieve for me, but be calm and resigned ; show that you are Germans who can bear suffering ; German parents who give what they value most for that which is of most value—our glorious Fatherland. For in spite of all the tragic things that I have experienced and of which I have heard, I still believe in the future, and for a new, a greater and a better Fatherland I gladly sacrifice my young life.

I am going into the battle quite calmly and am not in the least afraid to look death in the face, for I feel myself safe in the Hands of God. Jesus Christ, whom after wandering long astray, I was at last graciously brought to acknowledge as my Saviour, is to me too the Resurrection and the Life. Perhaps you do not share my convictions, but I have found some appropriate words in my book by Lhotzky : ' Many roads lead from men to God, but from God to men only one.'

One thing more : If in the old days I vexed and pained you, forgive me. I was often self-willed and have followed wrong paths, but believe that I am sorry and forgive me. And now there is nothing more for me to say except, in spite of everything, ' Auf Wiedersehen ' !

Your
HEINZ.

Psalm 43, 5 : Cor. 13, 13.

JOHANNES HAAS, Student of Theology, Leipzig

Born March 12th, 1892, at Erfde, Schleswig.
Killed June 1st, 1916, before Verdun.

The Farm of Mareuil, March 24th, 1915.

IT is Sunday morning. Behind our farm the valley rises gently in rich meadow-land towards the hills. The high plateaus fall away on either side. Thus we have a triangular, flat, sloping depression, and here our Field Service was held. The Chaplain's desk was fixed up under a solitary tree and decorated with flowers and shrubs. What a morning it was! I draw a deep breath when I think of it. No wind, the sky so blue, the sun shining so warmly—' Oh, thou clear blue sky!'—and larks just like those at home, offering their most beautiful morning hymn to their Creator.

The Chaplain can have been only recently ordained, but there was nothing of the ' pale young Curate ' about him!—a thorough officer in walk and bearing. He succeeded in diverting attention from the fine morning to himself. He preached quite a simple, excellent sermon on the divine institution of sacrifice. Then we sang some verses of ' Oh, wounded Head '. We separated slowly and thoughtfully. We did not feel at all worked-up, but more like the peasants at home, who on Sunday after service go nodding along the road saying, ' Ja, ja,' and then think over their pastor's words as they follow the plough during the week. Good seed had been sown.

(197)

In the afternoon I had to play 'skat' with some comrades, but I was rather absent-minded over it. Pictures of old days were passing through my mind. One of the players is Bergman of the Mansfelds, and he is talking about Rostock—Rostock, where I spent a winter of seeking and doubting ! That little bookseller with the spectacles and the many books, I wonder what has become of him ? . . . The corner there, just like the beach at Heiligendamm. Heiligendamm, one morning, an icy-cold wind, rain, snow, and myself, bare-headed, because I didn't know what I was doing, wandering for seven hours along the coast. I did not come home till 1 o'clock in the morning, having had nothing to eat all day, and how tired I was !—tired out, but ' no forrarder ' !

Skat again. A passing comrade shows some French postcards which he ' captured ' in Belgium ; their vulgarity sickens me ; that sort of thing even here ! A monoplane in the sky ; one of the skat-players, an artificer, begins telling once again the story of his monoplane : the German Government refused it ; the French bought it, but only paid half the money. That gives one pecuniary and patriotic reflections. At last the skat is finished and we go home. Our afternoon coffee is diluted with ' Love-Gift ' rum.

Towards evening. I must be alone for a bit. I'll go out. There is little W. looking like a gipsy. ' Yes, yes, Comrade, my eldest. Born in the middle of August. We hadn't a bite in those days, and always Englishmen, Frenchmen or black devils on top of us. Yes, yes, if it were but all over ! Otherwise he'll be able to walk before I see him ! ' W. is war-weary like most of those who have been here from the start. There is no enthusiasm, such as you at home imagine—no enthusiasm, but blind fury which makes no prisoners and yet is sorry for those who have also got a wife and children at home.

. . . I am alone in the fields. My thoughts keep wandering homewards and dwelling on the past and the future. And what about the present ? Oh, at present it is delightful to be alone ! I feel just as you do, my dear little brother, shivering out there in Russia with your machine-gun. We agree in that as we do in everything else. I have never been so much alone as I am here, except in Berlin, when I was absolutely by myself, struggling through the crowded corridors of the University to Erich Schmidt's lectures. One feels equally solitary as one marches along with the rank and file, hour after hour, abandoned to one's own thoughts. And I sometimes felt like that in the students' cafés—as if the whole atmosphere were somehow alien to me. If I could only begin my student-days all over again ! But I won't let myself think that. After the war everything will be different, and then I *must* begin again, anyhow.

The question is : shall I be a clergyman or not ? The old question, the old uncertainty, the old struggle ! Here one has time to examine oneself, to prove one's attitude towards God. Many people have found themselves able to make up their minds about such things here, but I find myself more doubtful than ever. I see nothing but question marks. What is the reason of everything ? How is that possible ? Questions that go round and round in a circle, and find no answer. . . .

It is getting cold outside now. I will go into my tent. I am thinking over the great ethical problem of the war. Preachers in the pulpits at home dismiss the question much more easily ; for us here the war remains a most difficult matter for one's conscience to decide about. When one is actually fighting the instinct of self-preservation and the excitement drown every other feeling, but when one is in rest or doing nothing in the trenches, then it is different. One looks with astonishment and horror at the more and more cunningly elaborate means devised for destroying the enemy. One is torn between the natural instinct which says, ' Thou shalt do no murder ', and the sacred obligation, ' This must be done for the sake of the Fatherland '. This conflict may be temporarily suspended sometimes, but it always exists. It often occupies my mind after we come in in the evening. The opposition between the two principles is emphasized when one looks out upon such a peaceful valley as this that lies before me. The white-owl, the ' bird of death ', screeches from the alder-clump, and the thunder of the guns grows louder again. Then all is still. It is night. Slowly I prepare for bed.

April, 1915.

The most trying part of this *mole's* war is that one can never have a real straightforward fight. When the first larks soar and, undisturbed by shells and whistling bullets, sing their morning hymn, then the guns begin firing aimlessly into the dawning day. This murdering is so senseless. The one consolation is that one is doing one's duty. I do think that we Germans have, more than any other nation, a stern sense of duty. And we stick to that in this ghastly war. The justification for militarism, which from the ordinary human point of view is detestable, is that it has helped to encourage and strengthen this sense of duty. Of course there are some shirkers here as everywhere else—' it takes all sorts to make a world '—but those who have this sense of duty do not ask : ' Is it dangerous ? Are the guns firing ? ' No : one shoots, one stays awake, one is constantly on the watch, burrows in the ground till 12 or 1 o'clock, and is at it again by 5 the next morning, simply because its one's damned duty and obligation. And all that is done just as a matter of course —neither willingly nor unwillingly—naturally, simply, just because it has got to be done. One may be a little braver or a little more skilful than another, but the same cheery tone prevails all through. Everybody does his best, one working for all and all for one.

April 27th, 1915.

You are dissatisfied because you are not, like the rest of us, actually risking your life for the Fatherland. You are right to feel like that. It is a magnificent thing to be an active participant in this world-conflagration, to share in the responsibility. For every sentry is responsible. If he were to fall asleep for a moment or cease to be on the look-out, that would involve at least the loss of our whole out-post, which in the case of an attack can do nothing anyhow but sell their lives as dearly as possible.

One becomes graver and more thoughtful here, in this position of constant danger and responsibility. I don't think that after the war I shall ever be able to waste a week, or even a few days, in mere loafing. I realize so clearly now how much I have missed, how much work I still have to do—work for myself and work in the service of the beloved German people. So let me say this to you, as a solemn warning at this time : Make use of the opportunity which is now given you for self-culture which shall be productive of results. We are young, and have so much, so very much to do for our own development. Let us work and strive gladly—only thus can we earn the right to enjoy the pleasures of life. . . .

Jouy, October 7th, 1915.

MY DEAR FATHER,—

How our little Konrad had grown, how strong and manly he had become ! With what greatness of soul he faced those difficult times with which I wrestled so feebly ! My dear Brother, your death has set me in the right way !

You see, dear Father, I am just like you now. I have none of that clap-trap, so-called ' patriotism '. But nevertheless I am full of pity and sympathy for

the sufferings of our dear German nation ; recogniz-
ing and wishing to help them to conquer their faults
and failings. And so I will not separate myself from
my own people, neither in thought nor in heart.
No, I must plunge into the middle of this great
distress and misery. I wish really to fight on behalf
of my nation ; to be free from all proletarian class-
hatred ; to take the field, with a heart bleeding with
love, in order to combat all that is not as it should
be in our people, both high and low. I want to
bear witness among my countrymen to the one thing
that can help them in every way, and which is now
scorned and derided in word and deed. See then,
Father, am I not on the right road, or at least on
one of the roads, by which alone I can find my chosen
profession afresh and for the first time aright ?
Father, my whole life will be a struggle, in spite of
my longing for rest and peace—a struggle against
myself and, in my own sphere of activity, against
all injustice, wickedness and meanness in our people ;
against—let us call it by the old, unfashionable name
—against Sin. And in that respect I have still so
much to amend in myself—may God help me to do
it ! . . .

It is late in the evening. My comrades are already
asleep. We are all packed up and ready to march.
There is no duty to-morrow because we may be off
at any moment. Where we are going we don't
know. There are all sorts of surmises : some say
Champagne, others Russia, perhaps Arras, or Serbia.
It doesn't matter. Wherever we go I shall be in
the fatherly Hands of God, and I trust that I may,

(203)

with His help, approach daily nearer to Him wherever I may be. Everything that I used to care so much about now seems petty and unimportant. When once we have brought this struggle to a successful end, I will never try to rouse fresh bitterness in myself or in others, but will fight honourably in that belief in my nation and its future which I still hold.

Champagne, October 10th, 1915.

. . . ' To the right, past Vouziers ! ' We knew then that we were bound for the ' Witch's Cauldron ' in Champagne. Now I am thinking of our little Konrad's last letter. The situation is the same. I think we are in for it this time. . . .

It is crowded in the little tent. Cold, too. The country is quite different here, still beautiful, but bare in some places and chalky. The houses look poor ; there are no bricks or slate-roofs, and the walls are generally of mud.

From the church come the soft tones of a chorale. I wonder whether we shall ever have a service again. Oh, Mother, how I wish I were just going to church with you, when Father was playing the organ ! That would be lovely !

I thank you, dear Parents, for all your love and devotion. Forgive me if I have often grieved you. I know that you love me too much to bear anything up against me. I have no fear of that or of the judgment of God. I commit us all with all my heart into His merciful Hands.

Champagne, November 27th, 1915.

. . . In what way have we sinned, that we should be treated worse than animals ? Hunted from place to place, cold, filthy and in rags, we wander about like gipsies, and in the end are destroyed like vermin ! Will they *never* make peace ! . . .

Champagne, January 29th, 1916.

A man called Reinhold in my section had a letter from his wife saying that she had pawned all the furniture except the indispensable beds. And then the Lieutenants wonder that the men don't want to go on fighting. The ' Champagne and Wine Johnnies ' are enjoying themselves while *we* are dying in filth, and celebrating Christmas with a spoonful and a half of ' plum-and-apple ' and fourteen pieces of sugar.

The only man who has any sympathy for or confidence in the Private Soldier is that ranter Liebknecht. ' Scheidemann and Legien should join the Agrarian Party ; they will never again be re-turned to the Reichstag as Social-Democrats.' That, and not the drivel of those who write dispatches, represents what the Field Greys really feel. I don't agree with the popular saying ' that there will only be peace when the bullets are aimed in the opposite direction ', but, all the same, there will be a fearful awakening some day ! It will be well then for those who can pass away into eternity still believing in the Fatherland, for that time will be worse than the war.

Champagne, March 3rd, 1916.

Dear Mother, don't be unnecessarily anxious. It is quite quiet where we are. And even if we ever do have to go into the thick of it—well, I feel just as my dear little brother did. His gallant words— ' Then you must be proud that you have been permitted to give me to the Fatherland '—come straight from my heart, too. And God only knows whether He intends me to be united with Konrad in a French grave, or whether He is preserving me for some other purpose. For God is the God of History, and in a small way we are all His co-workers in the History of the World. That is a sublime thought ! Dear Parents, of course I might have accomplished more in my life, but even so it has been well worth while to have lived ! And now one must put all thought of oneself quite into the background, for the sake of one's nation and one's Fatherland ; that is so very well worth while that it makes the most difficult things easy. . . .

April 28th, 1916.

Life is indeed beautiful ! To-day we had the exam. after the Course. I don't have to pass another to qualify as Platoon-Commander. This afternoon I have free. That is delightful. Dinner in the Cadets' Mess. Afterwards the musical ones gather round the piano. What a parting-celebration ! Beethoven's Sonatas ; Chopin's wonderful Ballades, Nocturnes and Waltzes ; and Schumann ; it was delightful ! And life, my Friend, is delightful ! Then I go out into the sunshine and dream.

The day after to-morrow I return to the Front.
Don't let's worry about that.   Life is worth fighting
and running risks for ! . . .

Before Verdun, May 13*th,* 1916.

MY DEAR, GOOD, OLD PARENTS,—

Here we have war, war in its most appalling
form, and in our distress we realize the nearness of
God.   Things are becoming very serious ; but I am
inwardly unalarmed and happy.   ' Let me go, I
long to see my Jesus so.'   It must be splendid to see
God in all His glory and His peace, after all that,
with human misunderstanding, one has longed and
struggled for !   I think often and joyfully of the next
world.   I do not fear the Judgment.   I am indeed
a poor, sinful creature, but how great is God's mercy
and the Saviour's love !   So, without fear or dismay,
I do my duty to the Fatherland and to my dear
German people.   I thank you, dear Parents, for
having led me to the Saviour ;   that was the best
thing you ever did.   I love you tenderly.   God be
with you !

HANS.

June 1*st,* '16.

DEAR PARENTS,—

I am lying on the battle-field, wounded in the
body.   I think I am dying.   I am glad to have time
to prepare for the heavenly home-coming.   Thank
you, dear Parents.   God be with you.

HANS.

(207)

RICHARD SCHMIEDER, Student of Philosophy, Leipzig

Born January 24th, 1888.
Killed July 14th, 1916, near Béthenville.

In the Trenches near Vaudesincourt, March 13th, 1915.

THE crucial point in the battle-area has long since ceased to be the right wing (Flanders), having been transferred to the neighbourhood of Souain-Perthes, in Champagne.

Anybody who, like myself, has been through the awful days near Penthy since the 6th of February, will agree with me that a more appalling struggle could not be imagined. It has been a case of soldier against soldier, equally matched and both mad with hate and rage, fighting for days on end over a single square of ground, till the whole tract of country is one blood-soaked, corpse-strewn field. . . .

On February 27th, tired out and utterly exhausted in body and mind, we were suddenly called up to reinforce the VIIIth Reserve Corps, had to re-occupy our old position at Ripont, and were immediately attacked by the French with extraordinary strength and violence. It was a gigantic murder, by means of bullets, shells, axes, and bombs, and there was such a thundering, crashing, bellowing and screaming as might have heralded the Day of Judgment.

In three days, on a front of about 200 yards, we lost 909 men, and the enemy casualties must have amounted to thousands. The blue French cloth mingled with the German grey upon the ground,

(208)

and in some places the bodies were piled so high that one could take cover from shell-fire behind them. The noise was so terrific that orders had to be shouted by each man into the ear of the next. And whenever there was a momentary lull in the tumult of battle and the groans of the wounded, one heard, high up in the blue sky, the joyful song of birds ! Birds singing just as they do at home in spring-time ! It was enough to tear the heart out of one's body !

Don't ask about the fate of the wounded ! Anybody who was incapable of walking to the doctor had to die a miserable death ; some lingered in agony for hours, some for days, and even for a week. And the combatants stormed regardlessly to and fro over them : ' I can't give you a hand,—You're for the Promised Land,—My Comrade good and true.' A dog, dying in the poorest hovel at home, is enviable in comparison.

There are moments when even the bravest soldier is so utterly sick of the whole thing that he could cry like a child. When I heard the birds singing at Ripont, I could have crushed the whole world to death in my wrath and fury. If only those gentlemen—Grey, Asquith, and Poincaré—could be transported to this spot, instead of the war lasting ten years, there would be peace to-morrow !

MARTIN MÜLLER, Student of Law, Leipzig

Born July 27th, 1892, at Blankenburg.
Killed July 20th, 1916, near Hardecourt-sur-Somme.

Tahure, Christmas Day, 1914.

A MERRY Christmas and a happy New Year ! May the New Year bring a satisfactory peace and let us all meet again safe and sound !

Yesterday—Christmas Eve—gave us a deep insight into the misery brought about by war, though we only viewed it from a distance. On the 23rd we had Brigade Exercise near St. Erme, from 7–9.30. Then followed an inspection of the Army Reserve Corps there, by the General in Command, till 12, with its accompanying thorough cleansing of the ' corpus ', brushing of the moustache, sewing on of buttons and darning of holes in one's trousers. After that, a banquet. I, determined to go a regular bust, selected roast-goose. Real, genuine roast-goose ! Topping ! Then I expended two of the little Mocca-bags in order to enjoy really home-like ' coffee and cakes '. After that I meant to write a letter of thanks to you, and then we were going to a Christmas service, followed by the Company festivities in the Convent cellar. Oh, we were all looking forward to it like children. But it was not to be ! A man suddenly rushed in with the cry : ' Alarm ! ' Well, we were used to that. It might very well be just a practice. But it seemed to me really rather ridiculous to give a dud alarm just before Christmas. Surely the Area-Commandant

(210)

wouldn't play such a dirty trick as that on us! Well, quick with all necessaries into the ' monkey '.[1] Besides underclothing, knitted-helmet, and the other things which have to go in one's pack, I crammed in a sausage, some gingerbread, the marzipan, and all the fags. All the rest—blankets, pillow, cape, jam, boxes, the little Christmas tree, and all sorts of other things—I chucked just anyhow into my kit-bag. I hastily buckled my Kodak on to my belt and—still with a great piece of cake in one hand —stuck Herr Grossmann's bottle of concentrated tea-and-rum into my bread-sack, seized the pop-gun, and rushed out ! I was one of the first. Soon the others turned up.

' Shoulder arms ! Out of step, March ! ' Off we go. And we didn't half march either ! It was about half-past three when we started, and we marched for one hour, two hours, and still the longed-for order, ' About turn ! ', did not come ! Only one subject was eagerly discussed all the time : the Christmas parcels we had left behind, especially the cakes ! And still we went on.

Night began to fall. Suddenly a shrill whistle pierced the darkness and we found ourselves facing a railway-embankment. An immensely long train was waiting there. ' Entrain ! ' Where on earth are we going ? Nobody has the least idea !

The dear little train puffs off. Our initial disgust is vanquished by a sort of brilliantly sardonic humour. One Christmas carol after another is

[1] The German knapsack was of rough, hairy skin : hence, perhaps, this nickname.

loudly intoned by husky voices. The train hurtles along ! A Corporal, who is a scene-shifter in the theatre at L., declaims some original doggerel verses which he had really intended to recite at our Christmas festivities.

The train comes to a standstill. ' Laon ! ' We all press inquisitively into the doorway of our cattle-truck—there are 46 of us in it, by the way. The wonderfully picturesque little city lies peaceful and brilliantly lit-up on its hill-top.

On we go again. It begins to get quiet in our truck. Soon one hears the regular breathing and snoring of weary sleepers. The pace at which the train is travelling has gradually increased to an alarming rate. I begin to doze a little too.

' All out ! ' The luminous dial of my watch shows that it is already half-past three. The marching begins again. All along the horizon on our left is the magnificent spectacle of a night battle. Flares, rockets, searchlights, the flash of gun-fire, the rattle of rifles. All things that we are accustomed to, but on a much larger scale. The whole night seems alive ! It is marvellous ! If only we knew what was happening ! Where are they shoving us to ? Especially disquieting are the countless motor-ambulances that keep tearing past and splashing us with mud. The road is almost impassable. Soaking wet ! It is raining. We are going at a quick march, without a halt, on and on. The dawn begins to break.

At last a village comes in sight. ' Halt ! ' Till 9 o'clock we stand here on the road in the deep mire. In the meantime it has begun to snow a little. It is devilish cold.

About half-past nine—at last—we are ordered to billets, and our Platoon manages to secure an uncovered yard with an elegant dung-heap ! Nowhere to sit down. Our officers are no better off. The place—Tahure—is crawling with soldiers. The Reserves of two Army Corps have collected in this completely devastated village.

And now the truth gradually leaks out : during the last three days the French have made the most desperate attempts to break through. All in vain. Appalling losses on both sides. Yesterday 1,200 French surrendered. On Christmas Eve a supreme effort was supposed to be designed against this place. The descriptions of the troops give us some idea at last of what war can really be like : madness ; awful agony ; ghastly terror. I have to put it shortly.

We lay the whole night in our princely quarters and froze. The Holy Night sank softly down upon the earth. And this was our Christmas miracle— we were not put into the line after all ! The enemy's main body was diverted to Verdun. To-night we are going back to St. Ermine. It is a pity I have so little time to write. I could tell you no end of interesting things about the last two days.

I will just describe Christmas Eve briefly. Towards 8 o'clock through the darkness sounded the sweet melody of ' Stille Nacht '. I went to see where it was coming from. On the other side of the road was an Estaminet where our 3rd Platoon was billeted. They had built up a big fire. Round it in a circle sat the singers. The song was ended. Then a slim young Coblentz Pioneer rose up from beside the fire and made a splendid speech about our Kaiser. Three rousing cheers rang out from our throats in the direction of the enemy. Then the Pioneer wished us a Happy Christmas and said we must have a look at their Christmas tree. I followed him. It was an unforgettable sight! A neat little dug-out. In the middle a table! And on it the lit-up tree, beautifully decorated with ' angels' hair ', little bells and gold and silver threads. It was very touching. And they were such good chaps! The one who had made the speech turned out to be a Corps Student from Jena. Talk about German hospitality! Everything you can imagine was simply forced upon me, and finally the best thing of all—in the tiny place there was still room for one more to sleep, and so I had the enormous luck to be better housed than even our officers! Thinking of you and your Christmas and of former Christmases, I fell asleep.

Oostkamp, March 19*th,* 1916.

An eventful month, this March of 1916. To-day the King has awarded me the Cross of the Albert Order, 2nd Class, with Swords. You'd think that would be almost a bit too much in one month, wouldn't you? Unfortunately this decoration is associated with a very tragic experience and the memory of what, at the time, I felt very much.

It was on the 28th of January. I had been back

for nearly a month in the Line, fortified by my glorious leave at home with you, and therefore feeling grateful and happy. When going the round in the afternoon, I was looking at the enemy wire and suddenly noticed that in two places it was broken and weak-looking—a few isolated ' Spanish Horsemen ' [1] presenting an obstruction which would be very easy to break through. I at once reported this to the Company Commander, for any reduction in the wire is considered very important, being generally the first sign of a projected attack. Our Artillery were also informed and must have been pretty sick with me, as they had to stand by their guns ' in Alarm Order ' all night.

I next told the Company-Commander that, in order to examine this thing more closely, I was going to send out a patrol. When, towards evening, I asked my Section Leaders for volunteers, the only one eligible as Leader who offered to go was Fahnenjunker-Corporal Strauss ; also a few Privates. As, however, Strauss had never been on a patrol before, I thought I had better lead it myself, if only to set my men a good example for a possibly similar occasion in the future.

About a quarter to eight we started—Strauss and Private Tschoppe with me. The latter had volunteered directly he heard that I was going. The distance between the trenches at this point was about 120 yards. The ground was perfectly flat and bare,

[1] A star-shaped framework wound round with barbed-wire, which could be thrown out on to no-man's-land from the trench.

so afforded but little cover. We scrambled over our own wire and then crawled noiselessly over the thin grass which covered the ground. I was in front with the two others behind me, in a sort of wedge. The stars were not yet out and the night consequently rather dark. From the enemy came the usual occasional shots, sometimes interspersed with the rattle of a machine-gun. Now and then a bullet whistled over us, but without troubling us, for here the trenches on both sides are built up above the level of the ground, and shots, being generally aimed at the parapet, don't often strike near the earth between the lines. Our side, having been warned about the patrol, were naturally firing seldom and always high.

We only advanced very slowly, as the enemy kept sending up star-shells, and then we had to remain absolutely motionless. It is not easy either to get along, crawling on the ground, and anyhow it is extremely tiring. Now we could see the flashes from the barrels of the enemy rifles. Tack, tack, tack, tack! . . . there stood a machine-gun, easily recognizable by the faint flash accompanying each shot. Suddenly from the left a narrow but brilliant beam of light pierced the darkness. Apparently the light from a dug-out as the door was opened for a moment. We now occasionally heard a slight cough from the trench. I myself had difficulty in suppressing a cough now and then, for the ground was very wet and during our long crawl my coat and trousers had absorbed a considerable amount of dampness, although we had taken the precaution of wrapping sand-bags round our knees and elbows.

Then suddenly, half-left of us, we heard them starting work on the wire ! That was the spot we were making for. So now our job began : we had to find out whether the enemy was removing the wire or mending the gaps. So we crept nearer. We could hear the chink of the iron pickets. Cautiously we crawled still nearer—now we were only 20 to 25 yards from the enemy trench, and we could see faint outlines of the working-party. Tzisch ! Up went a star shell ! We pressed ourselves even closer to the ground, but I still could see that a shining new wire was being stretched and that a number of new iron pickets were now standing in front of the ' Spanish Horsemen '.

Our task was accomplished. We could get back. I made a sign to the others ; they crawled up to me and I was just going to tell them the result of my observations when Tschoppe, who was close to me on the right, screamed out loud. A bad body-wound ! We two others picked him up as carefully as we could and crept a little way back with him. A few bullets struck the soft ground close to us. Another flare lit up the darkness with its brilliant white light, and we saw a small trench a few yards away from us : ' into it, quick ! ' Certainly we sank over our knees in mud, but for the moment we were safe. It is an old water-logged trench leading forward out of the English line.

Now I am able to examine the poor comrade's wound. It is a deep graze. We can't bandage it out here. He is in awful pain and whimpers softly. The English have quieted down again and aren't shooting any more. There is no time to lose. I take off my great-coat in order to lay the comrade on it and carry him in. But it is no good—the coat is too short. Also it is impossible for us two alone to carry such a heavy weight. I at last make up my mind to send Strauss for help. He vanishes into the darkness.

I am now alone with the poor chap, who is still groaning, and now and then cannot suppress a cry of pain. My luminous watch says 9.45. Fortunately the wound is not bleeding at all. Tschoppe leans his head on my knee and cowers down in a sitting position. Both my legs disappear gradually into the mud and go to sleep. I can't feel them at all. The poor chap realizes that his wound is a very serious one and is in a state of despair. He has been through the whole war and has never been hit before. The watch says 10.30. He tells me about his home, and then suddenly he screams again. The pain is too awful.

Now the attention of the English has again been aroused. They evidently know exactly where we are crouching and they are aiming straight at the edge of the trench. The dirt splashes up into our faces. We duck down as far as we can, but the trench is not very deep. And the hands move slowly round the luminous figures of the dial.

Every now and then the men over there have another bout of firing. I think to myself that now they are getting out of the trench and coming towards us and I grip my revolver tighter. But there are only six cartridges in it. Precious few !

And still the longed-for, anxiously awaited help does not come. Has anything happened to Strauss, or has he lost his way? It is so difficult not to go wrong in this featureless terrain.

Now it is 11.15. Still an occasional bullet splashes into the mud beside us. Still the poor man groans and moans, leaning against my knees—he is big and strong, but suffering horribly. I keep trying to comfort and encourage him. He feels that he is bleeding internally and gives me messages for his parents. I tell him about a beautiful Convalescent Home to which he will be sent when he comes out of hospital, and how after that he will go home till he is quite all right again. But he shakes his head and asks me to take a photograph of his grave and send it to his home. That is ghastly! And from up in the sky the stars look down so peacefully upon us! I thought: ' He who dwells up there will not forsake us ! '

And He did not, for after a long, long wait, there was a sudden rustle in front of us; at once I thought, ' The English are coming ', but a soft voice whispered my name, and Strauss and another soldier crawled into our trench. The watch said 11.50. The two had lost their way, just as I expected, and had only found it again through hearing the groans of the wounded man.

But now quickly to work! Our united efforts succeeded in dragging my legs, which were now completely covered, out of the mud and getting the life back into them. Then we laid Tschoppe as comfortably as we could on the ground-sheet, got out of the trench and struggled towards our line. Even for the three of us it was a heavy load, but we managed it. At last we reached our own wire, and there the ground-sheet tore. A new one was soon fetched and then we went on again. Getting over the wire was rather difficult and dangerous, as the chaps opposite began to shoot vigorously again. But at last, about 1 o'clock, we arrived, with our poor, mortally wounded burden, in the trench. Then he was tied up and sent to the rear. He was still fully conscious.

In the ambulance on the way to the hospital poor Tschoppe succumbed to his severe wound.

EDUARD OFFENBÄCHER, Student of Political Economy, Freiburg i. Baden

Born August 21st, 1895, at Mannheim.
Killed July 27th, 1916, on the Somme.

During the Battle near Arras (Loretto Hill), May, 1915.

WE had enjoyed two delightful weeks' rest in an idyllic little village of the Pas-de-Calais, where the cherry-trees were in bloom and the purple lilac peeped over the cottage walls. The dear little French children said good-bye to us with many tears and much waving of handkerchiefs, for they had quite ceased to think of us as ' enemies '.

After a long, hot march we arrived at Souchez, which was even then a horrible spot, at the foot of the hotly-contested Loretto Hill which we knew only too well. I sank blissfully down on the hard bed of straw prepared in the otherwise quite comfortably furnished cellar, and soon dropped into a deep sleep.

I don't know how long I had slept, when I was suddenly awakened by a clatter as of falling bricks and stones. It is daylight and the gun-fire very violent, my Vice-Platoon-Commander thinks it even ominous. A glance shows me that the cellar has, most imprudently, not been shored up. ' That must at once be——' But already the devil is at the door, in the shape of my batman : ' Orders from the Company-Commander. The Company is standing to ! ' H'm, the first day is starting well ! I think to myself, while outside the banging, whistling and howling and the deafening crashes redouble.

(221)

I have hardly shoved a few crumbs into my hungry maw, when we have to be off. Into the battle! Into the most awful battle that the regiment has ever experienced!

Two Platoons disappear into a communication-trench that opens right among the ruined houses. One has to follow it along the side of the slope, under heavy gun-fire, to the front line. It is simply called 'the Defile'—and, for the initiated, what horrible associations, closely connected with that of the village of A. above which it begins, that name has!

Just as the first section of my Platoon, which was the last, were starting, some men came rushing from the upper entrance to the village, with every appearance of terror, and while still at some distance from us shouted: 'The Frenchies have broken through! They're coming from up over there!'

The O.C. of the 2nd Baden Grenadier Regiment 110, Lieut.-Colonel von Blücher, standing bare-headed in his long cavalry cloak, passes his hand over his forehead as if to brush something away. 'Herr Leutnant!' he calls to me—'occupy Position $1\frac{1}{2}$ right and left of the railway-line with your Platoon! I rely on you not to let a single Frenchman pass!'— 'While I have a man left, not one, Herr Oberst!' The Colonel goes, with firm, deliberate steps, towards the lower entrance of the village, where the fatal bullet strikes him! . . .

Where is 'Position $1\frac{1}{2}$, right and left of the railway-line?' Nobody can answer, nobody knows! After a prolonged search, in a fearful hail of light and heavy shells; amidst the crashing beams, falling roofs and walls, splintering boards and spurting earth and stones ; in the midst of running, cursing, jostling men, with and without packs, with and without helmets ; in a chaos of wagons, horses, coils of barbed-wire and already constructed ' Spanish Horsemen ' [1] ; constantly looking back to see that the whole Platoon is following and nobody slinking off, as some are unfortunately inclined to do ; I at last find the communication-trench leading to Position $1\frac{1}{2}$.

I quickly decide the most favourable positions with regard to range, field of fire, observation-posts, etc., and send a patrol out to the foremost line where most of the Company are.

The left-flank outpost reports : ' Herr Leutnant, half-left to the rear, over there in Souchez church-yard, there are French in close column.' Damnation ! then the dirty dogs are through, curse them ! ' Herr Leutnant ! '—the telephone is working perfectly—' on the right, in the valley, there are three rows of trenches close together, and columns in the rear. The wood behind also seems to be full of red-legs.' I raise my field-glass to my eyes. Damn ! there they are again, sure enough ! And right behind us, towards the hill where the whole of our ' Heavies ' are posted, white clouds of French shrapnel are visible. They look like snakes' tongues as they burst. So our people have been driven back as far as that ! How we must be outdone in bombs and shells, and think what is at stake ! Our whole 21st Battery ! If they succeed—and they are only

[1] See p. 215.

(223)

a few hundred yards away now—they will be through ! And then we shall have no guns ! To have the enemy only about half a mile behind one is not a pleasant sensation. But things were to pan out differently.

The Patrol comes racing back quite out of breath : ' Herr Leutnant is to move forward at once with the Platoon. The Company is in urgent need of reinforcement. The French are attacking in great force. The 6th and 8th Companies are wiped out. Herr Leutnant must take over command, as the Company-Commander is dangerously wounded ! ' Cheerful ! Who is to hold Position $1\frac{1}{2}$? Well, it's no good thinking about that, and I give the order, ' Out of step, march ! ' and lead the Platoon through the communication-trench, which is quite blown in in several places and is being heavily shelled, to the edge of the village.

There was many a hold-up by the way—one serious one : it had been raining for a long time previous, and one man got stuck in the awful mud. We had no end of a job to get him out. I think eight men were hauling at him, and the language . . . ! Well, I was damned lucky to get back into the Defile with only a few wounded.

Two days later.

I am simply dog-tired and no wonder ! Two days without intermission in a half-blown-in trench, with every man keenly on the alert the whole time ; bayonets fixed day and night. Opposite, only about twenty yards away, the enemy, lying in wait.

Between us saps run out, guarded by barricades. A mountain of bombs lies ready to hand beside them. Right on top of one such barricade, but out of our reach, lies a comrade, his dimmed eyes gazing westward ; his trusty weapon in one hand, the other stretched out as he made ready to spring ; his once fair hair dyed dark red with blood. Many are lying like that outside the trench, friend and foe. Nobody buries them ; nobody has time.

The sun burns fiercely in a cloudless sky, making the foul smell of putrefaction grow ever stronger. The nerves of one's stomach are strained till one is nearly sick, but there is nothing inside the rumbling thing. I can hardly satisfy my raging hunger with the beautiful white bread from the knapsack of the young French soldier who lies there with a red patch on his breast. A bundle of mauve-tinted, scented letters is in my hands : ' Mon chéri, we are praying every day, Mama and I, that God will keep you safe for us. You, my one and only love . . .', etc. Always the same words, always the same woe ! And meanwhile I am munching his beautiful white bread and thinking : anyhow, they have nothing as good as this at home !

This morning we got a little rest at last. The body sinks exhausted on to the bed of straw, but the spirit wakes and listens for the cry of the sentry. We are a little farther on now, in the Defile itself.

' They're coming ! They're coming ! ' Blue-grey forms are bobbing up and down like Jack-in-the-boxes, but the Jacks carry rifles with bayonets, and they shout shrilly, oh so shrilly : ' 'Urrah,

'urrah!' All out, to the escarpment! Now a spring to the next! One more! Now it is only a few yards. One already hears the chink of metal, already bombs are rolling down the hill. Look out! Head down! A slight rise in the ground will protect me. But it landed close by. What is that man next to me doing? Oh, what a pity, it got him—instead of me! Minnies come oscillating through the air. It looks as if the French were presenting us with huge champagne-bottles, but the champagne contains rather too much carbonic-acid gas, it sends fountains of earth hundreds of yards into the air! and sometimes arms and legs of unfortunate human beings go too!

'Halt, look out!' There is a moment of awful suspense. A great commotion over there—bayonets moving about—talking in undertones—words of command. Is it an attack? ''Urrah! 'urrah!' —that sounds like a curse—ludicrous from those swollen red lips. There is a furious volley—first one and then another of our men screams—but we have looked calmly into those black, bestial masks and wiped them out!

A few moments' breathing space! I look back over the plain, glowing in the evening sunlight. A thick, black cloud of smoke hangs over the village down there, where only one pillar remains to show where the pretty little church-tower once stood. American shells fall unceasingly upon the homes of French peasants. The next one is just the same. Far, far away on the horizon are clouds of shrapnel, coming ever nearer. Can it be possible? Is there still hope ? Yes, our troops over there are actually gaining more and more ground. They have not forgotten our poor, little, almost isolated party on the Hill of Our Lady of Loretto. They have to thank us for holding that hill by our persistent blows, delivered from trench to trench.

'Herr Leutnant, they are coming on again!' Things look bad on the right. They are coming out on the flank. Damn, there they are on the left too, and our ranks are growing thinner. I must go over to the right flank myself. I leap up just in time to see a little 17-year-old fighting with a grinning, bloated nigger. Suddenly a stream of blood comes from my mouth. I press my left hand over it, so that the blood flows up my sleeve, and run to the right. I can't speak, but I wave my right arm and fire all the chambers of my revolver. Thank God, my brave fellows have held their own again, but at what a sacrifice !

Evening is falling. The red-gold sun stands in the west—a sun of blood ! Now I too can get a little rest. I must go and get tied up in the village or I shall loose too much blood.

The French did not come over again that night.

In the Line, July 14th, 1916.

The battle is still raging violently on all fronts ; the enemy still trying to gain a decisive advantage and emblazon victory on his colours. The heroic endurance of our troops deprives him of this hope and defies even the horrible weapons of present-day warfare. And in a few days, or perhaps weeks, the war will sink back into the old indefinite state of waiting while both sides prepare for further efforts and more gigantic losses, and devise yet more ghastly means of destruction for another struggle, which will again prove useless and will result only in a further loss of hundreds of thousands of young lives. And so it will go on, until—yes, until? And one is right in the middle of it all, no longer marvelling at finding oneself just a small wheel, without volition, driven by those who, fully realizing their responsibility, yet deem it their duty, for the honour and glory of the Fatherland, to send thousands of men to their death —dictating to thousands the way in which their loyalty and courage shall express itself.

What is the good of it all, considering that ultimate result of the war was decided long ago? Is it in order to pander to the pride and thirst for glory of a few men who, through the influence of the Press, drive whole nations into the arena? Is it a point of honour among those same nations, who, being so numerous, are ashamed to yield to the supremacy of a single one, while thereby still further exalting that one?—Have the German commanders made up their minds to gain some particular point, which they will not give up, and for the sake of which they think it worth while to sacrifice the wishes and well-being of the whole nation, and on which the enemy will not yield, having still too much faith in his own strength? Is a question of the continued existence of the German Empire, of Germany's position as a World Power, or have not our enemies long since abandoned the idea of the destruction of

Germany, and are they not fighting now only for an unattainable ideal (like the French) ; in the desperate endeavour to uphold their world-supremacy (like the English) ; or to prevent utter defeat (like the Russians) ?   In any case it is obvious that both sides must believe that they are as a matter of course and indisputably in the right, or they would not, after two years of an unprecedented struggle of millions against millions, still go on employing their whole strength, and making use of means which may well bring total ruin upon their national finances, confidently relying on the agreement of every individual that it is for the good of the State that they should continue to surpass themselves in these tremendous efforts.

One can only suppose, from past experience, that this will go on until complete exhaustion is reached —and that may not be for years !   One keeps cherishing the hope that it may be possible to find some way out of this miserable situation.   One keeps hoping that the enemy may be forced, either by military successes or diplomatic negotiation, to realize the true state of things.   That is the only comfort, but not a satisfactory one ;   for that reason I have acquiesced. . . .

Well, now I have expressed all the views I have about the future.   ' They are too gloomy,' you'll say. But think it over—are things otherwise ?   The nation, the great machine lubricated by filth from the Press, is beginning to think for itself.   People, both here and in other countries, are crying out for the war to end, and yet it does not end.   Who is responsible for that? No single individual or individuals. Human beings are not powerful enough for that. Nature governs all things and her laws are those by which men live. Is not the growth and decay of nations an anomaly? Why does Nature develop and then destroy them? It is just the same in little things. That is the history of life and death. Is there an ultimate purpose in the Universe? Or does everything just remain as it was and as it always has been? Perhaps in another life we may be given the key which will solve all these problems.

OTTO ERNST FRANKE, Student of Law, Rostock

Born February 26th, 1899, at Shanghai.
Killed August 2nd, 1916, near Martinpuich.

July 13th, 1916.

FOR the moment I am still at the depôt. They are pretty strict with us here. In consequence of several things that had happened, our lot were supposed to do extra drill every day for a week, from 7.30 to 9.30. Mercifully after two days we were let off. My telling you this is not meant for a complaint as far as I myself am concerned. I take the rough with the smooth quite cheerfully. But honestly I cannot think it right that old men, who have all got something more or less serious wrong with them, should be treated as if they were recruits being drilled into purely ornamental soldiers in time of peace—that they should be punished for not lying down quick enough, and things like that. It makes men, who anyhow didn't want to be soldiers, still more discontented. All the same I can't deny that all this drilling has great value. It makes us get accustomed to doing things we don't like over and over again ; to be blamed when we think we have done something well ; and to discover that when we imagine ourselves to have exhausted all our strength that that is just the time when we have to begin really to exert ourselves. All this will be of great practical use later on.

At the Front, Reserve Position, July 25th, 1916.

After accomplishing the greater part of the journey on foot, my new regiment was, during the course of last week, flung from its position near Lens to the Somme, where countless other regiments have already got pretty well knocked about, and where there is a good deal for us to put right.

The battles are extraordinarily fierce, as even older men who were in the attack on Hartmannsweilerkopf and know the Loretto Hill only too well, agree. The drum-fire is unusually intense, and the worst of it is there are very few dug-outs fit to use.

We are lying, for the time being, in the 2nd Reserve Position, which we occupied last night under fairly heavy shell-fire. It is a trench without dug-outs, which, after all, do give some protection against shrapnel, and we haven't had anything worse inflicted on us so far, thank God. But in the positions farther forward everything has been so foully smashed up that there is no cover left except shell-holes. No doubt we shall soon have to move up to relieve some of the others, for nobody can stick it for long. We are bound to have a pretty bad time, but I am still true to my principles and hope that I may remain free from the all too natural fear.

All the same, however, I don't consider it cowardice, in face of what we have to expect, to have done with the things of this life, and therefore, in case it should prove necessary, I want to take a tender farewell of you now. That is why I have written under such unfavourable conditions, here in the narrow trench. I shall not tell my parents where

or how I am situated, but you have a right to know.
' He who looks into the abyss, but with the eye of
an eagle, he has courage.' A Zarathustra is my
companion even here.   Good-bye !

MAX BÄSSLER, Student of Administration and History, Leipzig

Born February 19th, 1895, at Leipzig.
Killed September 12th, 1916, on the Somme.

Near Ypres, middle of May, 1915.

. . . The Lieutenant came and told me to see that our dead had proper funerals. They had already been temporarily buried by other hands, but we knew the places.

On the way back to Nuns' Copse, I noticed a field-postcard stuck up on the right of the trench, and on it was written : Rifleman Kurt Limke. A little farther on was a short post bearing the names of Beer and Lichtenberger.

I made the necessary arrangements at Polygon Wood the same evening, and got a day's leave from the regiment.

The work had to be done under the cloak of night, and before 3 a.m. Guck's rough voice called to me from outside the dug-out. In the opaque darkness stood the working-party with spades and picks. Silently we went our way. Outside the trench we divided up into small groups and I went with one to fetch Beer's body. We had to dig deeper than we expected. A horrible, sickly-sweet smell rose from the earth and we dared not smoke because of the enemy. First we found an infantryman who had been buried as a third in the same grave. Then we lifted poor Beer out. I helped carry him, four men remaining behind to dig out Lichtenberger.

(234)

We wrapped the body in a ground-sheet, and fixed poles at the sides to carry it by. Slowly the day dawned, palely red. It reminded me of Hauff's song. A dead man on such a primitive bier is rather heavy to carry, but on the edge of Nuns' Copse a wagon was waiting. Knoblauch and Hunger were already lying on it. The former, with his beautiful long dark beard, looked like a suffering Christ. Then they brought Lichtenberger, the only one who looked at all as he did when alive, and Zietzschmann, whose face was covered with blood. Lemke had not been found ; his grave was empty.

At our camp in Polygon Wood we had a short rest. Then we went on, by way of the old position and the old relief road, to Becelaere. There the Drivers were working at the graves, in the little Military Cemetery beside the church. We fetched some large glazed tiles from the roof of a summer-house to put round the graves, and picked some lilac-blossom and branches of red and yellow leaves to decorate them. Then we made the graves as much deeper as was necessary.

Meanwhile all who wished to take part in this last act of respect had assembled. We lowered the comrades into the earth. A Driver of the 248th, a Brother of the Rauhen-House in Hamburg, said a few moving words. The lilac gave out its lovely scent and the coloured leaves glowed on the fresh sods, but the earth crumbled as it were impatiently. Two big tears stood in old Böhne's eyes. Then we scattered the flowers and leaves over the dead, and began to shovel in the earth. The last service I was

(235)

able to render my dear Rudolf was to brush a little blue butterfly from his cold cheek. When I first saw him dead I almost envied him his unconscious state, but now, as I watched the worms and other creatures being shovelled in with the earth, and the last bit of ground-sheet disappearing, I was glad, after all, that for me the May sun still shone brightly, and that for me the lilac still bloomed and perfumed the air.

MAX GÖRLER, Student of Philosophy, Leipzig

Born March 13th, 1896, at Wittmannsgereuth.
Killed September 16th, 1916, before Verdun.

Leipzig, June 9th, 1916.

DEAR FATHER,—

I write to ask your permission to enlist as a War
Volunteer on June 17th. Since I met Scheidig again
in the holidays I have realized that I *must* be a
soldier. We always vied with one another at school,
but now what a poor figure I have cut, compared
with him ! He has only one brother left and he is
also at the Front. Up till now 270 students from
here have been killed. I understand the gravity of
the war, and I think it is shameful to allow younger
men to fight for one when one is capable of fighting
oneself.

How could I ever face a class of schoolboys some
day and teach them about Schiller and Körner, and
about history, without being obliged to tell lies the
whole time ! I want you to give your permission
in the same form which you have used before, leaving
the regiment to my own choice. I will join whatever
the doctor thinks me most suitable for. In any case
I shall not go straight to the Artillery, but only if it
seems, on consideration, the best thing to do. In
time of peace I should have chosen the Infantry.
Uncle Albert advised the Artillery because, he says,
' the Artillery has not such heavy losses as the Infantry " cannon-fodder " ; for example, the entire
XXth Battery has so far lost only 52 men, whereas

(237)

in the Infantry whole regiments have been wiped out.' If after that I joined the Artillery, it would be just as bad as if K. went off to Switzerland voluntarily. No, I shall go wherever I am most wanted !

OTTO HEINEBACH, Student of Philosophy, Berlin

Born August 14th, 1892.
Died in the Military Hospital at Frankfurt, September 14th, 1916, of wounds received before Douaumont.

In the Trenches, September 22nd, 1915.

MY DEAR FATHER,—

I write only to you to-day, because I have something terrible to tell you. Less than three hours ago, our dear, good H., my best comrade, was killed by a shell, which gave him a horrible wound in the body.

I was asleep in the dug-out when this awful thing happened. H. was on sentry-duty. They woke me immediately with the news. I hurried to the dreadful spot and found him lying in a pool of blood with his abdomen torn open. I went close up to him. He said nothing, though I spoke to him and he was quite conscious. When a comrade called his attention to my being there, he is supposed to have said : ' Nothing is any use ! ' I couldn't bear the ghastly sight for long, but I stayed near him, in the next bay, so that I could hear everything he said. He was in awful pain and uttered agonizing cries. ' Oh, my poor parents ! My poor parents ! ' he kept saying, and : ' Terrible, terrible ! '

When the stretcher-bearers and the doctor came and began giving him first-aid, he must have suffered horribly. I was told that he tried to prevent them from bandaging him, but begged for some sort of drug, which, however, could not be given—I suppose because of the injury to the intestine. The doctor and others tried to give him hope, but he didn't

(239)

believe them for an instant. He felt that he should not live to reach ' Point 80 ', where there is a dressing-station. The last words I heard him utter were : ' I can't see ! I'm fainting ! ' and immediately after that, as they lifted him on to the stretcher, he must have lost consciousness. He died on the way through the communication-trench to ' Point 80 '. His body is lying on a bier close to the dressing-station dug-out, and this evening it will be taken on a wagon to Hettencourt, where we are billeted, and laid to rest in the village churchyard.

Sometimes I can't realize that this dreadful thing has actually happened. Oh, what a passion of rage against this vile war rose up in me when I saw that dear, splendid man, who was so full of high aspirations and carried such a noble soul within him, lying there on the ground, hideously injured ! But let me be silent in face of the irrevocable ! At least our friend was spared more than a few minutes' suffering, and he had seen his home and his dear ones again, for he had returned from leave only five days ago. How glad I was to see him back, for he was the only one of my immediate companions with whom I was intimately in sympathy.

Last night we were on sentry-duty together three times—five or six hours altogether—and he was giving me news of home, and of you and the others. Together we saw the new day begin to dawn, and I softly quoted Faust's words. How often during the night he expressed his disgust at this stationary warfare, with its crawling underground, into the earth, its perpetual intimidation, its everlasting inaction. 'If only we could get on a bit,' he said several times ; ' I'm dead sick of this ! '

He would have welcomed death if it had come to him as it did to his brothers, in free fight, in the midst of the ' Hurrahs ' of an attack ; but that was not vouchsafed to him.

In his pocket was found a blood-soaked Reclam-Edition copy of the translation of Tillier's *L'oncle Benjamin*. He must have been reading it just before the end. He had had the book sent out to him on my recommendation, had only just begun it, and was talking enthusiastically about it while we were on guard last night. He quoted, among other things, a very clever passage about war. This morning in the dug-out he said to me : ' I am expecting a visit to-day, and I am so looking forward to it ! ' ' Why, who is coming ? ' I asked. ' My Uncle Benjamin ! ' That was the last pleasure the dear fellow enjoyed.

Achiet le Petit, December 30*th,* 1915.

Sometimes it seems to me as if the universal longing of all nations for peace *must* finally put an end to this murder. I heard yesterday, on good authority, that after the ghastly affair at Loos, there had been at one place on that Front an absolute cessation of hostilities, as if by mutual consent ; both sides walked about quite unconcernedly on the top, in full view of the enemy, who was only a few yards away, and not a shot was fired. I think such a state of things, whether it actually occurred or not, best represents the feeling on both sides, and I can imagine that the general war-weariness might at last

(241)

reach such a point that it might lead to a similar 'entente cordiale' between the opposing armies without any diplomatic preliminaries. Then indeed the World War, which began in such a flood of patriotic ardour, would end in farce; but I believe that the history of the world contains other tragi-comedies of the same sort, and that not every great mind is afraid to admit the fact; there are sceptics with a sharp eye for such absurd, grotesque and ironical situations, who do not attempt to gloss them over or explain them away.

Before Verdun, Friday evening, February 18*th*, 1916.
[*The day before he received his ultimately fatal wound.*]

In the dressing-station dug-out, where we are all lying for a day in reserve, it is stiflingly hot. The place is crammed with men. Outside it is raining as usual. A little while ago we heard that the attack had again been postponed for twenty-four hours, and just now came word that it was fixed for the 20th. That seems to be the final decision, though there is no sign of any improvement in the weather. Packs are to be worn, but everything not absolutely neces-sary is to be left behind.

I say good-bye to you, my dear Parents and Brothers and Sisters. Thanks, most tender thanks for all that you have done for me. If I fall, I earnestly beg of you to bear it with fortitude. Reflect that I should probably never have achieved complete happiness and contentment. Perhaps my life would, to the very end, have been cleft by the impossibility of reconciling desire and fulfilment,

(242)

struggle and attainment, yearning and actuality. This is the tragedy of moderately gifted natures, who, never being able to reach the heights of creative genius, come eventually, through constant self-criticism, to complete disaster—and I have always been of a melancholy temperament.

I say good-bye to you too, my dear friend, my Friedel. If I am killed, reflect that nobler, far finer men than I have fallen victims to the dark destiny of the race. You know that I would rather, far rather, not die, but the decision does not rest with me. We might have enjoyed many more delightful years together—now we may be called upon to renounce them. But you too must keep a good heart if you should have news of my death, and honour my memory by continuing to strive after knowledge, knowledge as we two have understood it, which does not shrink from the verge of an abyss and to which no truth is too appalling. May the intellectual conscience ever remain a disgrace in our eyes.

Farewell. You have known and are acquainted with all the others who have been dear to me and you will say good-bye to them for me. And so, in imagination, I extinguish the lamp of my existence on the eve of this terrible battle. I cut myself out of the circle of which I have formed a beloved part. The gap which I leave must be closed ; the human chain must be unbroken. I, who once formed a small link in it, bless it for all eternity. And till your last days remember me, I beg you, with tender love. Honour my memory without gilding it, and cherish me in your loving, faithful hearts.

HANS STEGEMANN, Student of Forestry, High School, Eberswalde

Born March 28th, 1893, at Wutzenow.
Killed September 20th, 1916, near Swinjuchy, in Volhynia.

France, about 60 miles from Paris, on the Cambrai-Peronne Road. August 28th, 1914.

. . . Our men, like heroes, did not yield a foot! Sergeant Struck, a good comrade, fell close to me, shot through the lungs, and died immediately. We buried him with Lieut. Lorenz in the churchyard at Caffenciers. I wrapped the bodies in pine-branches, as no coffin was to be had. We put up a cross over the grave. My Lieut. Rogge had a bullet through his shako; it grazed the top of his head and he fell to the ground, but he was only stunned and is now quite fit and back again in the saddle with us. Corporal von Heimburg fell saying, with a smile : ' We shall win all the same ! '

On the day after the battle I was in the church, which has been turned into a hospital. All the men with lung-wounds were getting on very well, almost better than the slightly wounded. Lungs heal quickly, and a clean shot makes only a small hole and goes right through. Their one and only question was : ' How are things going, Sergeant ? Is it all right again ? ' ' Lads, I've come straight from the line ; everything is going well, we have advanced a bit. The English haven't half caught it on the jaw ! ' Then they smiled and fell asleep like happy children. They are all perfectly calm and con-

(244)

fident, and suffer uncomplainingly, but it is dreadful to see the dangerously wounded, especially those who are raving in delirium.

I rode over the battle-field yesterday. There were about ten English dead to one of ours. I will write no more about the battle-field. It is difficult to imagine how anybody came out of it unharmed. One gets quite cold-blooded and indifferent.

All the armies are marching on Paris. We, too !

Coucy-le-Château, September 18*th,* 1914.

A cyclist comes sliding rather than riding down the steep hill on the right. Breathlessly he shouts : ' Order from Major—Jaegers out of ammunition ! ' I put spurs to my bay, swing him round and gallop back. I find some ammunition-wagons belonging to the Jaegers. ' Gallop ! Right wheel ! March ! ' Off they go at the gallop, flogging the horses ! Up the hill, on and on, through the heavy guns which are blazing away over our heads—we can see the great sugar-loaves in the air, because we are straight behind them, so that our eyes can follow their flight.

On we go ! ' Where are the Jaegers ? ' I shout to everybody. Shrapnel bursts. Wounded hobble and crawl back. There is a Jaeger, too, with a broken arm. ' Well, old chap, how goes it ? ' He smiled gaily all over his face. ' Jolly well ; we're giving 'em beans again ! Only they want cartridges, Sergeant ! ' ' Good-bye, good luck. Hope you'll soon be all right ! ' All this in passing—the last words shouted over my shoulder.

Another green coat. A Corporal on his way back.

'Hallo, what's wrong?' 'Not a single cartridge left!' 'Good Lord! here they come!' 'Thank God!' 'Hop up on the wagon. Now show us the way!' We trot a little farther and then, there they are! As they catch sight of me, they are just firing their last round. Now there are some more! I've got four thousand.

But meanwhile things are beginning to look black! The man who was sitting just now on the wagon is lying beside it with a smashed leg, which has since been amputated. I am still perched up on my horse beside an ammunition-column—six wagons as well as my cartridge-wagon. The enemy has got the range, and now the fun begins. Ssss . . . rrrr . . . sch! it goes, as if a giant were beating the foliage of the oak-trees with his stick. All the horses of the fifth ammunition-wagon—three on the right and three on the left—are lying struggling, with their legs in the air, though those of the next are untouched. The gunners are crawling about on the ground. Many have been killed. A moment ago the column was hale and hearty: now it looks as if somebody had brought an enormous fly-clapper down on it. My wagon was in the middle of it all.

The whistling continues. For the present I don't dismount. 'Who's hit, *is* hit!' my Jaeger says, and he is right. My men unload as coolly as if we were doing a Slow-March in the village-square at Görlitz on a Sunday: one hundred, two hundred, three hundred, four hundred, and so on, as they pile up the packages. The Jaegers come and fetch the little pointed things in quite a leisurely manner: the

English won't run away, and nothing upsets the composure of a Holsteiner. When a ' heavy ' comes whistling over they grin, and imitate the sound with their lips. On seeing my pipe one of them says, ' By gosh, that's a good idea ! ' pulls out a battered cigar and begins to smoke : ' that pretty nearly got spoilt in my pocket ! ' They are equally self-possessed. One takes off his shako, which is full of bullet-holes and looks at it : ' Well, as long as it don't let the rain in,' he says, and puts it on again.

' Now you've got cartridges, anyhow ! ' Suddenly my horse sinks beneath the saddle and founders. I have no time to see to him now, I am carrying cartridges to the firing-line. When I come back he comes to meet me, whinnying quite gaily, and snuffles at me. Three bullets have grazed his back, but only given him a fright. I have a bullet through my leggings, in the same place as last time. That will be the third pair I have to buy. A bullet has gone through the sleeve of my coat ; that can be sewn up, the precious skin is uninjured.

November 23rd, 1915.

At 7 o'clock in the morning we leave Novaja. It seems a pity, for I had settled in the Company so comfortably. The whole battalion assembles on the main road at Smielina and soon moves off, bearing to the north. Via Lautzensee (where our 6th Company is lying as cover for the Divisional Staff, and I get a ' stirrup-cup ') and Kompinischki, we continue northward.

For the moment we have perfectly gorgeous

(247)

weather. Russia shows a friendly face for once, but on the very same day its expression changes. In the morning the sun shines brilliantly and a blue sky stretches above the beautiful lakes and the dark pine-trees. Now and then we make a short halt. After all, it is quite pleasant to be on the move again. Even the future, which lies dark and mysterious before us, has a certain fascination.

We march on to Steinsee, where we halt for dinner. The roads have been getting worse and worse, the country being perfectly flat and the lakes connected by wide stretches of bog. The consequence was that my field-kitchen got stuck in a bad spot, where a stream crossed the road, and couldn't be got out. The other Companies had better luck, and got their field-kitchens up.

At last, after a long march, we found some billets : barns which were just deliberating in which direction they should collapse. Snow falling fast. Our poor chaps under open sheds on a December night, but they all crawl in as quickly as possible. Here and there a last cigar glimmers. Finally somebody starts a song, and the singing gradually increases in volume. It is my favourite song :

> In billets on the hard, hard straw
> I stretch my weary feet,
> And send a message through the night
> My far-off Love to greet.
> And I am not the only one,
> Anna Marie,
> They all are dreaming of their Loves,
> The men of the Companee,
> The whole 8th Companee.

We still shall with the Russian Bear
Have many a bloody fight.
The hour when we shall meet again
May not be yet in sight.
But maybe I've not long to roam,
Anna Marie,
To-morrow may come marching home
The good old Companee,
The whole 8th Companee.

And if a bullet shoots me dead
Just in this last long lap,
Then do not cry, my pretty dear,
But take another chap.
A tall and slim one, if you please,
Anna Marie,
It need not be just one of these
In my old Companee,
My dear old 8th Companee.

Plaintively the song dies away with a faint echo of :
' To-morrow may come marching home, the whole
8th Companee.' I seek a billet for myself. We all
take refuge in a Panje family. We greet them and
ingratiate ourselves with an initial present of rum,
which is drunk, with smacking lips and great satisfaction, out of a broken glass. After that we give a
cigar to the Panje, who is in a great fuss because some
of our chaps have removed part of his roof saying it
was their bed. The cigar pacifies him.

After the usual assurances that they have nothing
in the house—everything ' sabrali '—the Madja pro-
duces a samovar of excellent tea. In order to see
what she is doing, as she comes and goes in the
room, she carries a long chip of pine alight in her
mouth. There is not much to eat. We have to

make the best of what we have left. ' Laboriously
the squirrel seeks its food.'

I lie long awake. I can't sleep for worrying about
the field-kitchen. What will happen if there is
nothing to eat to-morrow? At last I send for my
dispatch-rider and write a letter to my Sergeant,
who is following with the baggage, telling him that
the field-kitchen must be brought in, dead or alive.
The dispatch-rider is just about to start with this
message when in the doorway appears the Sergeant :
' Herr Leutnant, I report field-kitchen present ! '

The Sergeant lies down alongside of us and soon
we are all sleeping the sleep of the just. Now and
then a child squeaks. The Russian cradle—a box
hanging by four cords from the end of a long, pliable
rod stretched right across the room—also squeaks.
A dog barks close by : the last cow moos and
bellows, and the last pig grunts. The Panje may
not be deprived of either of these two animals, for
Hindenburg has so decreed. So the night passes.
I have also just verified the presence of bugs and
fleas, which are not difficult to discover.

December 29th, 1915.

I am having such a good time here just now that
I never want to move ! If only the war does not
end before the snipe arrive ! It must be glorious
in these wonderful woods.

On Christmas Eve about 7 o'clock I had to visit
my Posts on the Dwina. Before that I was sitting
in a most picturesque corner of this incomparable
wooded country, with my pipe in my mouth. I
saw a lot of game, including actually an elk-cow with

her calf. It was an unforgettably beautiful evening. I didn't shoot at anything. It was the introduction to my Christmas. Perhaps my real Christmas service.

I then inspected the Posts with my Corporal Haupt. We stupidly had not put on our snow-cloaks. As I was standing with him on the Dwina and testing the strength of the ice to see if it would bear, a chap opposite began firing, and hit my Corporal with his very first shot. A slight flesh-wound through the upper arm and shoulder. It was bright moonlight and we were clearly visible on the snow. We threw ourselves down immediately, as there was a slight rise in the ground. First I sent a couple of bullets into the Ruski's listening-post, which we could see quite clearly on the farther bank. Whether I got him or not I don't know, but anyhow he shut up, so that I was able to tie up my poor Haupt properly in the shelter of a small trench. It was rather a difficult job, the lad had muffled himself up in an idiotic amount of clothes, and I had to cut them all away. Meanwhile my Double-Post had arrived, behaved very properly, and kept Ivan in order. After that we walked, or rather crawled, back to the N.C.O.'s quarters. I telephoned for my sleigh and it took Haupt back, as he was weak from loss of blood. Then I went from Field-Post to Field-Post. Every one had a little lit-up Christmas tree. It looked topping, especially from outside, through the window. There were plenty of 'Love-Gifts' too, and every man was feeling the glamour of Christmas, perhaps even more than in former years.

Afterwards, at 10 o'clock, my own Christmas started in my block-house. The senior-officers joined me and so did Lieutenant Gottschalk of my Company. A lot of champagne had been sent up and it was very cheery. Best of all was the lovely little Christmas tree which my batman had decorated. We sang Christmas carols to mouth-organ accompaniment, and everything was just as it ought to be at Christmas. Ruski remained quiet and kept the peace.

Malepartus-on-Dwina, April 13th, 1916.

We have been through some very trying days. This time it was not the Ruski we had to fight ; with the exception of a certain amount of Artillery activity and a few feeble patrols, he had not been attempting anything just here ; but the river sud-denly rose during the night of April 2nd with overwhelming force and rapidity.

The previous afternoon the water in the flooded meadows had already risen so considerably that I had had to send rations to posts about a mile away along the Dwina in a wretched boat. In the evening two of my signallers, trying to maintain telephonic communication, and two men with rations for advanced posts, started for Seikli by boat. They were caught by the flood with its accompanying floes of ice. The water rose five feet in an hour. The floating masses of ice, which were being carried swiftly along by the stream, capsized the boat.

It was a pitch-dark night. The water over-whelmed us at head-quarters too. We had to clear out of seven block-houses in a twinkling. An officers' dug-out disappeared under water.

We kept firing off light-pistols to guide the men who had been in the boat. We could not go to their assistance because the capsized boat was our only one. Several men and one officer swam out and ascertained that our comrades were clinging to a little tree, but were unable to help them on account of the flood and the ice-floes. Thank God, those who swam out got back safe, though utterly exhausted ; it was a mad thing to do.

Meanwhile the piteous cries of my men, who were shouting to me for help, grew gradually fainter. The Ruski was firing at intervals with guns and rifles, but we had to move away from the barbed-wire entanglement, being driven back by the water.

At last I established telephonic communication with our 7th Company who were lying a long way back. They had a boat, and Lieut. Jacobs at once started off in it to the scene of disaster, which I had meanwhile illuminated with a searchlight from the left side of my position, which lies high and was not endangered.

Next I managed to get forward again, as far as the edge of the forest, though I could only hold on there with difficulty. The men recognized my voice and answered. Sad to say, my little Corporal Mondry, aged only sixteen, had already been drowned. I shouted to them to stick it out for another hour, and tie themselves on with their braces ; a boat would be there in an hour. They understood and replied.

The situation got worse every minute as the water rose. I am thankful to say that, thinking it was best to be on the safe side, I had sent some of my horses off at 6 o'clock to fetch a boat from the Pioneer Park. That was the saving of us, for 30 of my men were still on the bank of the Dwina in little houses which had water up to their windows.

With great difficulty I managed to get back from the wire entanglement. Dahl was with me. I was absolutely frozen and done in. I quickly changed my clothes, drank five glasses of brandy and lit a cigar ; then I felt better.

By this time it was 2 o'clock. There came a boat ! Suddenly there was great jubilation on the hillock where the searchlight was : a boat with five heads visible in it ! Lieut. Jacobs, a Pioneer, and the three men they had rescued. Little Jacobs had really been fearfully smart ; with a miserable, leaky boat, and in that flood ! The three men were frozen absolutely stiff. I had them sent straight off to hospital. Jacobs I have recommended for a special decoration ; also the Pioneer. The three men have long since returned to duty.

Before dawn the boat I had sent for arrived. The flood was subsiding. By the time it was light I had all my men back, with the exception of poor little Mondry, whose body we were of course unable to recover. I felt his death very much, as I had had him constantly with me.

We fetched the men back from the Posts. I had ordered up the field-kitchen with hot grog, etc. And so all was well once more. I managed to find accommodation for the men whose dug-out was under water.

My whole position has vanished and in place of it we have a lake about two miles broad in front of us ! My Posts are out again in small isolated houses on little islands in the Dwina. We communicate by boat—at night, of course. We have laid a cable under the river and telephonic communication, etc., is all in order.

Unfortunately the troops on our right suffered heavy losses owing to the flood. Five men of our 5th Company were also drowned.

June 18th, 1916.

Fifteen miles north-west of Luck, shortly before the attack. Heavy losses day after day, but we are advancing grandly. We attack quite in the style of the old days, at the time of Frederick the Great ! Quantities of booty, etc. Morale excellent. It is fine to demonstrate the old strength which springs up afresh even in an old warrior like me ! Ruski has had appalling losses and is getting a regular drubbing. I haven't slept for four days. Send cigars ; I never stop smoking.

August 4th, 1916.

There was great rejoicing here at the news that Hindenburg (who is now at Brest-Litowsk) has taken over the supreme command of all the troops with the exception of the undefeated army of von Bothmer. Excellenz Litzmann from Neu-Globsow on the Stechlin has been appointed second-in-

(255)

command, under Hindenburg, of the Right-Wing-Army-Group, and was to have inspected us—his old bodyguard of the Masura battle—to-day. On account of the rain, however, the parade has been cancelled. Litzmann is said to have brought 40 Army Corps with him.

Hindenburg's appointment comes as a great relief to us, for he is said never to have had a reverse. I was quite astonished at my Hanseatickers, Mechlinburgers and Holsteiners, they were so wild with joy at the news.

No chance of leave for me, of course. I couldn't hand over my Company to anybody else just now. Moreover I greatly prefer the position of Company-Commander to that of Adjutant. I require the feeling of responsibility. An Adjutant is just an irresponsible go-between.

September 3rd, 1916.

Here at Schwinjuchy the devil has been let loose ! Fierce but victorious battles. I have been through some ghastly times. On the 31st of August the Company lost 3 officers and 50 men, mostly in hand-to-hand fighting. It seems miraculous that I myself should be still perfectly fit. Leave had opened again, but all the same I shan't desert my Company, as I am the only officer left. Just before the Russian offensive, which was a dead failure, I met Rudolf Nietsche. We are now in trenches. The Russians attack every day, but are always repulsed with terrific loss. ' Lieb Vaterland magst ruhig sein ! '

September 6th.

Still hale and hearty ! To-day Excellenz Litzmann decorated me with the Iron Cross of the First Class. He asked me to remember him to you, with his kind regards and thanks. His exact words were : ' Greet your parents, especially your mother, from me, and write this : " I congratulate you on the success of your son, who, through his smartness and courage, with the assistance of his splendid Company, has by his counter-attacks driven back the already demoralized Russians, and by storming Hill 259 averted what was a grave menace to my army-group." '

You may imagine how delighted I am at having earned this high distinction. I have been recommended for it three times. My men are almost more delighted than I am. I fully realize how much I owe to my Company, and not least to those who are now lying beneath the sod, still and silent, with clenched teeth ; their faces peaceful and almost joyous because in the very moment of death they knew that victory was ours.

One thing I learnt in those terrible days : even if we are killed death does not triumph over us, for the German soul will conquer, the German spirit is invincible throughout all eternity ! May God preserve our Fatherland !

At the Front, November 11th, 1916.

DEAR HERR PASTOR,—

Your letter of the 3rd inst. has just reached me and, sympathizing most deeply in your truly justifiable sorrow, I hasten to answer it at once.

(257)

On September 15th I changed places with another General, taking the position on his right instead of left, so that I had nothing to do with the battle on the 20th, but on the following day I heard about our terrible losses and of the heroic death of your dear son. I was quite overcome by the news, for your son had endeared himself to me as a perfect example of gallantry in defence of the honour of my troops.

It was an exceptionally great pleasure to me to pin upon his breast, in the presence of the Officer Commanding his Regiment, the sacred emblem of honour.

I wish to express my deep sympathy with you and your wife. You may both feel proud of your son, and may say to yourselves that you have offered up a sacrifice to the Fatherland the influence of which will be of lasting value to the brave 165th Regiment. Our heroes do not die in vain and they live on for us through their shining example. Lieutenant Stegeman, who held the recaptured Hill 259 for $5\frac{1}{2}$ hours against overwhelming odds with the greatest gallantry, and only after the last cartridge had been fired fought his way, with his little handful of men, back through the Russian ranks, will never be forgotten. If I ever publish my diary of the war, he will find a worthy memorial there.

Permit me now in spirit to press the hands of the parents of my dear young comrade as the truest sympathizer in your loss.

LITZMANN,
Infantry General and Army-Group-Commander.
(258)

ADOLF BECK, Student of Law, Leipzig

Born April 30th, 1894.
Killed September 21st, 1916, near Korytnika, Volhynia.

On the Serwetsch, August 17th, 1915.

WE are lying in the valley where we spent the first days of the advance. It is very pleasant here again. But how many of those who were with us before are gone!

The sun is shining gloriously. A beautiful late-summer, early-autumn day ! The time of broad, open fields and white clouds ; the time of ' Wander-lust ' and yearning. Summer seemed scarcely to have begun, and already autumn has stolen upon us. To-day I have already eaten some apples. The convolvulus is in flower too, which shows that summer is nearly over.

I have never seen so many flowers anywhere as here. All the land that used to be cultivated is now covered with the loveliest flowers—such as are usually called weeds !—Michaelmas daisies, camo-mile, cornflowers, larkspur, and Mamma's favourite yellow toadflax, all flaunt their gay blossoms. Böcklin-meadows, the Serwetsch flowing through them ; men bathing ; and above white clouds in a Böcklin-blue sky. It really is beautiful here.

We had a lovely evening yesterday. I went to visit Wilde's grave. In the stress of trench-warfare I had not had time to realize things before, but as I reached the quiet cemetery and sought among the graves till I found one with the inscription, 'Ser-geant Wilde, August 10, 1915,' a vivid consciousness

(259)

of the whole horrible situation came over me. Another young life cut short. Thirty years only had fate granted him. Thirty brief years, and already he had reached the end. It is all so incomprehensible, so senseless ! I still remember the last days in Strahlsund when we were with his little fiancée and all so merry. And of how she and Frau Jänicke stood on the railway-platform and we gradually lost sight of her little white figure. Narrow is now his bed ! I will make a wreath for him and take a photograph of his grave to send to his people as a last greeting from him.

I had a card from Jänicke. He is getting on all right. He says : ' I am sitting at a marble table having coffee and cakes, while you are lying out there.' This was the last straw yesterday, and I felt thoroughly depressed. It is not good to have nothing to do. I walked along by the Serwetsch and lay down in the flowery meadow. The green moon rose slowly. In the distance the rumble of a wagon. The Serwetsch ripples. All else is still. Not a shot breaks the silence. Slowly a harmonica begins to play, and the melancholy waltz-tunes of home melt into old folk-songs.

In the evening we got another reinforcement. A little Alsatian came to the Sergeant and begged to be allowed to join the 12th Company too, as four of his friends had been transferred to it and he was all alone with the 10th. ' We all joined up together and always shared a room.' The Sergeant said he was to ask if one of the others would exchange with him. He ran from one to another—like Elizabeth in *Tannhäuser*—but they all remained dull and indifferent. His childish face was full of anxiety. We told the Sergeant that he must see that the little chap stayed with the 12th, otherwise he would be all forlorn. I know how I felt, and still feel. Anybody who has had the same experience is bound to sympathize. And the Sergeant saw reason and said he would try and arrange it. Later I met the little chap and said, ' Well, so you're stopping with us ? ', and he beamed all over his face. On the same evening, two hours later, a stray bullet hit one of the reinforcement—it was one of his friends, who had served two years on the Western Front and was now fated to ' stop one ' here in Reserve. So one is gone already. Well, the poor boy will be wondering how long he will still have his friends !

August 18th.

A thunderstorm this morning and rain. Took a photograph of Wilde's grave. I feel the poor little chap's death very much. For some time past I have been trying to write poetry, and I sent the following to Jänicke and Menzel :

JOSEPH WILDE
Sergeant in the 42nd Infantry
Killed August 9th
before Skrobowa

They dug his quiet grave	And have woven a wreath
Mid the peace of the wood,	Of our happiest hours
And my sorrowful thoughts	To place on his grave
For his escort have stood	In the semblance of flowers.

*   *   *   *   *

(261)

July 24th, 1916.

At 7.30 came an order from the Company-Commander : ' Sergeant Beck to the Sap at once. Sergeant Jänicke is wounded.' I snatch a rifle and rush out. In the trench I meet Willem. His face is covered with blood. I ask : ' Is it bad ? ' ' Oh, not too bad.' I have only time just to shake his hand, for there is no Sergeant left in front and things are looking serious. How the bombs crash, and the artillery roars ! I hear that Sergeant Meier is also wounded.

After a time Ensign Brehmer arrives. I ask him to relieve me for a moment, as I do so want to have another word with Jänicke. I find him just going off. He has a head-wound in one temple, but it is not dangerous. So I am able to say good-bye to him. ' But I shall be jolly lonely ! ' I say. ' You've got Ensign Brehmer, anyhow.' We both have tears in our eyes. I must get back to the sap ! And I arrive just at the right moment, for the Panje is attacking. He comes in dense masses over the hill, but the bombs drive him back with heavy losses.

It becomes dark. It becomes quiet. Verey lights are going up constantly : sometimes it is bright as day, then gradually darkness falls again. It is a joy to see the men—each one perfectly cool and every inch a soldier. We feel sure that Ivan is coming over during the night.

Towards 11 o'clock the fun begins again. Appalling shell-fire once more. Our artillery shooting magnificently. We stand and await the attack. Absolutely calm because we know he won't get through. But he doesn't even try to. He no longer dares make the attempt. We only realize this when we see the Verey lights going up. Anybody who is going to attack doesn't send up flares. At 12 o'clock I am relieved by Sergeant Zeuck. Up till then I had sent up about sixty flares. No bombs. There is deathly silence once more.

Just then I hear that Ensign Brehmer has been badly wounded by a trench-mortar. I rush into the dug-out. There he lies with his head bandaged, groaning and talking in delirium. His thoughts are on the war. Once he says, ' Well, good night ; hope you'll be all right up there ', just as he often did when I was going out to the sap. He is wounded in the jaw, neck and shoulder. Towards morning he becomes sensible, says he is in pain, and gives his directions in his own quiet, decided way. I shall never forget the picture : A dug-out. On the bed the wounded man supported by his batman, who is sitting beside him. A tallow candle throws a flickering, reddish light over the scene. At 3 o'clock he is carried away. It is not so bad as it seemed. He will in all probability recover.

Now the last of our little circle is gone—Jänicke, Brehmer, Meier, Rossow—and I am all alone ! In July of last year Jänicke got his first wound, and now this year his second. If we now go back to our old position, how shall I be able to bear it ? Every free moment we had we spent together, talking about home and one thing and another. Now I have nobody at all here. I wonder if the others are there still ? Last night the 6th Company had nine killed. The 1st Battalion also has had heavy losses.

(263)

I am sitting in the sap again. It is 10.30 a.m. All is quiet. A Panje airman over us. Glorious sunshine. One already has a slight premonition of autumn.

I have just heard that Riedel was killed during the night, he is the first of our transport.

Evening of the 26th.

A wonderful summer evening. Quiet as it seldom is in the trenches anywhere. Not a shot being fired. On the Serwetsch wild-duck are quacking. It is our twelfth evening in this position. Our Company is the only one which has stuck it out so long. The others have all been already relieved. Our Regimental Commander has been praising up the 12th Company tremendously ; there is a big mail to-night and punch as well and we are all very cheery. In the dug-out, 10 feet beneath us, the batmen are sitting with a fiddler and singing old soldier- and folk-songs ; but Willem is no longer there, nor the jolly little Fähnrich—and everything goes on as usual. But when the wind blows over the heather it will look for you—and will not find you. The hours one passes here and the feelings one has are surely the most beautiful in all the world !

OSKAR GREULICH, Ph.D., Freiburg i.B.

Born December 8th, 1888, at Bruchsal.
Killed 27/28 September, 1916, near Swinjucki, in Volhynia.

Easter Monday, April 24th, 1916.

I HOPE you are having the same wonderful Easter weather at home as we are. All the time we have been here—and it is nearly six months now—we have not had such glorious days as these two Easter ones. Within two or three weeks the sun has simply worked miracles. One may say that if everything was frozen dead before, it is now all alive and kicking ! There are so many skeeters and froggies about that a certain person would scarcely be able to move without his vasculum. The clapper-stork has also arrived, in order to constitute himself to a certain extent watchman, and see that all goes well and is as it should be in his domain. Yes, he has become quite a friend of ours, has Mr. Stork, though no doubt he never stops puzzling over why we deliberately cage ourselves in with wire and play at being a Marionette Show, for that is how our wire-entanglements and trenches must look to him. Next time he is going to bring his Lady Wife with him, provided that she has finished getting the new home ready.

Our lake becomes more beautiful every day, and when once the trees are green it will be at least as pleasant here as it was last year on the Aisne. The change in the landscape has certainly not failed to make an impression on the Russians, who are

18 (265)

really much greater lovers of Nature than ourselves. For some time not a shot has been fired on either side, although everybody is calmly walking about on the top, and even taking an afternoon nap up there ! We keep an eye on one another, but we think it would be foolish to disturb one another by shooting. When the Russian sentry goes on duty, he thinks it necessary to inform his vis-à-vis of the fact. ' 'Morning, Auyoosht ! ' he calls across the lake, and he takes his leave in similar fashion.

Why the Ruski prefers to address the German as ' August ' I don't know. At any rate he means it more kindly than the French, to whom we are merely the ' Boches '.

At first ' Auyoosht ' did not respond and was extremely coy in his reception of these advances, or at most replied with an occasional bullet. ' Germanski damn ! Shoot nix ! ' sounded from over the way. The troops opposite are namely Lithuanians and Poles, and so understand something of our language. It is a good thing for the enemy that there is a lake between us, otherwise many of these men would certainly have deserted to us.

On Easter Eve they called out : ' Germanski shoot nix. To-morrow peace ! ' And this time Germanski was not ' damn ' and shot ' nix '. The Russian was grateful to him, and ever since early yesterday they have treated us to a most beautiful concert. An accordion and mandoline don't sound at all bad, and the vast forest in which the Russian trenches are situated resounds unceasingly with a magnificent ' Inihu ' as beautiful as any one could hear at Easter over in Eichelburg. In the evening the male choir strikes up, and solemn chants—no doubt Easter hymns—ring out into the night in three parts and sung by very good voices. Anna wrote to me a year ago about having heard the Russian prisoners at Titisee sing so beautifully, and it is just like that here.

Our men, not to be outdone, showed what they were capable of too, and gave some of their most solemn and moving songs, such as : ' This is the Day of the Lord ', ' It is Sunday ', and ' Alas, that we must part ', until cockcrow. Cockcrow ? Yes, we have even a cock, or at any rate what sounds like one. About 2 a.m., as it begins to get light, there is heard, either on one side or the other, a remarkable ' cockadoodledoo ' ; another, who can do it too, takes up the call, and hands it on, so that anybody with sharp ears can hear it repeated, farther and farther away, for a long while.

HEINRICH MÜLLER, Student of Theology, Heidelberg

Born May 30th, 1893, at Ebersbach.
Died October 2nd, 1916, in a Field Hospital near Bapaume.

A.I.P., August 6th, 1916.

Now you have got through your *Sekunda*,[1] and I hope that you will continue to be equally successful in your studies so that you may be a source of satisfaction to your parents and may develop into a capable, well-educated citizen.

Germany's future depends on you boys. The present generation is doomed to be offered up as a blood-sacrifice upon the battle-field. It will be your task some day to restore, in a time of peaceful culture, everything of intellectual and moral value which the war has trampled underfoot.

You see, one after another of our men here goes off to the Great Army. We are all prepared to do that, and we are looking calmly into the cold eye of death. It is simply extraordinary where the strength comes from, which enables us to go on so tenaciously withstanding an enemy who vastly outnumbers us.

[1] The 5th Form exam., which secured, among other privileges, that of One-Year military service.

KURT ROHRBACH, Student of Theology

Born August 21st, 1893, at Stettin.
Killed October 6th, 1916, on the Somme.

Flanders, July 26th, 1915.

IN this war, which obliges one to concentrate one's attention and exert one's strength to the utmost, I feel that I have lost many of the treasures amassed during a period of gradual, auspicious development, in time of peace. The knowledge which I acquired at school and at the University, the interests aroused in me by a civilian occupation, are lost to sight and memory, and only with difficulty will it be possible to regain them.

You know that having been too early forced to take a serious view of life, my youth was short ; I could not even fall in love properly ; but it is this awful war which has actually made an old man of me. Certainly here at the Front my body has become weather-proof and my muscles as hard as iron, but my mind has not developed. Everybody who looks daily into the cold eye of death, and gazes on so many dead faces bearing the stamp of suffering and renunciation, becomes certainly callous, but also old, very old. That is what saddens me, my dear old friend and war-comrade.

After having been so long away from home, my whole past life soon seemed like a beautiful dream to which one looks wistfully back. Even real dreams—those frail, shy children of refreshing night —which at first bore me on their delicate wings

(269)

far from the enemy land to my peaceful, beautiful, distant home, have gradually failed to bless me. The hours of sleep were all too necessary merely to restore the exhausted warrior. And so my home seemed to have slowly faded into the distance.

Then one day I happened to be talking to our Orderly Room Clerk, who comes from Berlin-Friedenau. He advised me to apply to Divisional H.Q. for home-leave. No sooner said than done !

One evening there was a call : ' Volunteers forward, for fetching a machine-gun out of the trench before Pilkem ! ' Of course I stepped forward. We did not get back to camp till 3 a.m., after a very trying march, and lay down quite exhausted. Then, just after sunrise, the Sergeant-Major appeared before my tent, woke me up and told me that I had been granted 8 days' home-leave and could start that same afternoon.

So at 4 p.m. I found myself, with very little luggage and a breast full of anticipation, at the light-railway station at Houthulst, and the little line soon carried me far away from that murderous region where the only aim of culture seems to be to devise new means of slaughter and destruction. My heart already felt lighter when, instead of barren stretches of heath, I saw around me fertile acres of corn, vari-coloured cattle in the meadows, and—instead of charred ruins—prosperous farm-houses, nestling among orchard-trees laden with fruit. The people here seemed quite unconscious of the fact that only a few miles from their homes an insane, gigantic struggle was going on.

(270)

In Courtrai I happened upon a leave-train, which was taking married men of the ammunition and baggage columns home on 14 days' leave. As I couldn't possibly get a fast train to Berlin, I joined this transport, but I regretted it later, for the journey consequently took 51 hours altogether.

How I rejoiced over the first German girl I saw, and over the German landscape which spread before my eyes beyond the Belgian hills between Herbesthal and Aix, but I was gradually possessed by such a longing to be home as soon as possible that I was oblivious of everything else in this one craving to get on and on. A secret foreboding, incomprehensible and irresistible, urged me towards my parents' house.

At last, in the early hours of June 14th, I reached the station, and changed into the Lichtenrade train. Here an interlude occurred : in order not only to be alone and not worried by inquisitive eyes, but also just for once to travel luxuriously— I hadn't been in a bed for 9 months—I went second class. At Papestrasse, a good-looking, well-dressed young man, in kid gloves and kid shoes, opened the door. Without glancing into the carriage he got in mechanically, shutting the door behind him, and only then did he look round—saw me, and with an embarrassed expression vanished into another compartment ! He had instantly recognized in me a genuine ' field-grey ' and was afraid of lice !

At last the train reached L. Everywhere familiar faces, even the guard was the same. As fast as I could walk, I hurried from the station towards home. On every side I was greeted by houses and villas which I had known ever since they were built, as if I were an old friend. Then, among the trees, appeared the dear paternal roof! With eager glances I scanned the familiar place. The little house and its garden lay once more before me, just as I had left them. Once again the trees bore their load of cherries, apples, and plums; the flowers bloomed and the scented, delicate green of the asparagus waved gently in the breeze. The golden morning light shone upon the high, bright gable, and up on the ridge of the roof sat the black-bird, just as he always did, singing his morning song. Within, all was still quiet; but just as I turned the corner of the street, the big front-door opened and my sister and brother came out to meet me, followed by Wölfchen, who barked loudly while they embraced me. In the doorway my dear mother put her arms round me.

As soon as they released me I said, 'But where's Dad?' and stepped towards the room where he had lain for months, ever since he was first taken ill. At that my mother fell into my arms: 'He is dead,' she said, 'he died two days ago. His last words, as the doctor laid a cool hand on his burning forehead, were, "There was a letter from Kurtchen to-day"—and then he died.'

That was my home-coming, my dear old Friend. Now I am back in Flanders in the trenches.

Flanders, August 26th, 1915.

Last night, towards 11 o'clock, my men and I were sent off as usual 'pumping'—that is to say, we had to go right up, in order to pump out the tiresome filthy water which is always trickling back into the communication-trench leading to the front line.

Armed with the heavy hand-pump we started. It was a lovely night. The full-moon shone in the sky and lit up the way, which on a dark night is hard to find owing to the many trenches and wire-entanglements. The Frenchies were keeping comparatively quiet, and only now and then there was the report of a rifle and a bullet whizzed by, or a missile struck a tree, ricocheted and flew on with a melancholy note. Also as it was bright moonlight very few flares went up. Far away on the left, probably near Ypres, the thunder of guns growled. Otherwise all was still.

Soundlessly we proceeded over the duck-boards along the narrow trench. When we reached the wet place the work began. My men took hold valiantly, and as there had been but little rain during the previous few days, the trench was soon pumped dry.

Suddenly one of the men said : ' Hallo, there's the pear-tree which the stretcher-bearers said was chock full of ripe pears ! ' And before I could stop them, the chaps had jumped out of the trench and begun—only 120 yards from the enemy—to pelt the tree with bits of stick and lumps of clay ! Imagine the scene—here in the moonlight, close to the enemy, these foolhardy devils running round with no cover, while bullets were whistling all about them, shying at pears! Certainly they were screened from observation by a fine white mist which was lying over the land. In a few minutes they had got every single pear off the tree, and, loaded with fruit, we started back.

Then as we were crossing a bit of open ground we heard a strange swishing, rustling noise, and as we got nearer we discovered some of our men mowing corn. Swung by powerful arms, the scythes were swishing through the ripe stalks. So much corn had sowed itself during the last harvest that, thanks to the rich soil and fine weather, there was quite a good crop. One must own that it contained a good many weeds, not only in the shape of thorns and thistles, but also of barbed wire, bits of entanglement-frame, and telegraph wire, and now and then the scythe got caught in one or other of these or struck the case of a shell, with a sharp, rasping noise. In spite of that, many a fine sheaf of corn was bound and so saved from rotting by German thrift and love of order. I don't suppose you ever heard before of such a harvest, garnered by moonlight and to the accompaniment of the weird music of elves, dancing their fairy measures in the form of ' blue beans ' ! [1]

[1] I.e. bullets.

ANTON STEIGER, Student of Theology, Freising

Born October 7th, 1896.
Killed October 14th, 1916, on the Somme.

July 17th, 1916.

THE last day before Verdun, and the most awful !
On July 11th our Company marched to Fosse
Wood, and, on the 12th, on to the Ablain Valley.
There the 2nd Platoon and one Section of the 3rd
remained. The 1st and 3rd Sections of the 3rd
Platoon—seventeen men, two Corporals, and a
Sergeant—(including me and my two old school-
fellows Steiner and Reifer) marched farther.

About 600 yards from our destination we halted
in a shell-hole in order to rest a little, as we had
come along pretty fast at the quick-march through
a fearful barrage. (You can best picture a shell-
hole by imagining the cavity left by a tree torn
up by the roots.) I had hardly lain down
when—ststst !—a shell pitched exactly in front of
us. There were screams, cries and yells, in the
midst of which a voice shouted : ' Up ! Up !
March ! March, those who can ! ' Summoning up
all my remaining strength I sprang up (we were
carrying all our equipment, of course), and didn't
walk the last 600 yards, but simply fell from one
shell-hole to another.

When we reached the dug-out, six out of the seventeen men weren't there. Three, including Reifer,
who had lolled on a school-bench beside me for nine
years, had been killed. One of the three wounded

managed to drag himself as far as the dug-out early on the following day. Our men were taking him back with them during the night when a shell fell on them, killing the wounded man and the four who were carrying him.

Our dug-out was an old, half-blown-in, French casemate, about 150 yards away from the fort of Thiaumont. From our side it had looked a mere hummock of earth. The entrance was like that of a fox's hole. At the end of a short passage some broken steps led down into the place we occupied for four days. Dead bodies were lying under the soil, one with its legs protruding up to the knees. There were three separate chambers down there : one was full of rockets and detonators ; another— as big as our kitchen at home—in which we were housed, also contained French ammunition ; the third was full of French explosive. It was pitch dark the whole time, as we had only a few candle-sticks. There was a horrible smell down there too —the reek of decomposing bodies ; I could hardly eat anything the whole four days.

On the third day the French artillery opened such an intense fire on the dug-out with 28c. guns that we thought it would certainly be blown in alto-gether.

On the fourth day, Friday, the heavy-artillery fire started again early in the morning and con-tinued till 9.30 p.m. Just think what that means ! Ten hours in a dug-out under shell-fire ; ten hours in the expectation of death either through being buried alive, or of being blown into the air if a shell should happen to fall where the explosive is stored. But things turned out otherwise.

One opening was already quite closed up by the bombardment ; through the other a man could just manage to squeeze without his equipment. Consequently, as our cellar was 6 yards behind the hole, and then 2 yards below the level of the ground, scarcely any air could get into it. Finally the French presumably fired gas-shells at the mouth of the hole. The Sergeant suddenly got up, feeling very ill. A few others also got up and then collapsed. Then the Sergeant shouted : ' Get up and out, all who can ! ' The rest, including myself, were lying with our heads on our packs. When we got up, we one and all fell over. Then there was a regular scrum. Everybody struggling for breath. Everybody trying to get out. One man fell down and blocked the way for all the rest. Some hadn't enough strength left to climb up. I was able to, thank God, and was even able to help one of the others. Out, and into the nearest shellhole ! We were all as white as a sheet !

We remained lying there and not moving in spite of the shells which were dropping to right and left of us. Some of us revived sooner than the others and went to fetch those who had not been able to climb out, and so all were saved. We had to use means to revive two or three of them.

After half an hour, at 10 p.m., we started on the return journey—that is to say, we staggered back. Nobody could walk properly—we had to halt every five minutes.

HUGO MÜLLER, Student of Law, Leipzig

Born May 5th, 1892, at Buchholz (Erzgebirge).
Killed October 18th, 1916, near Warlencourt, in the Ancre
Valley.

Before Agny, south-east of Arras, October 17th, 1915.

I AM enclosing a French field-postcard, which I
want you to put with my war-souvenirs. It came
out of the letter-case of a dead French soldier. It
has been extremely interesting to study the contents
of the letter-cases of French killed and prisoners.
The question frequently recurs, just as it does with
us : ' When will it all end ? ' To my astonishment
I practically never found any expressions of hatred
or abuse of Germany or German soldiers. On the
other hand, many letters from relations revealed an
absolute conviction of the justice of their cause, and
sometimes also of confidence in victory. In every
letter mother, fiancée, children, friends, whose
photographs were often enclosed, spoke of a joyful
return and a speedy meeting—and now they are all
lying dead and hardly even buried between the
trenches, while over them bullets and shells sing
their gruesome dirge. Lucky the few whom we or
those opposite have been able to inter with some
sort of decency—for fragments of human bodies are
still hanging in the barbed wire. Only a little
while ago, close in front of our trench, was a human
hand with a ring on one finger ; a few yards away
was a forearm, of which finally only the bone
remained—so good does human flesh taste to rats !

(278)

Ghastly ! The man who could never shudder and shake would learn how here ! I have learnt how *not* to do it ! When at night I go all alone through the trenches and saps, and there is a rustling here and a rustling there, and at any moment a nigger may leap out at one's throat—all in the pitch-darkness—that really is gruesome ; but I have gradually got used to it and have become as callous as our Landsturmers. War hardens one's heart and blunts one's feelings, making a man indifferent to everything that formerly affected and moved him ; but these qualities of hardness and indifference towards fate and death are necessary in the fierce battles to which trench-warfare leads. Anybody who allowed himself to realize the whole tragedy of some of the daily occurrences in our life here would either lose his reason or be forced to bolt across to the enemy's trench with his arms high in the air.

Before Arras, February 23rd, 1915.

. . . A few days ago we shot down a French patrol. We dragged one man in through our wire —a great fat brewery-owner from Paris. All he could say before he died in our sap of his bad body-wound was : ' Mon camarade, s'il vous plaît ! S'il vous plaît ! Mon dieu ! '

Before Armentières, December 30th, 1915.

Last night, when I came back from going the round, I unpacked the parcel ; stuck the fir-branches in the walls ; lit a few candles, and kept Christmas with my batman. Even the rats and

(279)

mice had a share in the celebration, nibbling the cake-crumbs and the eel's skin! That is the way out here, everybody expects a bit of whatever is going, and a sort of Early Christian community of goods prevails, which ordains the sharing of everything as one of the highest virtues. And that is quite as it should be, for every day the fable of the worldly possessions which moths devour, or laughing heirs snatch at, becomes a horrible reality here.

I am still feeling shaky after yesterday afternoon, when the English battered our trench with shrapnel and shells. More than one water-hole was dyed purple with the blood of those who were killed, and while I was on duty, patrolling the trenches from 3 to 6 o'clock, I was reminded of the old saga, where the heroes had to wade through the blood of the slain, while ever in my heart lurked the thought: 'the next one will get *you*!'

In the Trenches, March 11*th*, 1916.

I shall never forget that mine episode! Everything that I hadn't actually on me was buried. Everything not absolutely destroyed that I did not manage to grub out of the ruins with my own hands was sneaked by the Landsturmers,[1] who quickly take advantage of every such disaster. The next morning not even the posts and planks of the 'noble edifice' were to be seen; nippy little field-grey elves had been busy during the night, collecting firewood! Sad in one way, natural enough in another! We all become more or less callous and

[1] See note, p. 153.

unfeeling out here in this horrible war ; whoever
does not goes mad in the most real and awful sense
of the word.

I have just written a letter to the father of one
of my Platoon Corporals, who was killed the day
before yesterday. If the poor parents could have
seen their son! A shell had torn off his head
and we literally scraped up his brains with a spade.
Such incidents are by no means uncommon in
trench life ! The wagon which brings up the
rations to-night will take back these pitiful fragments
of once proud manhood.

ADOLF STÜRMER, Student of Law, Strassburg

Born April 13th, 1890, at Strassburg.
Killed October 23rd, 1916, on the Szurduk Pass, near
Petroseny.

Not far from Povorce, August 9th, 1916.

YESTERDAY I volunteered for the patrol that was
to blow up the bridge which the Russians had
thrown across the S. I knew the terrain from various
wanderings. When there are so many of you, you
can't swim over, because that would make too much
noise, so we had to manage with a raft. We lit a
small fire beforehand so as to see from which direction most of the bullets came, and immediately
realized that we couldn't get through on the right.
So we started off to the left, where we got across
the river and surprised the nearest Russian post.

It was funny how startled the chaps were ! One
great big bearded Hun especially ; Kramer was
going for him and he hastily made the sign of the
cross and then put up his hands. Then they were
all full of joy ; kissed our hands and coats ; tore
the cockades out of their caps, and threw down
their arms. They fell rather than walked from one
shell-hole to another while they were being taken
back to our lines.

However, we had made rather too much noise,
and as we advanced we were fired on. We threw
ourselves down and stuck our heads into the earth,
but we managed to reach the long bridge. The
Austrian sappers put the dynamite in position and

then : ' Back ! Quick march ! ' An explosion scattered earth in all directions, and again we took cover. One Austrian got a splinter in the head and bled like a pig. As we were tying him up I saw a patrol coming after us. Immediately : ' Right turn ! March ! ' and we found ourselves on a branch of the S. The ones in front tried to cross, but comrade Kramer sank up to his waist, and another man went in up to the neck in the bog and shouted : ' Halt ! I can't swim ! ' With some difficulty we pulled him out, and then proceeded along the bank.

At this point Senhöfer, a perfect comrade, promoted Corporal only to-day, was shot. He had been four years with the regiment. The bullet went in through his mouth and came out through the back of his head. I remained remarkably calm and cool ; one has got so accustomed to the thought of death ; one is on familiar terms with fate ; one must be hard—remorselessly hard ; but later on I felt it very much, for I was very fond of this comrade. I must admit though that I couldn't bear to look long at the dead man, with his face now so set, pale and covered with blood, when only that morning we had sat together, chatting and laughing. . . .

To-day I have had a rest. I went for a walk through the forest and across the dunes. On the way I stuck a bit of heather in my cap, and picked a whole bunch of it to send to my dear good mother at home.

When it began to get dark, I sat down under the birch-trees on the edge of the forest. From the neighbouring trenches comes the murmur of soldiers' voices : some telling long yarns ; some arguing about politics. Then everything becomes quiet. From the Austrians beyond comes the sound of singing : a single, beautiful voice rings out into the night. The dark forms of the trees loom above me like the shadows of giants and in the night-sky stars again stand so bright and near over my head. Suddenly I feel so buoyant and free from all earthly trammels that I could almost fly away up and down among the stars. And then I said a very earnest evening prayer.

August 28*th*, 1916.

I often think about Strassburg now. I got really to appreciate and love it for the first time during my last leave at home, in June. I realized for the first time what a beautiful city it is, and felt that it really was my home. I can't understand now how I have managed to ignore its beauties so long. I only knew the Cathedral and the old Kammerzell House. But this time I only needed to walk through the streets or along the Ill Straden to notice wonderful groups of houses, some timbered and covered with ancient carving, and some Gothic, with pointed arches, little towers, stepped gables, and steep roofs like those in Schwind's picture-books. The old black towers past which the Ill flows stand like a row of rugged giants, guarding the city. And then the splendid buildings of the French period ! One could hardly keep count of the beautiful houses, as one after another appeared. The buildings in few towns of Germany can be richer in interesting associations, among which shine the names of Gottfried of Strassburg, Tauler and Fischart, Gutenberg, Master Erwin, and Goethe. Strassburg bears witness to the time of Germany's greatest and most beautiful productivity. Why is all that dead and forgotten? Directly we realize it, it seems to revive, and one's home, which was almost unknown before, appears beautiful and lovable. That is what I often dream of nowadays when I am on guard in the trenches or lying, as at this moment, in the camp under the birch-trees.

FRIEDRICH OEHME, Student of Law, Leipzig

Born March 23rd, 1897, at Wurzen.
Killed October 25th, 1916, before Warlencour.

March 30th, 1916.

YOUR letter to-day has made me very sad. Many of my friends have already given their lives for the Fatherland, but I cared for none of them as I did for Otto J. You know what we were to one another. And now comes this terrible blow ! . . .

The Hand of God has fallen heavily on our class. My Otto is the eighth. In old days when we were having Religious Instruction, and the master, after we had read something like ' Who knows how near may be my end ', told us that we must always be prepared, and that nobody could tell who might be the first, we used to look at one another and think : ' Oh, there is time enough for that ! We are all so gloriously young ! ' And now already eight of us have passed into eternity !

June 16th, 1916.

What you say about my photograph is probably quite true. One does become older and graver out here. The constant proximity of danger must exercise a great influence over one. Also there is the continual feeling of anxiety about the spiritual and temporal condition of the Fatherland. I so often wonder what things will be like after the war ! It is no wonder either if all that one goes through every day here makes one look older. So much that I used to look up to is now dragged in the mire ; so much that used to seem glorious and splendid is proved to be foul and bad. The veil which, for the young, used to cover all that was evil, and which, in ordinary times, is only gradually raised as a man grows older, has now, with one wrench, been torn violently away from the eyes of us schoolboy War-Volunteers. Abominable things are revealed, and the contrast horrifies us. The period of time in which one would normally get accustomed to the change has been reduced, in our case, to a few months. And this is the reason why one has become graver. Nevertheless I do want to live. Like everybody else I am looking forward to the time when danger will have ceased and when I can work at whatever I like, enjoy what I like, when I shall be at home again. But how long will it be before then ?

July 26th, 1916.

A fresh east wind is blowing, which not only prevents all risk of gas, but is good for the harvest. I hope you have the same thing at home. And we have nothing to do ! Last night Eichler, who has a considerable dramatic gift, read Homer aloud to us. Our batmen listened with the greatest interest to old Heinrich Voss's fine lines, and time flew as we listened to two cantos. We thought about our Freshman year, and our Homer master, and wrote him a card. I wonder whether he'll answer.

On the Somme, August 21st, 1916.

Life here is absolutely ghastly ! I have been three days and four nights in the front line. It is horrible. On the evening of the 17th we had orders to occupy the 4th line. Soon we were moved up into the 3rd, and finally into the 2nd. The way up even so far is indescribable. It runs uphill past a shell-shattered convent. The whole sky is lit up with flashes and flares. The air is full of the thunder of guns, the crash of bursting shells, the howling and whistling of projectiles flying in both directions. The roads have been torn up by shells, but the holes have been filled up so that the motor-ambulances can be driven along them. Only one, a yard deep, is still gaping. An ambulance, loaded with wounded, has fallen into it.

The Company proceeds in open order, one behind the other, to reduce the number of casualties. Motors flash noiselessly by, to fetch wounded. One by one they return, crammed full. Ammunition-columns bring fodder for the insatiable jaws of the guns. Troops who have been relieved are hurrying back. We meet parties of wounded—walking-cases—each with a white label attached to his second button-hole. They are out of it now. They won't have to go up the line again. And so, in spite of their sufferings, they jog along quite merrily.

Gradually we enter the zone of continuous fire. Our march becomes a trot, or rather a gallop. Here and there a man who can't keep up falls out. Panting and sweating, we at last reach a village. Yes, it was once a village. Six weeks ago Martin-

(288)

puich was a pretty place, inhabited and secure. Now it is a region of horror and despair. ' Lasciate ogne speranza '—abandon hope—are the words over the portals of hell in Dante's *Divine Comedy*. I kept thinking of them as we tore through the village.

Next we took cover behind a house. Everybody lies flat on the ground. There is no guide and nobody knows what to do. Meanwhile it thunders and whistles, and bits of shell rattle against the walls. The men begin to get impatient. It is a desperate situation.

At last somebody arrives with instructions and guides us forward. It is well for you that you are not obliged to look on such horrible sights ! Quite apart from the bombardment, the mere appearance of utter devastation everywhere is enough to make one shudder. Not a house is left standing. Everything is completely destroyed—beams, bricks, and blocks of stone lie in the street. One shell-hole has filled up another. The chalky mud is splashed far and wide over everything. Trees, wagons, corpses, knapsacks, horses, rifles, tins, wire, bits of equipment, lie all about on the trampled paths between the craters.

Under the fiercest shrapnel and shell-fire the Company dashes forward—leaping over obstacles, tumbling into shell-holes, stumbling over bodies, or falling, wounded and unable to continue, still we go on till at last we are obliged to halt, and we lie, grinding our teeth, upon the road. When shall we get on ?

At last the mad chase is resumed. We reach the end of the village. There, close by, is the beginning of the front line. The opening is on the left of the road. We plunge in and find a shallow trough which was once a trench. A few men are already lying in the holes which are all that is left of the dug-outs. They look dully at us with cowed and desperate faces.

Now the men are divided up, one here and one there. They are simply crazy with fear. The shells keep falling. Splinters and filth fly through the air.

At last all the necessary dispositions are made and I can sit down for a moment. I meet a comrade of the 5th Company which has just been attacking with five other Companies. Owing to the fog the attack was frustrated by our own barrage. Now they were cowering despairingly here, these poor comrades, and were supposed to attack again, but they hadn't gone, they didn't know which direction to take.

Day now begins to dawn, and I hurry along the trench to see after the men. I realize with horror that before I had been walking over bodies, which were lying about in the water. The men are absolutely demoralized. They had been ordered to fetch bombs, but if I hadn't finally done it myself they wouldn't have had any. It kept getting lighter and lighter. Suddenly, just as the sun rose behind us, came the order: 'The 10th Company will advance 350 yards and dig itself in!'

We were lying in the second line, the first having

been captured by the English, and now we had to dig a new front line close to the English one.

I collect my men, so as to lead them forward all together under cover, and spring forward. When I look back not one, not a single one, has followed me. I go back, reason with them and order them to go with me. This time it has to be over open ground, as some parts of the trench have meanwhile been blown in. Now I spring forward again, leap through the shell-holes for about 50 yards, and throw myself down to get my breath. Two men have come with me. I advance farther. Rifle bullets and shells are falling all around us, but we are not touched and we have no time to worry about them.

At last we are far enough and we start digging. We work sideways, from shell-hole to shell-hole, so that a continuous trench is made. Another Sergeant drives the rest of the men forward with his revolver, until we have about 40, out of the 90 we brought with us, to occupy our 200-yard sector.

Work on the new trench now proceeded feverishly. The few men who have advanced did splendidly. We had scarcely finished when drum-fire started, and for two hours the new trench was heavily shelled, but no attack followed.

I had been on the look-out all through the two hours and was quite done in. Then came the order to report at once on the position at Battalion Head-Quarters. So, in broad daylight, I have to go back—down the slope ; past the reeking, fly-covered corpses ; past all the horrors which dark-

(291)

ness had concealed in the village. It was not easy !

At Battalion-Head-Quarters everything was in confusion. Nobody knew what was happening. Everybody had lost their heads. I learnt later that things were at that moment in an extremely critical state, though we didn't know it at the time, and that all important papers had already been burnt. Anyhow, I was glad to get away again. Meanwhile reinforcements had arrived for us, so I took them up with me. Fresh men to lead under fire. Out of 50, I got 30 up.

In rain and cold ; without overcoats or blankets ; without anything warm to drink (all we had was seltzer-water), we spent three days in the line. Spare me from giving any description of the condition of that company of men—frozen, dead-tired, and broken down by shell-fire. I conducted the relief myself ; therefore I had to go through all that fire and horror twice more. Now, to-night, we are at last back in billets.

HELMUT STRASSMANN, Technical Student, Charlottenburg

Born January 21st, 1893, in Berlin.
Killed November 5th, 1916, near Thilloy.

In Reserve, Forest of Roshan, July 24th, 1915.

SINCE June 1st small attacks have been made with the object of getting a good place for us to break through. With this idea our battalion, on June 15th, took the Cerwona Gora, a small hill near Jednorozek, during a night-attack, and the same thing has been done all along the Eastern Front. From July 1st small attacking-positions were being prepared everywhere—narrow trenches 100 yards away from the enemy, in which we put ladders and bombs ready. Moreover our plucky Pioneers, and also some Infantrymen, crawled out at night and laid mines, lit the fuse and so prepared the very necessary boyaux in advance. Then an uncanny amount of fresh ammunition arrived, and also heavy guns which started getting the range. Our airmen photographed the Russian position from above, so that every Platoon-Commander, and even every Corporal, knew exactly how it looked over there.

At last July 13th was announced as the date and with the pseudonym 'Wedding-day'. At 12.30 a.m. the Infantry occupied the storm-positions, each man being provided with a wire-cutter, five bombs, two iron-rations, and 200 cartridges. At 4.30 our artillery began their work of destruction. Shell after shell fell into the Russian trenches up till

(293)

8 o'clock. From 8 till 8.30 there was rapid-fire and from 8.30 to 8.41 drum-fire—the quickest of all. During these twelve minutes there fell into the Russian trenches, on a breadth of 200 yards, about 10 shells per second. The earth groaned.

Our chaps were as keen as mustard, and our blessed guns simply rushed them along. The Company was in the first rank and advanced in three waves. As senior officer I had to lead the first of these, so at 8.41 I scrambled out of the trench, made a sign to the men to come on, and we raced up the hill. Luckily we found several gaps in the wire, so we got through quite easily. We were 40 yards from the Siberians—a rifle-regiment. In spite of the devastating German shells they put up quite a good defence of rifle- and machine-gun-fire, but it was too late—we were on them! When our bayonets began to get to work the enemy surrendered or bolted. Very few got away, for we were so near that every bullet reached its mark. Our Grenadiers were perfect devils, wreaking bloody vengeance for four months in the trenches. The Company shot down quite 50 men and took 86 prisoners. Our own casualites were 3 killed and 11 wounded. One of our best men fell close to me during the attack, in the very act of shouting 'hurrah'. He was shot through the head, so had a lucky death, being killed instantly.

This attack, which Hindenburg directed from close by, succeeded along the whole front and brought in 13,000 prisoners and 17 guns. In the afternoon we were relieved and another regiment stormed the next Russian position, while we were rewarded by being moved back into Reserve.

By this second attack, which was carried out in exact accordance with Hindenburg's instructions, the whole Russian Front was completely broken and the Russians had to fall back on Warsaw to avoid being surrounded.

Late in the evening we were ' alarmed ', the Russians being reported again in full retreat, and —just as if there had not been trench-warfare here ever since the 1st of March—all the guns, wagons, and columns were immediately put in marching order and we started off in pursuit. The Cossacks set fire to the whole district, but our rapid advance saved many a village from the murderous torch.

On the 15th the Russians established themselves at Orzyc in a fabulously intricate quadruple position —four rows of barbed-wire entanglements, bomb-proof shelters, and the river as an obstruction.

The heavy task of storming it fell to our neighbour regiment, the 93rd Reserve. Three times they attacked, but in spite of frantic artillery-fire the Russians held on. At last, at the fourth attempt, the difficult job was accomplished and the Orzyc position, one of incredible strength, was broken through. This was, I think, the greatest achievement of the whole offensive. The Russians retreated before our regiment without showing fight, and we were thus spared any casualties.

On the 19th there was a final attack on a hill. This was also successful, and we found ourselves before Roshan, the fortress of the Narew.

Our Company was billeted for four days in a country-house—the villa of a Roshan doctor who had fled. It reminded me of Wannsee. When we arrived we found a half-finished meal on the tea-table from which the owners had fled. We had a delightful time there. There were four sitting-rooms ; beautiful sheets, free from lice, on the beds ; and—best of all—a German concert-grand piano. We were in the lap of luxury ! But on the 22nd the idyll ended, for orders arrived that the battalion was to storm the village of Miluny, a fortified position with 30 yards of barbed-wire entanglements. We were very sad at leaving our pleasant quarters.

The attack was fixed for 1.30 midday. Our infantry's task was lightened by a phenomenally intense artillery preparation—30.5c. Austrian howitzers, and even a 'Big Bertha', besides 5 trench-mortars. The 30.5's made a row as if hell had been let loose !

When we reached the 1st line the Russians had withdrawn, but were shooting all the more fiercely from the 2nd, which was also taken in ten minutes. Out of revenge the Russian guns dropped shells upon us without ceasing the whole day, till at last we got so used to it that we did not notice it.

At 6 p.m. I got an extra job—namely to occupy a flank position. With only 32 Grenadiers I had the luck to take 64 Russians prisoner, and I held the trench for three hours before the longed-for reinforcements, in the shape of three companies of Jaegers, arrived. Twice the Russians were about to attack, but each time our artillery-observers spotted them in time, and sent over a few salvos to greet the would-be attacking party. In the evening the Russians again attempted a counter-attack, which however was quenched at its feeble outset. At 1.30 a.m. we were relieved, and then I had to take over another Company whose Commander had been killed.

At 7 a.m. a mail arrived, bringing some splendid things and Mother's letter. She wrote that she was ' comforted to know that I was doing a Course and so was for the time being in a position of comparative safety '. Of course she couldn't tell that, on account of the Offensive, the Course had been cancelled and fighting had begun, but still it was funny to read that here. Afterwards I slept for 10 hours, and we remained for two days in Reserve.

To-day the Russians have blown up Fort Roshan and we have forced the Narew Line. The first of the Binnen Forts has fallen, and thus Russia's proudest line of fortifications is broken. Now we shall attack Warsaw in strength.

JOHANNES NOGIELSKY, Technical High School, Charlottenburg

Born March 4th, 1892, at Breslau.
Killed in an air-fight, January 22nd, 1917, in Champagne.

Dear Mother,—

When you read these lines I shall be no longer among the living : ' Be thou faithful unto death and I will give thee a crown of life.' Do not weep for me, for I am in the realms of light, so why mourn ? The war came and I also went like so many others to the Front and was faithful unto death. As I write these lines I know not where my grave may be ; do not trouble about my mortal remains ; it matters not if they rot in filth and fragments, for the soul lives on and is divine. May you live long yet in this beautiful world ! Greet all whom I love and who were my friends. Enemies I have never had, I hope. And now do not be sorrowful, for in a little while we shall meet again. I greet you all and am with you in spirit.

HERO HELLWICH, Student of Political Economy, Freiburg i. Br.

Born March 15th, 1896, at Bischofstein, East Prussia.
Killed December 20th, 1916, on the Somme.

(Lying on my tummy by candle-light, although it's daytime. This place lets in the cold and wind and rain all right, but not the daylight.)

DEAR PARENTS,—

If anything should happen to me, I hope that it will find me to some extent prepared. There is only one thing that worries me, and that is that I should leave this world as a mere 'silly boy'. Don't protest ; it can't be otherwise. I am straight from school and haven't yet had time to develop. The impression I have left upon you *must* be that of an immature lad, and that impression is bound to remain. I have never yet really lived, for life is struggle and toil, and I know nothing of either— life for me was nothing but pleasure and enjoyment, and if I have not always had those feelings of enjoyment, that was entirely my own 'silly boy's' fault.

The result of my short time here in Northern France has been to give me a feeling of gratitude towards the Creator that I was not killed on November 1st, nor on the 5th or 6th, like so many of my comrades.

If anybody should ask me to suggest an epitaph to be cut upon the tombstones of D. H. or E. H., I should not be at a loss. I should propose Hamlet's dying words : 'This fell Sergeant, Death, is strict in his arrest.' In Eichendorff's song 'In a cool valley' there occurs the passage : 'As a warrior would I hasten, straight into the bloody fight. By the quiet fire would I rest me, on the battle-field at night.' That is the romantic view of war, but in reality war is extremely prosaic—no waving flags, no blaring trumpets, no flashing blades accompany one into battle. It is an entirely different thing. One gets into a peculiar state in the trenches, physically and psychologically. Then comes the order to advance, and under the shadow of night we all creep and dodge forward, making use of every scrap of cover in the effort to give the deadly bullet as few chances as possible. I can't imagine anything less inspiring ! The dying Valentine says : 'Through death's dark valley I have trod, as a good soldier to my God.'

If I am killed it will be my parents' first great sorrow. It is not true that war hardens people's hearts. Anybody who comes back hardened, must have been hard to start with. The effect of war is much more that of purifying and deepening. One thanks God for every day that one is allowed to go on living. If through God's boundless mercy I should be permitted to survive the war, then I will endeavour—however poorly and inadequately I succeed—to prove myself worthy of that mercy. In war no one is master of his fate. Man's intelligence fails him. He can only say : 'Thy will be done.' I try to be always in such dispositions that, if a bullet or a shell should strike me, I may not die with vain thoughts in my mind. Remember me as I was when at my best.

WILLY HÖLSCHER, Academy of Forestry, Hannoversch-Münden

Born August 12th, 1893, at Münster i.W.
Killed January 31st, 1917, in Champagne.

In Champagne, February 20th, 1916.

THE weather is lovely to-day. If it keeps so, I shall ride over to our airmen this afternoon.

One thing more : Would you be so kind as to send me some flower-seeds? There is nothing very nice to look at round about my billet, and, as I don't know how long I may be stuck here, I want to grow some flowers. Please send me sweet-peas, convolvulus, sunflower, flax, mignonette, etc. I want to cover the unsightly earth with verdure.

Graudenz, April 7th, 1916.

Soon I shall be able to fly alone. According to my Instructor I am learning the art very well and easily. Then I shall be able to make over-land flights, which will be very jolly.

Now please be so kind as to send me at once my double-barrel gun and all accessories, cartridges and bullets, my dark-green shooting-suit, undress tunic, and the old shooting-hat, waterproof cape and rucksack. I want them because I have had the luck to get an introduction, through my Instructor, to a landowner here, who, not having time himself, has invited me to shoot his game, giving me ' plein pouvoir '. The first roe-buck he wants to shoot himself—the rest is all left to me.

(301)

April 25th, 1916.

To-day I have to go in for my first exam.—that of Pilot. I have to do all sorts of things in the air —make an ' 8 ', various landings, etc. Everybody here is astonished at my being already so far advanced and flying so well after only four weeks. I find it tremendous sport. Since I have been able to fly alone I have the sole use of a simply perfect machine—an Albatross bi-plane, with a 100-h.p. Mercedes engine.

A few days ago I was about 4,000 ft. up and about 1,000 ft. above the clouds, in the evening towards sunset. Down below, on the earth, the weather was dull and unpleasant, but it was a glorious sight when I rose out of the gloomy region below into the most gorgeous sunshine above the clouds which lay like an endless shroud over the earth. One could quite forget that somewhere down there there was a world where miserable human-beings were crawling about. I felt as if I could easily step out of my aeroplane and walk about on the clouds (I didn't try, however). It was quite unearthly. I pity the people who can't have such an experience. I should like to take you all up with me one day.

In Champagne, January 21*st,* 1917.

Things are fairly lively here, but we have the advantage over the French. The German aeroplane reported in the French newspapers as having been brought down by a French pilot behind Navarin Farm was unfortunately one of our squadron.

He was an exception in having bad luck. Whenever we come within range of the French anti-aircraft guns, they fire industriously at us, but it is very hard to hit. My machine has already got a few honourable wounds—once three, once four, and once one—but they are all harmless little holes which can be plastered over, date painted on, and all is well! There is still plenty of room on the wings for more!

HANS SPATZL, Student of Theology, Lyceum Freising

Born May 14th, 1891, at Surberg, near Traunstein.
Died March 16th, 1917, in a Field Hospital near St. Mihiel.

July 14th, 1915.

IN my yesterday's letter I described a scene of peace. To-day I have in my mind another unforgettable picture—that of the grave of one of our heroes. I often pass it, but never without uncovering my head and saying a Hail-Mary for the dead man. A faithful comrade buried him in the crater made by a heavy-shell; raised a proper mound and put up a pretty cross with a 'penthouse'. Two candlesticks stand at the foot. A big 7-in. shell dominates the grave, and flowers are planted on it. Nature runs wild all around— ears of corn and flowers of every colour hang over the edge of the shell-hole. An atmosphere of peace seems to reign there, and when I went by in the early morning, when the sun was sending its first rays flickering in golden flames over the grave, I pulled out my mouth-organ and played a hymn tune for the comrade in his grave.

December 20th, 1916.

I must send you a few lines before the coming season of tenderness, love and peace. I am looking forward to Christmas even more than I did last year, for I am in hopes that the dear Christ Child may have mercy upon us. If I could only be

(304)

quite alone on the Holy Eve, when night sinks down on velvet wings over the earth and the stars shine with quiet radiance like lights before the Tabernacle. May the dear Christ Child grant us a share in that burning love which brought Him from that heavenly throne, surrounded with the splendour of the sun and by choirs of adoring angels, to this accursed earth, to be our all. Let us kneel with the shepherds and the Wise Men from the East. We shall not rise without having received a gift. His love and His consolation will assuredly remain with us. May the dear Christ Child bless you.

WALTER SCHMIDT, Student of Natural History, Tübingen

Born October 12th, 1892, at Tuttlingen.
Killed April 16th, 1917, near Laon.

Firing-Position Elzbiecin, Grabowic, Sunday morning, July 18th, 1915.

I RECEIVED your nice letter of July 1st the day before yesterday. It flowed over me like a golden stream of beauty and the joy of youth, and innumerable vivid memories, which the rigour of war had swamped, sprang up again impetuously to the surface of my mind. It is good for you that you can enjoy such things without an afterthought, as if you were all children together. I doubt whether I should be capable of that now or could learn to do it again except by shedding the whole of my present personality.

Our Midsummer Night was also beautiful, and by way of bonfires the villages all around were blazing. Shrapnel whistled unceasingly, and in the distance we heard faint 'hurrahs'. The Russians were making a counter-attack in honour of St. John's Night, and were so absolutely wiped out that in the morning each of our Companies discovered 200 dead Russians.

All the same we had no time to admire the wild, stormy beauty of the night, as an attack in overwhelming numbers might be made at any moment, and in that case we should have been done for. Deserters stated that a brigade of Cossacks were standing ready to break through if the attack was successful, and if they had done so not a man among us would have been left alive. So all the time we went on loading and firing, loading and firing, dragging up fresh ammunition and firing again.

You can imagine that that kind of Midsummer Night leaves traces, and that is why I have said that it would be impossible for me to achieve the wonderful Midsummer Night's frame of mind of a ' Bird of Passage '. But I must cheer up—that will all come back when once we are at home again.

Fancy still dwelling on the thought of being at home again ! We have been disappointed so often ! First we hoped to be back by the end of October, 1914 ; then by Christmas ; then Easter ; then Whitsun ; then the 1st of August ; then Christmas, 1915 ; and now we are forced to admit that it can't be over before Easter, 1916.

These two years of war constitute a break in one's life, and are nevertheless a very important part of it ; but what the war is trying to teach us as human beings, we have not yet learnt and never shall. We hoped for an equalizing of social conditions as a result of having got to know one another better ; we hoped that our national ideas of pleasure would be ennobled and that there would be a return to simpler modes of life ; but these things have only come to pass to a very limited extent and are already being once more abandoned. We have not yet learnt to live entirely for the sake of others ; egoism is still the ruling passion at the Front as it is at home. Happy he who can at least feel that the war has had a good influence on him personally—the war that has deprived us of so much that we ought to have learned and enjoyed during these years of youth. Happy he for whom the habit of serving others and sacrificing himself for them without thought of recompense or recognition has become so much part and parcel of himself that it will remain with him after the war and he will live as one who does right without looking for a reward hereafter. Hopes and plans for the future are also denied us ; many who go home find misery awaiting them there—a neglected household, and a business which has gone down ; and we do not yet know what will be the ultimate fate of Germany and of us all. We only feel a secret longing for peace as something magnificent and sublime and an unconquerable resolve to fight on until we obtain it. One often also considers the possibility of deliverance from danger and privation by means of a sudden death, and this thought has become so familiar to us that it has lost all its horror. Our best friends, the most splendid men, have thrown themselves into the arms of this same death, and why should we avoid or dread it? It is the finest thing that can be granted one—and yet nobody wishes to die, because we cannot help feeling that we have not yet seen enough life, we still know too little of its depths and mysteries. . . .

Temessag, near Temesvar, September 27th, 1915.

' Stradom, De-lousing Station ! '—It was just beginning to get light as we climbed sleepily out of the train, dragging all our belongings with us, and stood shivering at the frost-covered barrier till the horses had been got into the other train.

The train which had brought us steamed off, back to the still lousy Front, while we, after having been *de-loused*, were transferred into a new, disinfected train.

As we stepped firmly towards the mysterious buildings, we could see in the morning light the distant tower of the Abbey Church of Czenstochau. There are six to eight *Lausoleums* on the Frontier, each of which cost a million marks, but they are obviously necessary for, according to some Professor's calculation, each Russian prisoner harbours some 9,000 lice on his person.

We officers went into one shed, the men into another. There were separate buildings for engines, disinfecting apparatus, bathrooms, sick-wards, and drying-rooms. We had to strip stark naked, give up uniforms and underclothing at a counter, also sleeping-bag and boots, lock up valuables, and then—in one's ' birthday-suit '—stand for half an hour under a hot shower-bath, rubbing oneself with liquid soap, to get rid of body-parasites which might be adhering to the skin. Then one dried oneself, put on a dressing-gown and went into a warm room, where, in classic simplicity of attire, we all sat round, from the General—who was cursing like anything because his under-clothes were so long in coming—to the youngest ' deputy ' from the Light-Column.

(309)

At last uniforms and under-garments emerged from the formalin vapour with which they had been treated, still damp and so reeking with disinfectant that one's eyes watered and a universal chorus of lamentation went up from the much-tried men, which, however, changed to laughter when one of them couldn't find his trousers, which had unfortunately got left behind in the boiler.

A good solid breakfast in the very nicely arranged canteen followed. After that we drove out to Czenstochau—about 20 minutes away—to do a lot of shopping, and there we once more came in contact with civilization.

A pretty boulevard planted with lime-trees, but very badly paved, runs right through the town up to the Abbey. Unluckily it was a Jewish holiday, and none of the Jewish shops were open, so we drove on up to the Abbey to see the Black Virgin. The imposing baroque building crowns a gentle slope, and with its moat and surrounding walls looks almost like a fortress. The fourteen Stations-of-the-Cross are represented in immense groups of statuary all around. Passing through several courtyards we reached the church, the interior of which is being restored. But, hark! through a side door we hear the muffled voices of a fine male choir. We walk towards the sound, which rings louder and louder through the aisles—the Latin chant of monks. Before the open door of a chapel our footsteps with their clink of spurs pause—there in the dimness is a kneeling throng and beyond, blazing in the light of a thousand candles, shines the golden altar with the Miraculous Image behind it. The chant is hushed ; the priest proceeds with the Mass, and at the Sanctus the choir breaks out again in a triumphant strain to the accompaniment of a burst of organ music. Truly one of the most impressive scenes witnessed during the war ! Here in the Heart of the Mother of God the suffering find comfort and succour and the afflicted a refuge ! Even we rough, matter-of-fact men, driven hither and thither by the winds of war, whose sole aim for a whole year has been the defeat and annihila- of the enemy, were wonderfully moved by the thought that there were still people who have nothing to do with all that, whose kingdom is not of this world.

September 28th, 1915.

It was already dark when we drove into Temesvar on September 25th, and at half-past seven on the following morning the sun of South Hungary was shining so fiercely on our faces that we got up as quickly as possible. We were greeted with the music of merry-go-rounds and all the hubbub of a Fair, and lo and behold, not 300 yards away from us, the Fair had started ! So after breakfast we went out in parties to visit the Pleasure Park.

I have seldom seen a spectacle more gloriously rich in colour. The background was much the same as in Tübingen market—two merry-go-rounds, boat-swings, shooting-galleries, photographers, cinemas, etc.—but here we had the addition of the daughters of Hungary in their extremely pretty national costume—snow-white bodices with gaily embroidered stomachers, dark skirts, silk head-kerchiefs, and coloured stockings. They wear aprons in front and behind. Most of the women and girls were pretty, with delicate features, slim figures, and a free and firm gait—quite different from the clumsy Polish women, with their flat, full-moon faces, and their waddling walk !

It was indeed a gay scene. There were a number of peasant youths too, also dressed in white blouses reaching to the knee and embroidered waistcoats, all remarkably clean and neat. Mingling with the crowd were gipsy women, with their unkempt locks interwoven with cords, beads, and ribbons.

The peasants had all driven in from the country in their farm-wagons, and there was a regular wagon-park of about 200 vehicles, some with very fine horses.

There was unfortunately nothing to buy but the usual factory-made town clothes and town goods such as one sees everywhere. The only things of any beauty were the water-jugs which are used all over the country and which still have the shape of the ancient Roman amphora, painted with very simple designs. A Southern Hungarian woman in her indoor costume with one of these amphoræ is a perfect classic picture.

We left the fascinating scene of gay life and colour, ardent glances and laughing maidens, slowly got ready to start, and then marched off at 12 o'clock to a neighbouring village to find billets. The way lay through the town where, as it was

Sunday, the bells were just ringing the people out of church, the shops were opening, and in the big Platz a military band was just beginning to blare as we passed. The many saunterers, who included a large number of Austrian officers, waved, saluted, and called out greetings to us—we were indisputably the sensation of the day in Temesvar !

Kragujewaz, November 2nd, 1915.

DEAREST MOTHER,—

The tide of war is rising high again. We captured Kragujewaz yesterday, and I am to-day occupying a most princely billet with my batman. I am inhabiting nothing less than the house of a Major, replete with mid-European comfort, including a gramophone.

Kragujewaz is in every way larger and more beautiful even than Semendria, and if it weren't for the cobble-stones it could compete with any of the Hungarian towns. The large number of cafés and public-houses testify to the dissipated life led by the Serbs. The shops—any, that is, that have not been looted—are shut and guarded by sentries so that it is impossible to requisition anything, but still one gets as much wine and poultry as one likes.

The best thing of all is that the whole arsenal, gunpowder factory and magazines, with any amount of war-material and light and heavy guns, fell into our hands.

My battery has been under fire on the hills above

Kragujewaz since this morning, the enemy aiming continually at his powder-magazine, but luckily not hitting it.

Some of the people here speak German, and most of them have stuck to their homes, which has proved a good thing for them, as inhabited houses have not been looted. My Major and his wife and family are naturally exceptions.

How delightful it is, after all the rainy days, when one has been plastered with layer upon layer of filth, urging the horses over steep hills and sleeping at night in a tent or a wretched mud hut leaking at every corner, to find oneself suddenly in the midst of cleanliness and luxury, eating at a table covered with a snow-white cloth and knowing that one has won it all for oneself! We certainly are still Huns and barbarians to revel in the startling and inexplicable variations of the war here as we do. I wouldn't exchange the ups and downs of this war for all the laurels and decorations gained by my comrades on the Western Front. One day we are in the depths of misery, rain, casualties, nothing to eat, the horses sick and over-driven ; on the next we have sunshine, a country like fairyland, villages and lovely vineyards clustering on the rugged mountain-side, and below them the town, into which the long coils of the war-dragon are winding their way. On the highest slopes the Serbs are still established, helplessly watching the progress of the gigantic force deploying below them. . . .

(314)

Bivouac, August 30th, 1916.

I received your nice letter of July 29th here on
the Somme, where we have been since the 1st of
August, in the Guinchy-Guillemont sector. What
I have been through during this time surpasses in
horror all my previous experiences during the second
year of the war. As a gunner I don't wish to com-
plain, and I willingly admit that the infantry in this
salient have had a far worse time, but the sort of
thing that has been happening in our firing-position
is quite sufficient even for anybody who had been
through a good deal.

You will no doubt have learned from the newspapers and other sources about how the English,
with the aid of their airmen, who are often 1,500
ft. above the position, and their captive-balloons,
have exactly located every one of our batteries and
have so smashed them up with long-distance guns
of every calibre that the artillery here has had
unusually heavy losses both of men and material.
Our dug-outs, in which we shelter day and night,
are not even adequate, for though they are cut
out of the chalk they are not so strong but that a
' heavy ' was able a few days ago to blow one in
and bury the whole lot of men inside. The gun-
emplacements are surrounded by a ring of shell-
craters and every day some heaps of 50 to 100
shells are blown up by a direct hit. When we are
firing a barrage the men have to cross a stretch of
open to get to their gun and then, without taking
any notice of falling shells, we have to fire as hard
as we possibly can. A few days ago the whole

(315)

detachment of an N.C.O. and three men were killed by a direct hit during the barrage. As nobody else wanted to fire a gun covered with corpses, the Fähnrich and I took on the job, and there, in the midst of dead bodies and blood and in full view of death, I was filled with a feeling of profound happiness because the attack had been frustrated. We have carried out our task if the enemy fails to break through, even if thousands of us have been killed. What does an individual life matter on such occasions, and can one spend it to greater advantage than in offering it up as part of the general sacrifice ? These are perhaps banalities and platitudes, but one often realizes their truth and value when one is put to the test. Death may be bitter, but we can conquer it in advance, and then the object of it—the salvation of the Fatherland—shines through all the blood and horror and one no longer dreads it.

HANS OLUF ESSER, Student of Natural History,
Freiburg i.B.

Born August 30th, 1894, at Elberfeld.
Killed April 17th, 1917, near Corbény, Chemin-des-Dames.

July 6th, 1916.

. . . Oh, you chaps, what sport I have had to-day !
I was supposed to have breakfast at 5, but I over-
slept and didn't wake till half-past 6, so that I
should have had to be off at once, but luckily it
was too misty.

At 8 I drove my machine out and waited to start
till there was something happening. At 8.25 two
dots suddenly appeared in the sky, and somebody
called out : ' There come two ! ' Off I started and
just at the last moment someone shouted that eight
enemy planes were approaching. Sure enough,
hardly was I over Vouziers, when I saw high above
me—at about 11,000 ft.—I myself being only 1,600
ft. up—a number of machines : first six, then eight,
then ten—more and more—all flying towards the
north.

I at once set off in pursuit, losing sight of them
several times, but keeping to the north. Then
suddenly I discovered the whole seventeen over
Charleville—a fine sight ! I was about on a level
with the lowest—1,000 ft. At that moment they
swooped down like birds of prey, leaving only a
few above as cover. There were twelve duplex-
engine Caudron bi-planes and five enemy one-seater
Nieuport fighting-bi-planes. I try to attack one

(317)

Caudron while they are all circling round in order to drop their bombs, but I have scarcely begun firing when I am driven off by the Nieuports. Finally they flew off again towards the south, while I followed them closely in case one should drop behind.

And that's just what happens. A Caudron, rather below me, hangs back, guarded, unfortunately, by a Nieuport. Seizing an opportunity when the Nieuport is a little in advance, I dive down, but the Nieuport is already back again. A vigorous fight ensues—most daring stunts on both sides. I am astonished how well I can do it, but the Frenchman can do it better still! He rolls, flies on his back for six seconds, shooting all the while; loops the loop—it's marvellous! However, he accomplishes his object only partially—he doesn't shoot me down, but I have lost touch with the squadron. After ten minutes he decamps, and I follow, thinking that he will try to rejoin his squadron.

Over Attigny, a little to the north of our aerodrome, I am again under the squadron, having unluckily dropped too low during the fight. Drawing to one side, I try to fire at them from below, and so I twice got quite close to a Caudron. Now came the crucial moment. Suddenly, from the Front, a Fokker comes dashing in between us, in pursuit of a Caudron. Two more Caudrons and two Nieuports swoop down from above upon the Fokker, while I rush to help him. I attack the hunted Caudron, which comes at me to within 30 yards, as if it wanted to ram me, but I slip through underneath. Then I find myself face to face with a Nieuport, and fire at him. He banks, makes a steep spiral and drops from 8,000 to 2,500 ft., finds me close behind him and tries to escape straight ahead. But I am in front of him and fire. Another nose-dive, another attempt to escape, then another dive, and so on, till I lose him. He was very well camouflaged.

Suddenly I see a shadow skimming along the ground, so I know that he can't be more than 325 ft. up. I immediately fire down, and already he is preparing to land, seeing that it is all up with him. I fly round him several times, waving my handkerchief, and he also shows a white flag. I then make a beautiful landing beside him, just in time to stop him setting fire to his machine.

He came up to me and said in German, 'You are surely no N.C.O.?', and then introduced himself, 'Lieutenant Jean Raby'. I did the same, and we shook hands. He and his machine were quite uninjured, he had only had an attack of nerves and at the same moment his machine-gun jammed. He expressed his gratitude to me for his being alive, and said I flew very well. In the afternoon we were both invited to coffee with the Flight, and smoked the pipe of peace. A very pleasant young man, from Saubnes, near Longwy, studying engineering in Paris, and very intelligent.

So now I have got my first, and I am very glad to have brought him down quite safe and sound.

FRIEDRICH GEORG STEINBRECHER, Student
of Theology, Leipzig

Born May 3rd, 1892, in Dresden.
Killed April 19th, 1917, near Moronvillers (Champagne).

March 13th, 1916, before Pontavert.

WENT through the captured position. A swampy
stretch of forest, consisting of shell-smashed trees
and battered trenches, surrounds the hill. The
whole place looks as if it had been ploughed up.
Blown in dug-outs. Huge shell-craters. Fragments
of wood and clothing ; corpses ; rifles ; knapsacks.
A field and wood of horror.

March 14th.

Had a stiff job : getting ammunition and material
into the line. Gas-shells polluted the air. Men
got buried. Attempts at artificial respiration. A
fearful squash in the dug-outs. Only half can lie
down at night, the rest have to sit or stand. I
managed to do without going to the latrine for four
days. Then it had to be risked. The strain on
the nerves is terrible. Many break down altogether.
I haven't been able to eat or sleep, from exhaustion.
Yet I am forced to admire the way in which many
a delicate chap keeps up. Germans have a damned
lot of backbone. A man can always stand a bit
more than he thinks he can. The time passes
quickly. At night I am woken up suddenly by
shells which keep me lively.

March 15th.

Every movement must be executed at the double. Every trip to fetch rations is an act of heroism, a matter of life and death. We badly need to be relieved. I am quite fit again. On the 14th there was a partial attack. Successful.

March 17th.

Relieved to-night. At last. We had cleaned up the battle-field fairly well. Sights which I shall never forget. Sickening—sickening is the only word. But it has to be.

* * * * *

Officers' Convalescent Home, Marchais, July 3rd, 1916.

Only faint rumours of the great events happening to our comrades on the Somme penetrate into the quiet solitude of this old cathedral city.

I am alone to-day. The Staff-Doctor and the Jaeger officer, who are the only others here, have driven over to Sissonne. I sit in the library and dream myself back into French history. Rays of sunshine are playing on the dusty, leather-bound volumes. They sparkle on the gilt edges and are gone again. Outside roses are nodding in the breeze. All is still.

Opposite me—I think—the Bishop and the Abbot of Notre-Dame de Liesse are sitting playing chess. There is a faint cough—the rustle of clothing—the sound of delicate ivory figures being gently set down. Otherwise silence. A sound of footsteps. A servant enters : ' Your Lordship is implored to lend a

gracious ear.' Oh, no, it's an Orderly saying :
' Cocoa is served ! '

I pass noiselessly through the great saloons and
see myself coming and going in tall mirrors. The
Bishop and the Abbot have vanished. The chess-
board has been pushed aside. The figures lie prone
with bored expressions. I draw back the heavy
curtain and let the sun shine on the Gothic panelling.
Birds are twittering in the ivy. Roses kiss the
window-panes. On the other side of the room the
cocoa is steaming in a service of English china.
The ancestors look indignantly down upon the
new master of the house. The scent of roses steals
through my blue salon and the blackbirds are giving
a concert as I write.

April 12th, 1916.

Somme. The whole history of the world cannot
contain a more ghastly word ! All the things I
am now once more enjoying—bed, coffee, rest at
night, water—seem unnatural and as if I had no
right to them. And yet I was only there a week.

Life is a gift. If only I had not seen all that !
We only gradually realize who is no longer with us.
So many have gone. Some so soon that they are
already forgotten. Those who fell beside me I
shall never forget. Only a fifth of my platoon is
left ; all the best have been killed.

At the beginning of the month we left our old
position. During the lorry and train journey we
were still quite cheery. We knew what we were
wanted for. Then came bivouacs, an ' alarm ',

and we were rushed up through shell-shattered villages and barrage into the turmoil of war. The enemy was firing with 12-inch guns. There was a perfect torrent of shells. The last days had been stiflingly hot. Sooner than we expected we were in the thick of it. First in the artillery-position. Columns were tearing hither and thither as if possessed. The gunners could no longer see or hear. Verey lights were going up along the whole Front, and there was a deafening noise: the cries of wounded, orders, reports.

At noon the gun-fire became even more intense, and then came the order: 'The French have broken through. Counter-attack!'

We advanced through the shattered wood in a hail of shells. I don't know how I found the right way. Then across an expanse of shell-craters, on and on. Falling down and getting up again. Machine-guns were firing. I had to cut across our own barrage and the enemy's. I am untouched.

At last we reach the front line. Frenchmen are forcing their way in. The tide of battle ebbs and flows. Then things get quieter. We have not fallen back a foot. Now one's eyes begin to see things. I want to keep running on—to stand still and look is horrible. 'A wall of dead and wounded!' How often have I read that phrase!—now I know what it means.

Day melts into night. We are always on the alert. We can't establish communication with the rear without casualties. The wounded are in a makeshift dug-out. One has to sit by without being able to do anything for them. Deserters come in. French wounded crawl into the trench with shining faces. In a moment I got to know dozens of men. I had men belonging to three different regiments. I felt then what it is to be in command. It means responsibility, over life and death. The men cling to one like children.

I have witnessed scenes of heroism and of weakness. Men who can endure every privation. Being brave is not only a matter of will, it also requires strong nerves, though the will can do a great deal. A Divisional Commander dubbed us the 'Iron Brigade' and said he had never seen anything like it. I wish it had all been only a dream—a bad dream. And yet it was a joy to see such heroes stand and fall. The bloody work cost us 177 men. We shall never forget Chaulmes and Vermandovillers.

September 29/30*th,* 1916.

When one has come through a bad time, one puts up with a great deal to which one used to object. Work and worry and again work and worry. One learns to be unexacting and grateful. I have often felt the same before. It doesn't last long, but for the time being it does one good. Such experiences change one's nature and one no longer asks for thanks or reward, for what one has been through is too sacred to require payment. When all thought of reward ceases, the region in which God lives is reached. Those are no doubt the holiest moments in life which reduce one to silence.

November 3rd, 1916.

At last I have had good news of Hans. He is farther back and out of the racket, but I also am in a quiet position. To-day I have been wandering with my Corporal and my dog over brook, rock and ruin, to a spring which we use by day and the French by night. That shows you that the situation is pretty peaceful. But it is not like it once was. The poetry of the trenches is a thing of the past. The spirit of adventure is dead. We are now oppressed by the reflection that we have seen what a battle is like and shall see it again. We have become wise, serious and professional. Stern duty has taken the place of a keenness sometimes amounting to passion—a frigid, mechanical doing of one's duty.

When one has seen how brutal, how degrading war can be, any idyllic interval comes like a reprieve from the gallows. My dog is snoring and the coffee has got cold. Formerly the walls were adorned with pictures—now they are covered with maps, orders, and reports. Formerly the men christened their dug-outs, trenches, and houses—now they are numbered 1, 2, A, B, etc. I sometimes feel so wintry inside. The war which began as a fresh youth is ending as a made-up, boring, antiquated actor. Death is the only conqueror. We are all disillusioned, at least as regards what is called world-philosophy.

RUDOLF KRÜGER, Medical Student, Berlin

Born May 9th, 1897, in Berlin.
Killed May 3rd, 1917, near Rheims.

April 23rd, 1917, near Rheims.

YESTERDAY, that is to say on April 22nd, I received
my baptism of fire from enemy Artillery. We had
to occupy a Reserve Position again, but this time
we had to go up over open ground. It was not
long before the enemy guns spotted us and scattered
some very heavy crumbs for our benefit ! Just at
this spot four of our Company were killed by direct
hits. I did not wink an eyelash and was not in
the least uneasy or upset, though the beastly things
often landed quite close to me, but all the same I
thanked God in the evening when we were out
of it.

Here we are living in an absolutely uncivilized
fashion—no houses or beds, and no means of washing or shaving, and look like wild men of the woods.
My own sweet face is adorned with a yellowish-red
beard, the colour of pickled-cabbage, a yard long !
In the morning one cleans one's eyes with ' spit '
and then spits on one's handkerchief to do the rest
of one's ' washing '. The whole business is beautifully simple and accomplished in a few movements
of the hand. And yet how I long to get back to
decent conditions, where one could also get the
rags off one's body and a proper night's rest oftener
than once a week !

A mail has just come in after a long interval,

and I have got letters. I am glad to hear that you have seen the *Evangelimann* at the Opera. I once took part in it as a supernumerary, and ran from left to right across the stage carrying a long pole as a fireman during the burning of the church. I still remember distinctly how beautifully the rising of the moon was represented. Oh, what a glorious *motif* that is : ' Blessed are they who are persecuted for righteousness' sake.'

What wouldn't I give to be able to do a theatre once again, or—what would be simply ideal—to spend a few days with you ! I simply long to make my 'cello sing for joy during a trio-evening. But brace up ! All will yet be well ! Besides, Papa has taken immense trouble in copying out a whole lot of beautiful well-known musical themes for me. By that means one can listen, if only with one's mind's ear, to the glorious old melodies which have so often thrilled us.

KARL SCHENKEL, Theological Candidate, Marburg

Born June 18th, 1892, at Murr.
Killed May 5th, 1917, near Douai.

On the Arras Front, April 20th, 1917.

You know that the situation here was anything but rosy when we arrived. The English had broken through to a distance of 5 miles in one push. There was a thin line of infantry in front of us, and the English were just where our heavy guns used to be. All that had been saved in the rear of our section was five heavy howitzers and a few field-guns. This was the state of things when we took hold. The enemy had tanks, cavalry, and thick swarms of infantry, while we were entirely dependent on rifles and machine-guns ; but we were perfectly cool from the start. ' If those chaps were worth anything at all—if they were Germans—they'd have broken through long ago ! ' we all thought. Day and night, with a calmness and determination which is characteristic only of Germans, our reinforcements arrived. After two or three days we had collected such a lot of guns that no English attack had any success.

Wonderful to relate our morale remained perfectly good in spite the intense bombardment and its ensuing casualties. That ought to be a cause of deep gratitude to you at home, not gratitude to us—we do our duty and are not responsible for our morale—but to God.

You must realize that the time now approaching must and will require that we should shed rivers of blood—he who would gain so great an object must throw his all into the balance. Who knows how soon the last hour may strike for us or for someone we love ! What then ? One thing I do earnestly beg of you : do not be anxious about me. And if the supreme sacrifice should be demanded of us, then do not give way, do not indulge in vain lamentations, for it is just at such moments that war is the test of our faith. Sorrowful we must indeed be—that we cannot help—but two things are still possible to us : we can transform our suffering into a blessing and we can set an example to others.

WILLI BOHLE, Student of Mathematics, Freiburg i.B.

Born November 2nd, 1897, at Hamburg.
Killed May 26th, 1917, near Arras.

Erre, April 15th, 1917.

THANKS, thanks be to the Lord God for having protected me through the terrible days which now lie behind me !

We went into the Line on April 10th. The whole night of the 10th–11th we were digging ourselves in, in order to get cover from the fire. Then came the morning of April 11th. Never shall I forget the 11th of April ! The English had been firing on the front line all night and in the morning they attacked, and our troops went streaming to the rear. Our Company it was which swarmed out into the open and, under shell-, shrapnel-, machine-gun- and rifle-fire, dug itself in again, and in spite of heavy casualties, brought the English advance to a standstill. That was at 5 a.m. From then till 3 p.m. we lay only 6 yards from the enemy. Then fresh troops arrived, counter-attacked, and won back all the ground that had been lost in the morning. We were again masters of the situation.

How I felt, dear Mother, all that day, that you were thinking about me ! And how lovingly I thought of you all ! My one prayer, which was, ' Dear God, not my will but Thine be done,' gave me strength to bear everything. And yesterday, when I came out of the zone of fire, I simply did not know how to express my joy and gratitude to God—

whether to laugh or to cry ! My whole self was one prayer. What superhuman strength God grants to those who have found Him. I am so rich, so safe, so happy ! Many found the march yesterday, after having had only about ten hours' sleep between the 9th and 13th of April, very trying. In spite of all fatigue I was full of joy and gladness. I had sufficient strength to carry a comrade's rifle for hours, and to sing when everybody's spirits were drooping from sheer exhaustion.

To-day is Sunday—that means a general clean-up ; for through all those wet, snowy, cold days we were lying, wet through and with chattering teeth, in the mud and filth of holes which we had dug ourselves in the ground.

Darling Mother, darling little Mother, and you too, my brother and sister, I am ready to endure anything for your sakes, so that you may never see what ruined villages and shell-destroyed fields look like ; so that you may never learn what the word *war* really means. Be thankful, my Gretel and Erich—although you are still so young and know nothing of the serious side of life—that our little house is still standing ; that you can sleep in beds ; that you have a roof over your heads ; that you are not tormented by vermin ; that you have your meals at the proper times ; that you do not know what thirst and hunger are. Be thankful ; fulfil all your little duties conscientiously, and never grumble !

The day after to-morrow we move farther back, into a quiet spot. We have done our duty in the Arras battle.

FRANZ VON DRATHEN, Technical Student, Charlottenburg

Born April 15th, 1898, at Charlottenburg.
Killed June 10th, 1917, near Senhey.

Segrshe, May 3rd, 1917.

. . . We have again had a little march-like walk to Fort Benjamin. The sun shone on the dusty country road, from the edge of which the Narew's waters had long since subsided. The six graves have been left thickly covered with mud, and broken trees and crooked bushes testify to the strength of the swollen river's current. The tarred-felt casing of the wooden breakwaters has been peeled off by the impact of the racing ice-floes, and ragged black pieces, with protruding nails, wave fantastically in the wind which kindly blows the dust away from the column.

The peasant is busy ploughing, harrowing and scattering manure. Bare-footed boys herd the grazing cows, which stare in astonishment at the Company. The sows are wallowing in the village pond, surrounded by innumerable little pigs of all sizes— the smallest, seeking nourishment from the alluring mother, look as if they had been polished by her tongue. Those of an older litter are more independent, but they are still in their mother's care. Others no longer pay much heed to their parent, but are frolicking and romping about on their own. It is all just like it is with human beings! Among other animals are mares with their foals, such awkward, fragile creatures that they look as if they might get broken at any moment. The spotless ducks are too dignified to take any part in this turmoil, and are having a big wash on the surface of the water. Larks are trilling high up in the sky and dropping suddenly to earth in the fields. There are swallows on the banks of the river. The bird-family lure one to the forest, and there on the edge of it—in front of the work of destruction—is a purple crocus ! A message from home ! Oh, memories ! Out of the green grass rise the grotesque ruins of the Fort, blown up by the Russians. Colossal masses have come crashing down, it would take ten wagons to deal with them. The thickest iron bars have been broken like straws by the force of the explosion, and yet how innocent that murderous chasm in the earth looks ! It is all covered with grass. Trees are growing out of the casemates. I found the first blossom of an unknown white wild-flower there, and thousands of gnats were dancing their ever-varying spiral measures.

Hattonville, May 28th, 1917.

. . . Whit-Monday is nearly over ! The reddish rays of the setting sun play about the ruins of a castle high up on the top of the hill. A road which cuts diagonally across the dead, trampled vine-stocks runs steeply straight up the overgrown cliff. On Saturday I climbed up it, puffing. With every step the view became more extensive. Now I can already follow the course of the railway-line to Vionville on the far side of this hill. Just in

(333)

front of the village, which has an undamaged church, there is a meadow of rich, rippling gold. Horses and cows are grazing in it with lowered heads.

Now I can see all over the green plain : fair-sized woods are dotted about, showing up against it in darker shades of green. Beside every 'Bois' is a village. Many of them have been destroyed, and the black roofs of wooden shanties are to be seen among the ruins. Broken spires, and here and there a whole one, point towards the sky.

Now I'm up ! Brambles are rampant all over the stonework, displaying the Hamburg colours of red and white, mingled sometimes with the brilliant yellow of laburnum clusters on which falls the shade of a walnut-tree. Birds are playing among the branches of an oak. The chestnuts are in bloom. Pansies and forget-me-not are beginning to flower in the deserted garden. A sword-lily shows the symbol of fidelity. Glistening insects run about between the stones. Everywhere there is movement and a reawakening life.

In the castle cellar there is also life—stimulated by a glass of beer ! The gunners are having an evening out and are enjoying themselves to the strains of a gramophone.

I step through the stone gateway. Shaky-looking walls menace the street and the broken stonework has a bizarre effect in the evening light. A house, on the wall of which one can still see the chimney, is barricaded. To the left is the church. A bomb has made a hole over the altar. On the roof of the nave stinging-nettles are growing luxuriantly.

The concussion has smashed the stained-glass windows and broken the heads off of the terra-cotta Stations-of-the-Cross. The saints from the apse are standing round a new altar which has been erected in the body of the church. A strip of red velvet hangs behind the crucifix. The Madonna has lost her halo. The porch is colourless and cold, the walls are white, as if they had been frightened to death. I climb up into the tower. The bell has been removed and every opening is boarded up so that one gets no view. I cautiously retrace my steps. A Way-of-the-Cross leads to the castle where the Staff is lying. In the dusk I clamber back into the valley.

3rd Line, June 1st, 1917.

. . . The valley lies bathed in the golden evening light. Long shadows stretch themselves at the foot of the trees. Clouds drift by and the grass quivers in the gentle breeze. The vintner who is at work in the only remaining vineyard hacks away indefatigably at his stocks until darkness falls. The rays of the slowly sinking sun are caught in the foliage of the tree-tops. It is nearly 8 o'clock.

Now there are signs of life in the huts. Field-grey figures, laden with knapsacks, and hung round with all sorts of straps, bags and bottles, emerge, rifle on shoulder. For the last time for a month, probably, they line up between the withered vine-stocks ; the Captain gives a few instructions ; then the Lieutenant takes over the Company and leads them to the baggage-wagon ; there is one such receptacle for each platoon ; the knapsacks are neatly packed in ; we sling our bread-sacks round our necks, hook up our cartridge-bags which would otherwise press too heavily on the hip-bone, and march off.

Slowly, with heavy tread but without a halt, the column trudges along the excellent high-road. Here and there on the far side of the ditch is a wooden cross, a fenced-in mound, a stone with a chiselled inscription. On the left rises the wooded hill crowned by the castle. Its battered grey walls still defy the weather and peep out through the blossoming chestnut-trees ; brambles and golden clusters of laburnum flourish at its feet.

A township appears in the valley and there we strike the Grande Chaussée, a model Roman road and example of construction carried out with due regard to nature. We are going up-hill all the time. The road is absolutely straight. Far below, on the left, is the Russian Gorge. Magnificent beeches and tall elms lift their shady heads out of the depths and look patronizingly upon the woodland flowers and small bushes. Manifold nature clothes the slopes to right and left. On the far side of the ' Russian Camp ' the field-railway nestles against the friendly hill-side and stretches its iron rails through the forest, sheltered from the eyes of airmen by the trees. Half-way up over there a red streak of light vanishes just above the tree-tops—it is the last greeting of the departing sun which has already sunk behind the hills.

Now the half-moon gains in brilliance and shines

(336)

mildly down upon us. The song of the birds is hushed. We have reached the top of the hill and now we are on the direct road to Verdun. Green walls rise on either side of the ' Great Glade ' ; the trees take advantage of the clearing and stretch themselves out into the open. Stars appear dimly, half drowned by the moonlight. It gets darker ; one can hardly distinguish between the different trees ; blacker grow the shadows. The road dips a little and then rises again. At such places an overhead screen woven of rushes and boughs stretches from side to side and hides us from view. One of the larger cemeteries lies to the left ; bracken is springing up among the graves. The undergrowth becomes denser, and now there are also protecting screens on both sides. Many a tree has been robbed of its crown just when in full beauty— it stands maimed but still erect and is putting out roots from its young shoots, though but little foliage remains on the lopped branches.

There is a sound as of rushing water in the air and a sharp report—our artillery is firing. From the other side also comes an occasional shot. Then all is still again. A deathly silence reigns. The wagons halt. Faint whispers are heard as the packs are distributed, quickly slung on, and then in double file we climb down into the Brigade Gully. It is a good thing that the moon is shining as we silently scramble downward over roots, stones, tree-stumps, through pools and across furrowed cross-ways. Far below a cooking utensil rattles. The heavy tread of the troops thuds on the stone under foot. One man slips sideways.

At the bottom—yes, we have reached the bottom—there lies a meadow veiled in mist. A dim figure carrying a water-bucket goes mournfully across it.

Now we mount, to the right, up the steep boulder-strewn hill, feeling our way in the shadow of the great firs and beeches—puffing, sweating, clattering. Nobody tumbles down ; each man gropes his way carefully along. The moon is veiled. There is another crash. We halt a moment and sit down. The sweat oozes from every pore and soaks one's coat so that the pay-book in the pocket is wet through and can't be taken out or it would tear.

Well, sitting down makes one feel the pressure of the steel-helmet, so we move on, and now enter a trench cut in the solid rock. Rifles can no longer be carried on the shoulder on account of the over-hanging wire, briers and bushes. We still have to pick our way among stones, and be damned careful. Shell-holes in the ground are covered with logs which have sometimes been tipped up by a false step.

We descend some steps and on the left a ray of light comes from a dug-out. Everything is rock—hewn, chiselled, or, sometimes, built-in. One must not forget to duck or one will get caught in the wire. Electric-wires—only for the telephone—run along the wall. We are in the 3rd line, farthest from the good enemy, and there at last is our dug-out ! It is 1 o'clock.

We stumble downwards for some six or eight yards. A candle flickers below. We often bump our steel-helmets. The ceiling and walls, partly stone and partly corrugated-iron, are black with smoke. On the left is a table for a half-section, with benches round it. On the right are the beds, which are merely bare—or, rather, dirty—boards. They are intended to accommodate six men, but we are twelve who squeeze in, half on the shelves and half on the floor below. . . .

One's limbs feel as heavy as lead. Fully dressed, buckled up, with gas-masks at hand and helmet and rifle within reach, my mates are soon snoring. I gaze at the flickering lamp. Only the breathing of the comrades and the nibbling of the rats break the silence. No sound penetrates from above. I am astonished at such stillness and tranquillity so close to the enemy. Then I too slumber for a few hours.

At 5 o'clock coffee has to be fetched. I am first on the roster, and with the five tins, holding nearly ten quarts, I barge off. The journey to the kitchen is delightful. The birds—every variety of tiny voice—are singing for joy in the greenery above me. It is like the Saxon-Switzerland in miniature, the bushes meeting above a narrow, rocky gorge. The branches hang confidingly over the sides of the trench, and insects are humming in the foliage. After going about half a mile one turns to the left and emerges into the forest, and so reaches the kitchen. Then comes the same pleasant walk back. Broadly smiling one gaily says 'good morning' to faces still heavy with sleep, and then, sitting on a bench outside the cave-dwelling, enjoys the steaming ' drink of the Levant '. The only thing lacking is a bit of bread, but no food is issued till 10 o'clock at night, so till then one has to do without.

Next I go sound asleep and sleep till 11. Then I clamber out into the sunshine and sit on the bench again, amusing myself with two short stories by C. T. A. Hoffmann, while a bird sings close to me. Insects are numerous, diverse and cheeky! They crawl over my trousers and book, and buzz round my ears. The centipedes find the spot as pleasant as I do. The sun shines down into the trench.

Water is fetched, we wash ourselves, and I ' de-flea ' my shirt. . . .

KURT BERGTER, Electrical Student, High School,
  Darmstadt
Born February 6th, 1893.
Killed June 20th, 1917, near Het Sas.

You must know that we are waging three different
wars here : one against the lousy Russian ; one
against the Russian louse (which is now attacking
me with greater violence) ; and—one for the ' thick '
in the camp-kettle ! Living in the open of course
one gets a tremendous appetite, and when there is
pea-soup all the dear comrades fight for the honour
of being the one to fetch rations for every eight men.
Do you think that is out of Christian charity ? Not
much ! It is the same thing with peas as with
people : the empty heads are superficial ; those with
something in them go deep into the matter, which
in the peas' case is the kettle ! My partner comes
back and sadly announces that he got nothing but
' thin ', and to prove it lets me just look into the
can but *not stir it*. Then, very carefully, ' so as not
to spill any ', he pours the soup into my mess-tin ;
but I make a quick dive into it and spoon out my
share of the ' thick ', amid a torrent of abuse from
him : ' Greedy pig ! No sense of comradeship ! '
etc. This battle, which is all the fiercer because so
far we have only got rations at night, is fought daily,
and the same comedy is played everywhere. I, as a
young recruit and one who is accustomed to simple
student's fare, don't think anything of it ; but I
wonder how men accustomed to grand table-d'hôte
meals in a restaurant feel when they have to join
in the battle for ' the thick in the kettle ' !

(341)

EUGEN RÖCKER, Student of Theology, Tübingen

Born October 9th, 1893, at Ravensburg.
Died June 21st, 1917, in the Military Hospital, Bremerhaven.

November 3rd, 1915.

I HAVE now watched the development of trench-warfare for a whole year. The progress made is gigantic. The art of trench-making was in its infancy a year ago, although I used to write you enthusiastic letters about the wonderful achievements of our troops in the front line and communication-trenches. It all goes on now on a grandiose scale —communication-trenches are sometimes miles long, and they are all floored with duck-boards. We should have arrived in the front line with our feet quite dry yesterday, if we had not had to wade through mud and puddles before we got into the communication-trench. Every musketeer now has a better dug-out than a Battalion- or a Company-Commander in those days. Certainly in those idyllic times in the Argonne, when trench-mortars and shells (with the exception of light-shells) were unknown, it wasn't necessary to have bomb-proof shelters, but anyhow we didn't then know how to make them. However, as more and more powerful weapons have been invented and constantly improved upon, it has become necessary to burrow deeper and deeper into the earth. The war becomes more and more of an underground business and the troops are better and better provided for, though it must be admitted that the enemy also *provides* for them better and better! And so the strange fact is established that the more intellectually developed war is the more horrible it becomes—for while fighting in the open is a much more primitive institution, it is at the same time much less dangerous. In our present advanced state of civilization it is quite possible to be killed while sitting at ease in a beautifully arranged dug-out. In a mobile war one may possibly have to sleep in a damp meadow on a foggy night and be terribly cold, but still one is out of the reach of danger. So it is difficult to choose between the two evils!

The time passes surprisingly fast. When I think over the past month I am tremendously glad to have spent it at the Front, and the greater part of it in the Line. I wouldn't have passed this month in the safety of Weingarten for a good deal. You also would, I am sure, rather know that I have got safely through a month at the Front than that I had spent four weeks in the peace of Weingarten. Now I have nearly a year of war to my credit. It has not had the slightest ill effect on my physique, and the nine months in the trenches have given me time and opportunity to deepen the impression made upon me by mobile warfare. The effect upon me of the time from November 1st, 1914, when I arrived in the Argonne, up till the service in the big new cemetery the day before yesterday has been —I can say this to you because you will understand that I am not boasting—a wonderful development of manliness and religious faith. Shall I ever again in my whole life experience a year so rich in ups and

(343)

downs, in joys and sorrows, in privations and pleasures, as this last !

December 12th, 1915.

We have now happily survived the muddiest days of the whole mud season in the trenches ! The weather has been perfectly foul. Dread of the enemy is as nothing compared with dread of the mud, but with sardonic humour we adapt ourselves to the new conditions of existence. . . . In my dug-out I can't lie down on the bed because it is under water. I have just been sleeping for a few hours on a poor sort of bench. One's boots are full of the wet *mud-soup,* and inside them one's feet are standing in it, and though during the day the sensation is rather pleasant than otherwise, yet, during the 15-hour night, the *soup* gets cold ! I should be glad to walk up and down in the trenches during the night in order to keep warm, but the mud is too awful, although innumerable hands have been feverishly at work upon it to-day. You have never seen anybody whose clothes are so stiff with mud as mine !

I am now quite accustomed to having my feet wet through. I have got acclimatized to life in a bog. A fish is always wet, and why shouldn't a man learn to be so ?

In a few hours we shall be in huts. One can hardly imagine anything so glorious ! . . . The remembrance of these days, when human beings were degraded to the level of animals living in mud and filth, will be a constant joy to me by and by.

Anyhow, there are two things which the mud has failed to do : pull the lace-boots off my feet and prevent my enjoying the war ! The only thing I mind is that our poor musketeers feel all the hardships so dreadfully. And it rains and rains and never stops raining—not a good downpour which will soon be over, but a persistent gentle drizzle, which soaks through everything and lasts for ages. . . .

MARTIN HIEBER, Student of Law, Tübingen

Born June 18th, 1891, at Tuttlingen.
Killed July 6th, 1917, near Brimont (Rheims).

December 4th, 1916.

. . . I have always disliked hearing people talk of
the aviator as the ' Conqueror of the Air ' ; of his
pride in having fulfilled the dream, the longing of
humanity ; of the sublime sensation of being able
to accomplish so much more than the feeble little
beings crawling about down there on the earth,
down there among the trees, roads and meadows.
So much in the descriptions of those who had once
' been up ' seemed to me exaggerated, or like the
bragging of a scorching ' road-hog '. The flying-
man who really flies does not talk about his feelings,
for when one knows that everything depends on such
small details, then the super-man attitude vanishes.
One has a roaring engine in front of one which
effectually prevents any sensation of ' boundless
space and solitude '. Only gradually does one get,
in addition to the consciousness of forming part of
a branch of war-service where the individual man
does still count for something, a real appreciation
of the beauties which are continually revealed during
a flight. And another feeling may be bound up with
this—that of having a pull over the rest of mankind,
who can't see all these things, just as the Alpine
climber prides himself on being superior to people
who can't reach such heights as himself.

The sensation of conquest is also, I think, only

acquired by degrees. The Pilot is haunted at first by the stories of Dædalus and Icarus ; but later, when he gains in self-confidence, he is certainly more to be envied than the Observer, who after all, during a flight, occupies more the position of looker-on. My heart swells when I look down on the sunlit earth and see the mountain ranges stretched below me and the streams finding their way through the marvellous colour-scheme of green woods and meadows, dark blue sea, violet mist on the vanishing horizon, and pink cloud. The almost flat landscape here on the Somme is exceptionally beautiful from above. The broad valley with its shimmering marshes ; the villages with their lush meadows ; the yellowish-gold of cornfields ; the roads pencilling delicate lines through this mosaic ; the intervening shadows of hills : all this constitutes such a wealth of colour and form that one can hardly take in all the details at once.

But beyond the Somme and farther north—the raging battle ; the churned-up earth ; the blazing and smoking ruins ; the never-ceasing flashes and explosions of shells ; the suddenly rising columns of smoke ; the constant roar of drum-fire which smothers everything in dirt and smoke : this is a gruesomely beautiful spectacle.

One only receives these impressions by degrees ; the war-picture, especially, only develops quite slowly because it takes time and leisure to grasp it all, and both these conditions are only possible on the Somme during ' lucid intervals '. For here the feeling of ' boundless solitude ' does not exist. About fifty

(347)

aeroplanes are always whizzing about in the air. From one side a squadron of five machines is approaching ; and there flies one of our Leader-Planes ; there are so many observations to be made, and one must not lose touch with the rest of the Flight. Moreover it is all at the rate of 250 miles an hour. Over on the enemy's side Caudrons and Farmans, Nieuports and B.E.'s are flying round. One can hardly distinguish friend from foe. A one-seater fighting plane goes up—one is on the alert to see if he drops—an anti-aircraft shell bursts close to one and one has to bank—four Nieuports are rising skyward, so one must get the machine-gun into position and signal to the Leader—a Nieuport is attacking a German plane—away to help him—a Halberstadt is swooping down on a Frenchman—one must have one's eyes everywhere at once. And while a fight is going on in the air—when one hears the rattle of bullets—when a Nieuport is right on top of one—or (what has only happened once so far) when he is hit and hurtles to the ground—Hurrah ! —one has not much time for enjoying the ' boundless space and solitude ' !

ERWIN SELLO, Student of Engineering, Charlottenburg

Born September 23rd, 1894.
Killed July 22nd, 1917, near Krewo (Smorgon).

February 25th, 1917.

ON the morning of February 21st we marched to Stoj and there entrained in goods-vans. It was lousy cold in the vans, so most of us lay full length, rolled up like mummies in our coats and blankets. The route was via Wladmir-Wolynsk, Kowel, Grodno, Wilna. It was not much good attempting to sleep in the vans : the hardness of the boards and the cold soon roused one again. On the evening of the 24th we detrained, dead-tired and shaking all over with cold. Our hope of getting into billets and having a chance of making up our lost sleep was disappointed, for we were immediately packed into another train : this time on a field-railway in open trucks. There were fifteen men to each truck—that is to say fifteen men's baggage, for though some of the fifteen were forced by sheer exhaustion to take a turn of riding now and then, in such cold it was impossible to stick it for long. The march beside the train, which travelled at a fair speed, lasted seven hours. It was ghastly ! I was so done that I actually managed to fall fast asleep several times on the truck, in spite of 36 degrees below zero. In the open it would have been several degrees colder owing to the bitter wind. When we detained from the field-railway one of the men remained lying, frozen, on the truck.

(349)

Whether he is still alive I don't know. We looked like ghosts. Our hoods and coat-collars were a mass of ice. The tears which the wind brought to one's eyes were instantly frozen, so that I could hardly see out of mine. But our Way of Sorrow was not yet ended, for from the place where we detrained there was still a good two hours' march, this time with all our equipment, and this march was the absolute limit ! Ever so many men fell out. Even the fear of being frozen to death couldn't keep the chaps going. They were past caring what happened. If the march had lasted any longer I think I should have felt the same : after all one could but die of cold, and that is said to be quite a pleasant sensation.

At last we reached the camp in the forest. But I was not to get a rest even then, for I was ordered to take part of my Platoon, occupy a newly dug trench in the 2nd line and prepare it for defence. It was about a mile and a half farther on. That may not sound very far, but think of the weary, frozen limbs, and the snow-drifts which the wind had heaped up into veritable mountains ! Every few yards one sank up to one's belt in the snow and had to be helped out. It took us an hour and a half to cover that mile and a half. Then I noticed that my left big toe was frozen, but I found that I was the fifteenth man suffering from frost-bite !

LUDWIG ELSNER, Student of Law, Freiburg i.Br.

Born March 11th, 1895, at Dresden-Neustadt.
Killed August 5th, 1917, near Berezanka-on-Zbrucz, Eastern
Galicia.

Treskowring, Hill 108, *January* 12*th*, 1916.

. . . In the afternoon of the day before yesterday,
at the Platoon-Commanders' Conference, Lieut.
Brox, the Company-Commander, said : ' Gentlemen, please see that to-day all work ceases between
2.30 and 4 o'clock. Pioneers and Miners must be
at the listening-posts ! ' That told us what was up !
So from 2.30 to 4 a deathly silence reigned in the
whole sector. Then began the usual afternoon bout
of artillery-fire on my Section, which is particularly
beloved by the Channellers [1] because of my two
earth-mortars, one trench-mortar and one machine-
gun, and where we counted about 30 to 40 shells
every day, while on some days there were as many
as 60.

About 6 o'clock my night-sentries were posted—
trench-posts, crater-posts, alarm-posts. Then suddenly, at 9.10, an orderly from Lieut. Brox dashed
down the steps into my dug-out : ' Order from the
Company-Commander : all advance-posts to be
withdrawn ! ' (that means all who were out in front
of the 1st line), ' the French have charged their new
mine-galleries and they may go up at any moment.
Our trench-mortars to commence firing at once ! '

[1] Apparently a nickname for troops preventing the German
advance towards the English Channel.

Hardly had he said this when the first German trench-mortar exploded in the French trench with such violence that everything shook even on our side though we were 100 to 120 yards away.

'Hasler, all listening-posts in at once! Working-parties to take cover in the mined dug-outs!' Hasler, my orderly, rushes off.

My trench-duty Corporal then appears: 'Herr Feldwebel,[1] splinters from trench-mortars on both sides are falling all over the trench . . .' 'All right. Everybody except three Double Posts, into the mined dug-outs. Zimmer, order everybody to stand to!' Zimmer, my batman, hurries out to pass the word to all the men in my platoon dug-outs. And all this time it is howling and crashing, everything is shaking and the dirt is being scattered in all directions. The concussion from the explosions is so great as actually to put out our candles—only think! five or six yards underground!

Hasler comes back. 'Listening-posts all in!' 'Right.' Now we have to sit still again. The whole dug-out is full of men, as the working-parties have had to take refuge in the mined dug-outs. Now there is nothing to do but wait and wonder when the gentlemen opposite are going to send up their mine!

Eleven o'clock came; 12 o'clock; nothing happened beyond the continuous cannonade. Then came an Orderly from Lieut. Brox: 'Working-parties out! Everything to be finished!' 'Right!' 'Hasler, take the working-parties through the

[1] Sergeant-Major.

(352)

" Lung-tester " to Steinbruch—only show them the way ! ' The working-parties disappear. We wait and wait—nothing happens ! At 12.30 the [gun-fire at last begins to slacken, and as I haven't slept since the previous morning, I lie down for a bit. ' Nothing is likely to happen to-night now, but if it should wake me at once ! Men can sleep, but with belts buckled and rifle and gas-mask handy.' That's all right and 10 minutes later I had dozed off and slept till 4.30 a.m.

' Everything suspiciously quiet ! ' my half-platoon Commander reports. I take over the watch and pay a short visit of inspection to the posts. True, it *is* suspiciously quiet ! But 7 o'clock comes ; I write the Early Report ; the Channellers are pretending to be dead ! The morning dawns. I order all necessary work to be begun—the entrance to one mined dug-out is entirely destroyed, the 2-inch thick iron plate in front of it rolled up like a piece of paper by a French 100-lb. ' minnie '. Quick, fill up the shell- and trench-mortar-holes on top of the dug-outs before it is daylight ! So it appears that the Channellers' mine is not going up after all ; one of ours once went wrong too.

All day nothing particular occurred, only the inevitable shelling. At 6.30 some working-parties arrived from Infantry Regt. 192. I distribute them in the sector. ' Bothe, I am going to lie down now. Wake me at 11.' I had hardly lain down full length when my dug-out began to quake as if it were a wave-bath. ' Up, everybody, stand . . .' But already my voice was drowned by the fearful

(353)

bombardment in which not only all the French guns of the sector took part, but doubtless a number of flying-batteries ! Everything groans, shakes and rocks, one concussion after another. Suddenly Egyptian darkness !—a shell from the gentlemen opposite has cut off my electric current—and just then the working-parties come tumbling in again : ' Steady, don't sit down, there's room for all of you ! Corporal Grund, fetch the listening-post in at once ! Trench-posts into the special observation-posts, nobody must show themselves in the trench ! ' Exit Grund, in spite of the appalling fire. ' Hasler, just see what's wrong with the electric light.' Hasler hops out—close to the entrance the wire has been shot through—within twenty seconds it is mended with a little bit of telephone wire. Hasler hops in again : ' Herr Feldwebel, our alarm signal-bell is also shot through, that is to say the connection above.' ' Let's leave it till to-morrow ; everybody is to stop under cover now ! ' Then the listening-post come in, plastered with layers of filth : ' The mine went up farther to the right.' The post were only able to get back by rolling from one shell-hole to another.

Corporal Grund comes back : ' Order carried out. Nobody visible in the trench ! ' Well, that was very necessary, for what those wretched Channellers sent over passes all description. We could only count by several at a time—it was the most intense kind of drum-fire !

Although I was feeling pretty shaky I managed to light a cigarette with apparent nonchalance, and puffed away as if nothing on earth mattered beyond the inexpressibly exquisite enjoyment afforded by that cigarette ; I also, with ostentatiously amiable ceremoniousness, produced the box of chocolate-tablets you sent me : all in order to try and steady the trembling men, which I succeeded in doing to a certain extent. I would rather not know how much money was shot away both by those opposite and ourselves yesterday. The wasteful, aimless firing went on till half-past 10, and then I quickly sent off the working-party from Infantry Regt. 192.

Lieut. Brox now sent again to ask whether anything had happened to us. No, thank God, apart from our agitation we were quite all right. No casualties ! On such days the war-news simply states that ' in several places on the Front there was artillery and mining activity '.

It was not my first experience of such days—on the contrary I have known bigger and more numerous mine explosions when I was first at the Front, but on previous occasions I had not been in command and responsible for the lives of the fifty men under me. And even though the world would not have laid the blame for any possible losses on me, still one feels responsible towards oneself and towards God. In old days one had only to look out for oneself, but now it was a question of seeing that nothing happened to the already weakened Platoon. But the very increase of responsibility helps you ; you feel that you are of some importance, your own individual worth is at stake. Well, if the good God goes on helping us as He did yesterday and the day before, then we shall be all right !

July 29th, 1916.

. . . Early this morning—7.30 a.m.—I had to take the Company back to our dear Menneville for the funeral of some of our comrades. We had a glorious march. It was already very warm, although the landscape was still veiled in mist, and only gradually did individual trees emerge from the grey mass. Slowly the light brightened over the wide stretch of country ; the sun climbed higher and higher, gilding the whole scene by slow and sure degrees, so that when we mounted the last hill to the resting-place of so many brave comrades there was a blaze of golden sunshine and summer radiance ! It was a parable of life and death : leaving the grey of past uncertainty for the golden light of knowledge ; passing through life's sad days to reach the freedom—not of death's night but of death's victory ! We have witnessed nature's resurrection—may God grant us an equally glorious one !

Everybody, even the most apathetic of the Landsturm, seemed to feel the influence of the moment. They were all silent the whole way—thinking of the dead and sympathizing with those who during the darkness had been so suddenly snatched away by a treacherous mine ; they were all reflecting on what it would be to die just now when we are surrounded by all the glory of spring, the richness of summer.

Up on the cemetery hill stood the regimental band and a number of officers, including even the Colonel, and to the strains of ' Jesus my Refuge ' the funeral ceremony began. After the burial, when I had already fallen in the Company, the band began to play the ' Song of the Good Comrade ', and once more all helmets were doffed in a last farewell greeting to the departed brothers of our great family ! Then the regimental march rang out and to its lively strains we marched back to the front line, towards the enemy ; not sorrowing any more, but vowing in our hearts to preserve the memory of the dead by honouring—and revenging them !

HANS FINK, Student of Law, Marburg

Born May 10th, 1893, at Hünfeld.
Killed August 31st, 1917, in Flanders.

May 27th, 1917.

On account of our continual losses the Company-Commander has the difficult, unceasing task of fitting reinforcements into the Company. There are no old, experienced men left—nothing but Deputy-Reservists and recruits. The officer has himself to create an efficient body of N.C.O.'s. And what soldier nowadays has any self-reliance ? All impetus must come from the officer, whose influence is more important than it ever was. Although I am no longer in command of the Company I do believe that my influence had a good effect, and that Prometheus feeling is the finest thing about being in command. It is quite a novel sensation to find that just with one glance one can make chaps advance under the fiercest fire.

GERHARD   GÜRTLER, Student   of   Theology,
    Breslau

Born December 21st, 1895, at Breslau.
Killed August 14th, 1917, in Flanders.

At the Front, August 10th, 1917.

WE spent the whole of the 30th of July moving up
to the wagon-lines, and that night, at 2.30 a.m., we
went straight on to the gun-line—in pouring rain
and under continuous shell-fire ; along stony roads,
over fallen trees, shell-holes, dead horses ; through
the heavy clay of the sodden fields ; over torn-up
hills ; through valleys furrowed with trenches and
craters. Sometimes it was as light as day, sometimes pitch-dark. Thus we arrived in the line.

Our battery is the farthest forward, close behind
the infantry, so that we can see the English position
on the left. Our position is a perfectly level spot
in the orchard of a peasant's ruined farm. In the
square of trees, on each side of the road which runs
through the middle, stand two houses. One is a
mere blackened heap of bricks ; the other has three
shattered red walls still standing. The whole place
is in the middle of arable fields reduced to a sea of
mud, churned up to a depth of 15 feet or more by
the daily barrage of the English 6- to 8- and 11-inch
shells, one crater touching another. To this the
never-ceasing rain adds a finishing touch ! Nothing
can be seen far and wide but water and mud. From
the position the hill gradually rises to the front line.

In order to have some cover our two guns stand

(359)

under a tree to which extra green boughs have been added. We can't have a proper dug-out because the ground is so soft and wet, only a sort of rather superior wooden hut, covered with tarred felt, sand and leafy branches, so that when it rains, as it generally does, we simply have to lie in the water.

Then the work began, for there has to be something behind the trails to prevent the gun from running back too far, so we had to dig, bale out water, and drag tree-trunks into position. That went on all day and all the next night.

'We joyfully marched full of hope to the war,
Our companion was ardour, his banner we bore,
And gay youthful voices sing out as they roam :
"Little birds in the forest, we'll soon be at home!"'

But we new arrivals were disappointed at first, all the same.

Towards the afternoon the fire increased noticeably until it developed into a regular barrage. And then came what is the worst thing of all in our life here—the lugging up of shells. In themselves the baskets aren't particularly heavy—70 to 80 lb.— but when you have a hundred, a hundred and fifty or two hundred of them, it's no joke. The ammunition-columns usually arrive at night, so that one has to be as quick as possible, because of the English fire and one's anxiety about the horses, and what with the darkness and the slippery ground it isn't easy.

At last we thought we were going to have a rest —and then the great Flanders battle started ! Nothing is so trying as a continuous, terrific barrage such as we experienced in this battle, especially the intense English fire during my second night at the Front—dragging shells and dragging shells, and then the actual artillery duel in the rain and filth.

Darkness alternates with light as bright as day. The earth trembles and shakes like a jelly. Flares illumine the darkness with their white, yellow, green and red lights and cause the tall stumps of the poplars to throw weird shadows. And we crouch between mountains of ammunition (some of us up to our knees in water) and fire and fire, while all around us shells upon shells plunge into the mire, shatter our emplacement, root up trees, flatten the house behind us to the level of the ground, and scatter wet dirt all over us so that we look as if we had come out of a mud-bath. We sweat like stokers on a ship ; the barrel is red-hot ; the cases are still burning hot when we take them out of the breech ; and still the one and only order is, 'Fire! Fire! Fire !'—until one is quite dazed.

And now came the most dangerous time for me. It was just getting dark when suddenly our bolt jammed : ' Gürtler, you must go to the other Section and fetch the battery-artificer.' Through the darkness, through the enemy barrage of 6- and 8-inch shells, to No. 2 Section. That was the night of the great Flanders battle. I leapt from shell-hole to shell-hole while fresh shells fell to right and left of me, in front and behind. The nearest one burst only three yards away, but I escaped the splinters as I was lying deep in the mud of a crater. The mud I naturally did not escape ! Thus I proceeded for half an hour into the void—not knowing the way, not knowing the position, but only the direction. In one crater I found a wounded infantryman, and crouched beside him for quite half an hour. It is not pleasant to await the arrival of an 8-inch in the slimy yellow water of a shell-hole ! Will it get you, or will it not ?

Then on again. Sometimes I thought I should get stuck. Once when I dragged my foot out of the mud, my high boot remained behind ! At last I reached the Battery, delivered my message, and then came the journey back ! And once more the bringing up of fresh ammunition, hauling shells, making up and collecting cartridges, removing empty cases, until the artificer arrived and we could go on firing till the end of the English attack. Then the gun-emplacement had to be cleaned up and aeroplane-camouflage procured—that is to say, grass mown and branches cut.

Half the morning had already passed, and now came the sequel which follows every battle—and the battle of Flanders not least : a long file of laden stretcher-bearers wanting to get to the chief dressing-station ; large and small parties of slightly wounded with their field-service dressings—some crying and groaning so that the sound rings in one's ears all day and takes away one's appetite, others dumb and apathetic, trudging silently along the soft, muddy road in their low, heavy boots, which look like nothing but lumps of mud ; others again quite cheery, knowing that they are in for a fairly long rest : ' For at home, for at home, we shall meet our friends again ! '

(362)

Their thoughts wander back into their past lives like stray birds that do not know the way. Some figure appears before their mind's eye : perhaps a little old mother, holding a tattered letter close before her eyes—a fresh young girl stroking the narrow gold ring on her finger—a boisterous small boy ' presenting arms ' with a stick.

And those men who are still in the front line hear nothing but the drum-fire, the groaning of wounded comrades, the screaming of fallen horses, the wild beating of their own hearts, hour after hour, night after night. Even during the short respite granted them their exhausted brains are haunted in the weird stillness by recollections of unlimited suffering. They have no way of escape, nothing is left them but ghastly memories and resigned anticipation. . . .

My gun is the only one which has had no casualties. ' Haven't you got a bullet for me, Comrades ? ' cried a Corporal who had one leg torn off and one arm shattered by a shell—and we could do nothing for him. Of us new ones from Jüterbog, two have already been killed—a one-year man and a bombardier—not to mention sick and wounded. And we have no news of the other batteries, all communication being cut off. . . .

The battle-field is really nothing but one vast cemetery. Besides shell-holes, groups of shattered trees and smashed-up farms, one sees little white crosses scattered all over the ground—in front of us, behind us, to right and left. ' Here lies a brave Englishman ' or ' Bombardier ——, 6.52 '. They lie thus, side by side, friend beside friend, foe beside foe. In the newspapers you read : ' Peacefully they rest on the spot where they have bled and suffered ; where they have striven ; under the eyes of the dear comrades with whom they marched to war ; while the guns roar over their graves, taking vengeance for their heroic death, day after day, night after night.' And it doesn't occur to anybody that the enemy is also firing ; that the shells plunge into the hero's grave ; that his bones are mingled with the filth which they scatter to the four winds ; and that after a few weeks the morass closes over the last resting-place of the dead soldier, and only a little, crooked, white cross marks the spot where once he lay. . . .

HELMUT ZSCHUPPE, Student of Philosophy, Leipzig.

Born December 29th, 1898, in Vienna.
Killed September 18th, 1917, near Maronviller (La Neuville).

No. 11 *Field Hospital, October* 25*th,* 1916.

IT doesn't do one any good to spend one's time between going on guard every fifth and sixth hour and sleeping in a mud-hole or a half-finished dug-out at the far end of which the air is so bad that a candle won't burn. And after an attack in a trench with bombs and flame-throwers one's very soul is seared. By the time I was wounded my nerves were in such a state that I had to make a great effort to control myself even though it didn't hurt. ' There's no need to get in such a fuss, you silly ass ! ' the staff-doctor said, and no doubt he was quite right. One must keep perfectly calm in body and mind. Therefore instead of sympathizing with the sufferings of others, I have become as one of them—looking on death with indifference because I myself may die at any moment, and no longer sickening at the sight of wounds and of dark-red blood on pale, yellowish skin. Pity must be left to the angels.

We moved up at night, under shell-fire, into the front line. The next day there was drum-fire for eight hours. I lay in a so-called ' rabbit-hole '—a burrow under the firing-step—there were only four dug-outs for the whole Company. Thank God I was quite calm. The air was rent with bullets and shells. There was a wild medley of a thousand different whizzing, whistling noises, buzzing like bumble-bees all around us. When the fire is most intense

(365)

it is impossible to distinguish between the crashes. The shapes of the splinters too varies in a fantastic manner such as no power on earth could devise. During the attack I looked round for my rifle—the smooth, shining barrel, which was lying close to me, had been torn open without my noticing, and was hanging in jagged strips. One heard a dull, metalic hammering noise, like that made by central-heating. Our shells were flying one above the other like flocks of birds. As the shells pitched nearer, one could calculate the chances of being covered with earth. I kept wonderfully cool. I suddenly remembered the words, ' God and myself ', thought how fitting they were, and smiled. How wonderfully were the saints protected—the stake fell and the fire was quenched !

Military Hospital, Cologne, November 13*th,* 1916.

. . . The Cathedral. Great halls of stone. In a dim corner gleams the little red light ; worshippers kneel before it. The gold of the open Shrine begins to glimmer through the dusk, only the red in the garments of the figures depicted on it is visible— dimmed by age and veneration. There is a dark brown organ in an alcove. Perhaps a note is sounded. The painted windows are dark and con- fused. Suddenly one colour comes into its own, and shines out as the nimbus round the head of a saint; the wintry sun throws a yellow-and-red patch upon the stone ; a long ray pierces the mist of dust and dreams. Dividing grilles become visible. Pillars renew their youth ; they lean towards one another but never fall ; theirs is no dead, stiff, erect, encompassing of space. . . .

The Holy Ghost is captive in the Cathedral. In the form of a dove He must hang, with outstretched wings, above the nave. Far below stray a few human beings—lost in the vastness.

One should never stand still to look at the outside of the Cathedral, but should walk round as one gazes ; then one realizes how one harmony melts into another. Gargoyles jut out in their primitive isolation and inaccessibility into the air.

September 5th, 1917.

I rejoice in the beauties of Nature ; in this summer-like Renoir autumn of the canal and the Aisne ; in the ever-shimmering, ever-rustling avenue of elms. The hedge-bordered meadows take on a bluish tinge from the rising mist on the brink of the water, and a faint, blue-green reflection is mirrored below. This green, flourishing wilderness is woven in summer's threads of autumn-tinted, soft-toned wools. One can hardly look into the dazzling blue sky. In the tangled grass blooms—an exquisite miracle—the autumn crocus. Long, slender, pale-lilac flowers, with their wonderfully varied length of petal, and the pistil, thickly coated with scented yellow pollen, shining through the frail calyx. Their delicate stems are snow-white. The ruins of the town are pastel-white in the heat. Sometimes one sees here the ' classic ' landscape of Poussin or Böcklin. I realize how art is determined by landscape. I have drunk all that my eyelashes could encircle of the world's golden superabundance.

Military Hospital, Rethel, September 10th, 1917.

I have reported fit for service. I am restless. I hate the kitchen-table at which I am writing. I lose patience over a book. I should like to push the landscape aside as if it irritated me. I must get to the Front. I must again hear the shells roaring up into the sky and the desolate valley echoing the sound. I must get back to my Company. They are all now very much reduced in strength ; and, worn out and over-tired, have to be on guard the whole time in the Front line. I must get back into touch with the enemy. I know far too well what the danger is, but I must live once more in the realm of death.

September 14th, 1917.

Yesterday the Iron Cross of the Second Class was sent to me. The pleasure this gave me was some small compensation. To-morrow I start back to the Company. To-day I am in the Convalescent Section getting ready. Well, and what now? When one thing is over one begins to ask, what next? I wait for what fate may bring ; am low-spirited, pale, and love the dusk. It seems as if many sleepless nights had made one ultra-sensitive. When I was left alone for a few minutes with the Cross, I had quite different thoughts from those that were in my mind before. It seemed as if the Cross were made of shell-splinters—black blood congealed on a yellowish dead face with open mouth—bandages encrusted with pus—the strangled cries of hoarse voices—flaccid, gangrened flesh on the stump of a leg. But all that shall not make me hold back ! And I am comforted by the thought of your prayers and your love.

JOHANNES PHILIPPSEN, Student of Philosophy, Kiel

Born April 19th, 1893, at Dollerup (Angeln).
Killed September 20th, 1917, near Poelkapelle.

Saarlouis, July 22nd, 1917.

THE time of waiting is over. I received my marching orders to-day and am off to-morrow. How different this departure is from the last ! and how different, again, from the first in December, 1914 ! Things have become more and more serious, and, in spite of all our victories, the burden presses more and more heavily upon our country. And that impatient longing to fight, the wild joy at the idea of being on the spot when the enemy got his *coup de grâce,* that cannot be expected from anybody who knows what life in the trenches is like and who has experienced in his own body the full gravity of the situation. I am delighted when I see such feelings exhibited by our boys, and I should think it an outrage to try and quench them by cold-blooded sarcasm ; but we, who have seen the dark side, must substitute for that enthusiasm a deep-seated determination to stand by the Fatherland whatever happens as long as it has need of us. We know that death is not the worst thing that we have to face. Thoroughly to realize everything and yet to go back, not under compulsion but willingly, is not easy. To try and deceive oneself by working oneself up into a state of excitement is, I hold, unworthy. Only genuine self-command is any use to me.

(369)

I know that I have been permitted by a benign fate to drink deeply of the clear spring of the German nation's courageous attitude towards life in itself. On wonderful journeys my eyes have been gladdened with the sight of Germany's beauty, and I have a home that I can truly love. This shows me where I belong when it is a case of defending that land. That was how I felt when I went to the Front for the first time, and it is just the same now.

A new chapter of life is beginning, and I must learn afresh to face the end with calm. One must not omit to examine oneself as to one's merits and deserts in the past. We do not practise auricular confession, but one must honourably clear these things up in one's own mind. One thing I must say to you, anyhow : I shall most certainly be fully conscious of all the kindness and comfort and friendly sympathy which I have met with even where I did not deserve it. For your large share in this I thank you from the bottom of my heart. Don't grieve because I have to go out again. My place is at the Front. That you must recognize.

EDMUND KNOELLINGER, Student of Philosophy,
Giessen

Born August 20th, 1892, at Budenheim, nr. Mainz.
Killed October 16th, 1917, at the Chemin-des-Dames.

On the Western Front, August 15th, 1916.

GERMANY is beautiful, oh so beautiful ! You must
have had a lovely time in the Harz and afterwards
at Lahnthal.

. . . My Mother made an application to the War
Office, stating the case about my brothers, who were
both killed in France, and asking that I might be
transferred to the Base, so that at least one son
should be spared to her. She did this without my
knowledge or consent. The War Office at once
granted her request and telegraphed instructions
to the Regiment. It was then proposed to transfer
me to a Recruit-Depôt or an Officers' Training
Camp, or possibly to some place in Germany. I
flatly refused to leave the Front. It is a matter of
honour with a young officer to remain at the Front
as long as it is anyhow possible. It is no lack of
love for my Mother which makes me say this, I am
merely stating my conviction that one's first duty
is to one's country.

I know perfectly well that most officers at the
Front have not such a strict sense of duty as I have,
and that probably everybody will blame me, but
I am absolutely certain that I am doing right. My
brothers went to their death like heroes, and shall
I try to escape ? Never !

(371)

KARL GORZEL, Student of Law, Breslau

Born April 6th, 1895, at Breslau.
Killed March 21st, 1918.

Slype, October 1st, 1916 (*after the battle of the Somme*).

Now that the horrible affair at Thiepval lies like a bad dream behind me, I will tell you in broad outline how I have been faring on the Somme. . . .

As we were passing through Cambrai we saw Hindenburg and greeted him with exultant cheers. The sight of him ran through our limbs like fire and filled us with boundless courage. We were going to feel the need of him too !

On the evening of September 11th we relieved the 5th Guards (Regulars) in the Thiepval position. The march up was awful. The nearer we got, the more intense became the gun-fire and the flatter the communication-trenches, which at last disappeared altogether. Then we had to advance in spurts through the murderous shrapnel- and shell-fire. Even there we had heavy casualties.

The next morning the English attack began and the guns were not silent for two hours during the day. At dawn I looked around me : what a ghastly picture ! Not a trace of a trench left ; nothing but shell-holes as far as the eye could reach—holes which had been filled by fresh explosions, blown up again and again filled. In them we lay as flat on the ground as if we were dead, for already flocks of enemy aeroplanes were humming over us. We were absolutely at their mercy, and with remorseless

(372)

accuracy they directed the English heavy-guns, shell after shell, into our line, and themselves fired with machine-guns at everybody who made the slightest movement below.

Hour after hour passed. The wounded lie helplessly groaning. The supply of water runs out. The day seems to stretch itself maliciously to twice its usual length. The fire increases to such bewildering intensity that it is no longer possible to distinguish between the crashes. Our mouths and ears are full of earth ; three times buried and three times dug up again, we wait—wait for night or the enemy ! Oh that waiting !—it scorches the brain and drives one frantic. And the bursting shells' dance-of-death becomes ever madder—one can see nothing for smoke, fire, and spurting earth. Feverishly one's eyes seek to penetrate the curtain of fire and detect the advancing enemy.

Suddenly the barrage lifts—the shells are falling behind us—and there, close in front, is the first wave of the enemy ! Release at last ! Every one who is not wounded, every one who can raise an arm, is up, and like a shower of hailstones our bombs pelt upon the attacking foe ! The first wave lies prone in front of our holes, and already the second is upon us, and behind the English are coming on in a dense mass. Anyone who reaches our line is at once polished off in a hand-to-hand bayonet fight, and now our bombs fly with redoubled force into the enemy's ranks. They do their gruesome work there, and like ripe ears of corn before the reaper the English attacking columns fall. Only a few escape in full flight back through the boyaux.

We sink down, dazed, upon the tortured earth, and tie up the wounded as well as we can, while awaiting the coming of a second attack or of the night. The machine-guns are buried in soil and smashed by shells ; the stock of bombs is almost exhausted ; the fire becomes more violent again ; it makes one's head ache and one's lips burn. The issue lies now in the Hands of God. There is only one thought in every mind : ' They shan't take us alive ! ' But the Tommies have had enough ; they won't come back to-day. It gets darker and the fire becomes normal. I light a cigarette and try to think—to think of our dead and wounded ; of the sufferings of humanity ; to think back to—home ! But away with such thoughts ! The present demands its rights—it requires a real man, not a dreamer. Food arrives and drink—*drink* ! The stretcher-bearers carry the wounded back as far as they can. Reinforcements arrive, things are cleared up and the dead buried, and a new day breaks, more horrible than the last !

Such is the battle of the Somme—Germany's bloody struggle for victory. This week represents the utmost limit of human endurance—it was hell !

HERMANN LABUDE, Student of Philosophy

Born February 12th, 1894, at Breslau.
Killed March 29th, 1918, near Beaufort, before Montdidier.

Before Dünaburg, December 8th, 1917.

AT the moment we are having an armistice, from December 7th to the 17th, here. In my Division it started on the 2nd. The first rumours began to circulate on December 1st. On the 2nd I was occupying an observation post which is exceptionally near the railway, in order to make a sketch from there. I saw that the telegraph-wires along the railway embankment were being mended. That told a tale, and I was further enlightened by the arrival in the 2nd line of several motor-cars.

At 4 p.m. there appeared upon the railway-line which runs between the Russian trenches the white smoke of a locomotive, and through the storm-gaps in the barbed-wire entanglements came the Russian delegation. There were about 32 people—officers in uniform, civilians, and—prepare for a shock— one female! A thaw was in progress, and in their elegant clothes they hopped valiantly through the deep mud and in and out of the shell-holes which were brim-full of water.

Behind our front line they were joined by our Excellencies. Farther back they travelled a little way in our light-railway until they and their dispatch-cases were received by a pullman-car which was awaiting them. In one of the big H.Q. towns they met our Bavarians and the Austrians.

(375)

During the past years we have often, as a joke, asked anybody who came in from a forward observation post : 'Well, Comrade, did you see Peace passing by?' Now, on this Sunday, I really did see her, and this is what she looked like : telegraph-wires, dispatch-cases, and a special train !